"BUCHWALD IS, AS ALWAYS, DOWNBEAT
AND ZESTY!"   —PUBLISHERS WEEKLY

"America's funniest scores again!"
                              —THE SUNDAY OKLAHOMAN

"Nothing is sacred when Buchwald is loose with a
typewriter . . . Buchwald at his best."
                              —GRAND RAPIDS, MICH. PRESS

"Amusing, wise and witty as ever."
                              —MACON, GEORGIA TELEGRAPH & NEWS

"Great fun!"

                              —COLUMBUS, OHIO DISPATCH

Berkley books by Art Buchwald

THE BUCHWALD STOPS HERE
LAID BACK IN WASHINGTON

LAID BACK IN WASHINGTON

ART BUCHWALD

BERKLEY BOOKS, NEW YORK

This Berkley book contains the complete
text of the original hardcover edition.
It has been completely reset in a typeface
designed for easy reading, and was printed
from new film.

LAID BACK IN WASHINGTON

A Berkley Book / published by arrangement with
G. P. Putnam's Sons

PRINTING HISTORY
G. P. Putnam's Sons edition / November 1981
Berkley edition / February 1983

All rights reserved.
Copyright © 1978, 1979, 1980, 1981 by Art Buchwald.
Copyright © 1981 by Los Angeles Times Syndicate for columns first
published in 1981.
This book may not be reproduced in whole or in part,
by mimeograph or any other means, without permission.
For information address: G. P. Putnam's Sons,
200 Madison Avenue, New York, New York 10016.

ISBN: 0-425-05779-8

A BERKLEY BOOK ® TM 757,375
Berkley Books are published by Berkley Publishing Corporation,
200 Madison Avenue, New York, New York 10016.
The name "BERKLEY" and the stylized "B" with design
are trademarks belonging to Berkley Publishing Corporation.
PRINTED IN THE UNITED STATES OF AMERICA

To that lady in Chicago Ronald Reagan kept talking about during the entire campaign because he said she cheated on welfare. I hope she's better off today than she was yesterday.

Contents

PART II

PART III

PART IV

PART V

PART VI

PART VII

By Way of Introduction

"Where do you get your ideas for your columns?" the blonde girl asked me as she smoked a cigarette after an unbelievable night of lovemaking at a Quality Inn Motel.

"I was afraid you'd ask me that," I said. "Can't you leave well enough alone? We had a wonderful evening. Why do you have to spoil it with questions?"

She pouted and punched the pillow with her fist. "Is that all I mean to you? You're no different from every Washington pundit I've ever known. All you're interested in is my body. You don't care about my mind at all."

"That's not true," I said. "I do care about your mind. But I don't want to hurt you. If you knew where I got my ideas for my columns, you would think less of me."

"You're wrong," she said, as tears welled up in her eyes. "I love you and nothing you say about your work could change that."

"All right. I'll tell you where I get them. But remember, you were the one who pressed me."

"Oh my darling," she said, clutching me tightly. "Tell me."

I braced myself. "I steal them from the newspapers."

Her eyes opened wide in surprise and alarm. "Oh, *no*!"

"That's right," I said bitterly. "I read the newspapers and I grab a story from the front pages and run with it. I've been doing it all my life."

"But you don't seem the type who would steal from the papers."

"What do you know about writing a column?" I asked contemptuously.

"You think all I have to do is call up the Secretary of State and he's going to give me an article? It doesn't work that way, baby. You have to take an idea anywhere you can get it. I get mine from the newspapers, because whatever is on the front pages is far funnier than anything I could possibly make up."

I could feel her body go stiff and cold. "Why didn't you tell me before?"

"Because I knew this is exactly how you would react," I said, turning over on my side with my back to her. "We had something good together until you started prying into my professional life. Sure I steal from papers, and from television too. I've gotten column ideas from Dan Rather and John Chancellor and even Barbara Walters."

"Not Barbara Walters!" she said, aghast.

"When you're in this business, everyone is fair game. I've even stolen from my kids. Now you know the kind of guy I am."

"But why?" she said.

"Because," I shouted at her, "that's where the money is —stealing ideas from the headlines. I vowed when I started out in this business I would never be a reporter living on a pauper's salary all my life. I wanted a flashy car, beautiful girls, a condominium in Far Rockaway. I wanted people to look up to me. I knew I'd never make it with my imagination, so I started taking things out of the newspapers. First, it was petty items about the National Rifle Association, the Teamsters Union, and Spiro Agnew.

"But then I got into grand larceny, stealing my ideas from Watergate, Jimmy Carter, and now Ronald Reagan's administration. I mainline on Al Haig and supply-side economics. Once a guy goes down this road, there is no turning back."

She got out of the bed and slowly started getting dressed.

"Where are you going?" I asked, as I stared at her beautiful naked back.

"Who knows?" she mumbled. "Who cares? But I could never sleep with a man who steals from Barbara Walters."

"Suit yourself, kid," I said, lighting a cigar. "But nobody changes the way I write this column—nobody."

Once fully dressed, she headed for the door. As she put her hand on the knob, she turned around. "I just want to ask you one more question."

"Ask anything you want," I told her.

"Does your wife know what you're doing?"

"What the hell are you talking about?" I screamed. "YOU ARE MY WIFE."

Part I

"Trees" by Ronald Reagan

The Reagan forces were sitting back relaxed at headquarters. Ronnie was sticking to the script as they had written it for him, and everything had been going well. Then, suddenly, out of the blue, Reagan decided to ad-lib his opinion on the environment, and the sulphur dioxide hit the fan.

One of the aides rushed in with a wire story. "Ronnie just announced the battle for clean air is over, and attacked the volcanic eruption of Mt. St. Helens."

"Okay, can the jokes. The election isn't won yet."

"I'm not kidding. He said in Ohio that Mt. St. Helens had released more sulphur dioxide into the air than had been released by automobiles in the last ten years."

"Automobiles don't pollute with sulphur dioxide."

"Well, don't get mad with me. I didn't tell him to say it."

"Get him on the phone . . . . Ronnie, where are you? . . . You think you're over Los Angeles? Aren't you sure? . . . You can't see because it's all brown smog down there? Ronnie, why did you get into the clean air thing without checking with us first? . . . I know it sounded like a good idea comparing Mt. St. Helens with pollution, but, Ronnie, you got it all wrong. Cars pollute with nitric oxide, carbon monoxide and other gases. Mt. St. Helens' sulphur is peanuts compared with what man-made pollutants are doing to the atmosphere. . . . I know you're not a scientist, Ronnie—but people want their President to have the facts before he speaks.

3

Can you see the airport yet? . . . You can't see anything but dirty clouds. . . . Los Angeles isn't going to like what you said about the battle for clean air being won.

"Ronnie, remember how you promised you would not say anything unless we put it on cue cards for you? . . . I know how much you hate EPA. Everyone hates EPA, but you're not going to win votes attacking it when no one can see Los Angeles.

"And while I've got you on the phone, why did you have to attack trees? People love trees. . . . Yes, you did attack them. You said that 93 percent of all nitrogen oxide pollution comes from vegetation. You got nitric oxide mixed up with nitrous oxide. Trees give off nitrous oxide, which is harmless and non-toxic . . . I'm not loading you down with a lot of chemistry, Ronnie. But this is the kind of stuff the other side can throw at you to prove you don't know what the heck you're talking about. Now all they're going to be asking you for the next week is what do you have against trees. . . .

"What are you coughing for? . . . The smog is getting into the plane. . . . No, it's not from trees, Ronnie—it's from the automobiles down below that you can't see. You are going to have to make a statement when you land. . . . You want to say everyone is nit-picky and just trying to get away from the real issue? . . . That's the best you can come up with? . . . Why don't you say you are still an environmentalist at heart and your words were taken out of context? That should give us a couple of days to come up with something better. . . .

"By the way, did you really say the oil slicks off Santa Barbara are good for people's health? . . . I was afraid you did. . . . Yes, Ronnie, it could present a problem. . . .

"Ronnie, people don't like oil slicks, whether they're natural or man-made. . . .

"Please don't talk about oil slicks again. . . . We'll send you new cue cards so you won't have to deal with the clean-air issue at all.

". . . Of course you're your own man, Ronnie, and you have a right to say anything that comes to your mind. But stay away from trees unless you know the difference between nitric oxide and nitrous oxide.

"Are you still trying to land? . . . You're going to in spite of the smog? . . . Okay, Ronnie, good luck. But for heaven's sakes stay indoors while you're there. We don't want you to get sick from the pollution. . . . Do I have any good lines for you as you get off the plane? . . . How about this: You come off smiling, not coughing, and you say, 'I think that I shall never see a poem as lovely as a tree. . . .' No, don't memorize it. Write it down, Ronnie—write it down."

God Doesn't Vote

God is really getting a workout during this election year. There was a time when the TV preachers devoted their programs to telling us how angry God was with the way we were behaving in our private lives, which of course is their business.

But now we're being told that God has a vested interest in whom we put into public office, and some Fundamentalist sects, known as the Moral Majority, are spending wads of money to defeat anybody whose voting record doesn't go along with their interpretation of the Bible.

They are calling for a holy war against those who are for the ERA, pro-abortion, school busing and are against the B-1 bomber.

I always thought the nice thing about God was that he stayed out of American politics.

But after watching the TV shows for the past few weeks, I was beginning to wonder.

So when I spoke to God the other night I asked, "Whom are you going to vote for this year?"

God seemed very angry. "I never take sides in an American election."

"But there are a lot of people down here who say you want Reagan."

"That's ridiculous. I hardly know the man, though I have seen his movies."

"But the Bible thumpers keep quoting you all the time. They say you've definitely made your mind up and we'd better all go along with you or we're headed for damnation."

"With all due respect to these people, they don't know what the devil they're talking about. I've told them time and time again that I don't give political endorsements. If I did, I wouldn't be God. I have a good mind to sue them for using my name without my permission."

"I don't blame you," I said. "And I for one never believed them when they kept quoting you on the political issues."

"What scares me," God said, "is that these TV ministers are

not only telling the American people whom I support, but they're raising all their money in my name. They keep warning the viewing audience that if they don't send in their checks, I'm going to be very upset. I don't deal in money—never have and never will. But they're telling those poor souls out there that if they don't come up with a contribution, they won't have any salvation. I'd appreciate it if you put the word out that anyone is free to send in any amount of money to a TV minister, but the money isn't buying them a place in heaven. It's buying limousines and private airplanes and $500 suits for the people who are making the pitches."

"God, you sound mad."

"I *am* mad. I'm trying to keep the whole world from blowing up and those preachers down there say my only concern is to defeat George McGovern in South Dakota."

"I wish you could somehow get the message over that you aren't for or against anyone running in our elections this year. It would certainly clear the air for all of us."

"I can't do it. I believe in the separation of church and state. I've stayed out of American politics since 1776 and that's why you people are still around. I'm sorry. I have to go now, I have the Moral Majority on hold."

The Boys on the Bus

"The Boys on the Bus" is the title given to newspaper people who travel with presidential candidates. The phrase was made famous by Tim Crouse in his excellent book concerning the McGovern-Nixon campaign.

At the beginning of this year's presidential race, there were quite a few buses to choose from. The top political writers and TV commentators had first choice of which bus they wanted to take. Everyone wanted to get on John Connally's bus because it looked as if he had the best chance of beating Reagan for the Republican nomination. George Bush's bus was half empty before Iowa, as was Howard Baker's. Bob Dole had a mini-bus, and if you wanted to follow Anderson around, you could always get a ride with him in his Volkswagen.

On the Democratic side, there was a serious bus problem when Teddy Kennedy got into the race. The pundits had predicted that as soon as he challenged Carter, the nomination would be his for the asking. So all the media stars fought to get on Teddy's bus.

Before Iran, President Carter was supposed to campaign, and because he was President, as well as a candidate, *two* buses had been set aside for his press entourage. Then he decided to stay in the White House and send surrogates to campaign for him instead. Nobody fought to get on Fritz Mondale's bus, so there were always plenty of seats.

Well, after Iowa, some of the newspapermen started to doubt that they were on the right bus. George Bush's win had given him "momentum." Connally didn't show any, so the big-shot scribes asked their editors for a transfer.

The second-team reporters who had been assigned to Bush, because no one thought he had a chance, were angered that they were being kicked off the bus just when the Bush campaign was rolling.

But that's life, they were told, and they could either climb on Reagan's bus or get off the campaign trail.

While this was going on, Teddy stumbled in Iowa. But no one wanted to get off the bus, because it was still a good story

8

as to how badly he was doing. Besides, if they did get off, there was no other bus to get on except Jerry Brown's, and you never knew if you'd be sharing it with a rock band.

So everyone took their buses to New Hampshire. The people on Bush's bus were filled with optimism—mostly fed by George Bush. The ones who rode behind Reagan thought it was a hopeless cause.

Teddy's bus had standing-room-only because the big question in New Hampshire was, "Could a Kennedy win a primary in his own backyard?"

A few more souls rode along with John Anderson, so he had to replace his Volkswagen with a van.

Well, much to everyone's surprise, Reagan clobbered Bush in New Hampshire, and every by-line reporter piled out of Bush's bus and demanded seats on Reagan's. Once again, the second-team reporters protested, but to no avail.

They were told to get on Anderson's bus.

Since Anderson didn't have a bus, they had to hire their own to follow him.

But after Massachusetts, John Anderson suddenly started catching on with the public. Immediately, many of the top correspondents on Teddy's bus said they wanted to get off and ride with the congressman.

Once again, the second-team reporters were told the story was too big for them and they should take another bus. With bitterness, some hailed Howard Baker's bus, and a few thought maybe Connally's bus might be worth a ride in South Carolina.

But it was too late. Both Connally and Baker had run out of gas.

So now, for all intents and purposes, there are three buses worth buying a ticket on: Ronald Reagan's, John Anderson's and Carter's, if he ever takes it out of the White House garage.

You may be wondering what happened to all the second-team reporters who kept being shunted from bus to bus as the primary picture evolved. They have just been ordered by their editors to come home—by train.

The Answer Man

Every presidential candidate has a style uniquely his own. Ronald Reagan is now developing a reputation for getting all his facts wrong. One of his more recent misstatements was that Vietnam veterans "were not eligible for the G.I. Bill of Rights with regards to education or anything."

Mr. Reagan is very angry about the press reporting on his factual flubs, and claims the media seem preoccupied with his mistakes.

I believe the only way he can fight this is by holding a weekly radio and TV show, along the lines of *The Answer Man,* in which people could call in and ask him questions so that his answers would not be filtered through the people who are covering him.

It would go something like this:

"Governor, could you tell us how you would resolve the energy crisis?"

"There is more oil under Three Mile Island than in all of Saudi Arabia. But because of bureaucratic foul-ups in the Department of Energy and the EPA, our oil companies have not been given permission to drill even a test well."

"Mr. Reagan, do you think the United States is in a strong defense posture at this time?"

"I certainly do not. When the Chinese bombed Pearl Harbor, this country was unprepared to go to war. I believe we are in the same position now as we were then. This nation has to say to the Kaiser of Germany, if you go one step further in trying to dominate the world, we will blockade Cuba."

"Mr. Reagan, you've taken a strong stand against the government getting involved in the lives of its citizens. Can you give us a specific example of how it is doing this?"

"Yes. When this country was founded, if someone was sick, that person could go to any barber and he would bleed you with leeches. But now, HEW has ruled that barbers have to be licensed before they can do it. Most barbers refuse to fill out the paperwork required of them, and instead of the American

10

people getting better medical care, it is costing them five billion dollars more a year."

"Governor, what would you do about farm parity?"

"I would let the farmers raise their own parity, rather than have Washington tell them what crops they can, or cannot, grow. Nancy and I both like parity, particularly as a dip with potato chips. Some people hate parity with anything. But in a free economic society, I don't want some pencil-pusher in the Department of Agriculture telling me what I am allowed to eat."

"Mr. Reagan, I'd like to ask you a question about the MX missile. Do you think the U. S. should build it?"

"Yes, I do. There are six million, five hundred and twelve people who would rather take their welfare checks from the government than figure out how to make the MX missile work. I say we should tell them, they either get a job in research and development on the MX program or forfeit their welfare payments."

"Governor, are you for the boycott of the Moscow Olympics?"

"Yes, I am, providing our American athletes are permitted to participate in them. We must let Khrushchev know that we mean business."

"Political Tours Available"

"Media Travel Service. Can I help you, please?"

"Yes, this is Henry Kidney. I'm planning a tour for my political candidate, and I was wondering if you could advise me of some good places where the media would be likely to cover him."

"We have a gastronomic, ethnic food tour which is very popular. You can visit an Italian pizza parlor, a Jewish delicatessen, a Mexican carry-out shop, and wind up eating at a Soul Food restaurant in the ghetto. It's one of our most popular trips for a political candidate. Your man gets to eat a pizza, a dill pickle, a tamale, and red beans, which are included in the price."

"Don't you have a Polish restaurant you can recommend? My guy is very interested in the Polish people ever since they had their strike in Gdansk."

"We do have one, but it's very hard to get a table. Everybody running for political office, from the presidential candidates on down, wants to be photographed with someone of Polish descent. I may be able to book you into a Polish bar in three weeks."

"What else would you recommend?"

"We have a slum tour which all our clients are crazy about. We arrange for your candidate to walk through ten blocks of burned-out buildings, talk to a mother on welfare, and sit on a stoop with six unemployed youths who have no future."

"How much is it?"

"Five hundred dollars, unless you want us to arrange a demonstration of the people in the neighborhood."

"Wouldn't that be dangerous for my man?"

"Not really. But it will guarantee him getting on TV that night. Cameramen love demonstrations, particularly if water hoses and tear gas are used."

"What about a tour of an automobile factory? Do you arrange those?"

"We have two tours—one where the employees are work-

12

ing, and the other where the factory is closed and everyone is out of work."

"Which one would you advise?"

"Frankly, the unemployed-worker tour is more popular. Our guides will take your candidate to an auto worker's home, and give him an opportunity to eat cornflakes, and talk to the entire family. It also gives him a chance to discuss the economy and attack the importing of Japanese cars. The last time we sent a client to that home, he was on Cronkite, Chancellor and Frank Reynolds all in the same night."

"We'll take it. What about my man standing in front of a coal mine, early in the morning, and shaking hands with the people as they go in?"

"I wouldn't recommend it. It's become too much of a picture cliché, and you'll never get your man on the air with it."

"Do you have something that's really different?"

"We have a deluxe tour to a disaster area. If Mt. St. Helens erupts again, or a hurricane hits the coast of Texas, we'll take your candidate to the scene in a private jet, give him a tour of the ravaged area, and arrange for him to speak to a man and woman who have just lost their house and all their possessions."

"That sounds like fun. Send me the brochure."

"You also might think of visiting an Indian reservation. For $3,000 we can arrange to have your candidate become an honorary chief of the tribe and participate in a tribal war dance. It's a surefire photo for *People* magazine."

"I must say you have a wide selection."

"By the way, we are also in the Hertz Rent-a-Baby business. For $35 a day, which includes free diapers, we'll supply a baby for the candidate to hug on any of his stops on the tour."

"Do we have to keep the baby?"

"No, you can drop it off at any Hertz office after your man has finished kissing it, at no extra charge."

Why Are People Mumbling?

It may be my imagination, but more and more people seem to be talking to themselves during this election year. All you have to do is walk down the street and you can hear someone mumbling. I was curious to hear what people are saying, so I followed one man who was muttering. This is what I heard:

"I can't vote for Carter—anyone but Carter. . . . But then I can't vote for Reagan either. . . . If I go for Anderson, I'll be throwing my vote away. . . . I better vote for Carter. But Carter doesn't seem to know what he's doing. He got us into a recession, and in four more years, he could get us into a depression. . . . I better vote for Reagan. . . . Reagan will get us into a war. It would be terrible to be in a recession and a war at the same time. . . . I better vote for Anderson. . . . What do I know about Anderson? I voted for Carter last time because I didn't know anything about him. I won't make that mistake again. . . . I better vote for Carter.

"I'm not sure I could stand the Georgia Mafia for another four years. I better vote for Reagan. . . . But if I vote for Reagan, I'll be voting for simple answers to complicated questions. He hasn't said anything original since *Bedtime for Bonzo*. . . . Maybe I better vote for Anderson. Why should I vote for Anderson? He seems honest—but they all seem honest at the beginning. I'll bet underneath it all, he's just another politician on the make. . . . I think I'll cast my ballot for Carter. What am I saying? The reason I'm having all this trouble deciding who to vote for is because of Carter. He hasn't solved any of the problems we're facing. . . . He says one thing one day and another the next. . . . It looks as if I have no choice. I have to pull the lever for Reagan. . . . But if Reagan gets in, he may have two or three Supreme Court appointments. I couldn't live with the people Reagan would appoint to the Supreme Court.

"It's obvious. I have to forget the two-party system and support Anderson. . . . Hold it. . . . Anderson can't win. All he can do is spoil it for the other two and then it will go to the House, and they'll probably give it to Carter. I might as well vote for Carter in the first place. . . . My wife said she'd never talk to me if I voted for Carter again. She says she's had it with Born-Again Presidents. . . . I don't think Reagan's been born again. I wonder if she'd want me to vote for Reagan? . . . I wish she hadn't left home to take a job in California so I could ask her. . . . I guess it has to be Reagan. . . . No, it doesn't have to be Reagan. He never gets his facts straight. That's all right when you're running for office—but it could be real trouble in the Oval Office. . . . I better think Anderson. . . . Anderson? Is he just a media star who will burn out once the election is over? . . . Where did he come from? What do I know about him except he looked different from the others? . . . I have to come to my senses. I'm not happy about it, but I'll go for Carter.

"But if I vote for Carter, we'll get the whole damn family in the White House again. . . . I'm not sure I can put up with Amy in her teens, and I know I've had it with Billy. At least with Reagan we don't get a family. . . . It's obvious what my decision is. I'll vote for Reagan and take my chances. Some people say he was a good governor of California. Come to think of it, he's the one who said it. Others say he fudged his record. . . . Maybe I should vote for Anderson and forget about the whole thing. But Anderson's record in the House isn't all that hot either. He says he's changed his mind on a lot of things. . . . Well, if he can change his mind, so can I. At least I know what I'm getting with Carter. If anyone asks me, I'm a Carter man. . . . I can't say it with a straight face. Can I say I'm a Reagan man with a straight face? Nope, I can't do that either. I can say I'm an Anderson man with a straight face. Look at my straight face. It isn't straight? I was afraid of that.

"So where does that leave me? Maybe Carter has learned a lot in the first four years and will be a good President in his second term? It's happened before. When did it happen? How do I know? . . . If I vote for Reagan, he said he'll only stay for one term. . . . That's in his favor. But then again I have to consider his age. Of course, his hair is dark. Anderson's is white. I wonder why Anderson's hair is white. . . . Can the country survive with a white-haired President?

"There has to be a solution to my problem. . . . Wait a minute. I think I have it. Why didn't I think of it before? I'll move to Chicago and vote for all three."

The Thrill Is Gone

"Let's have an early dinner and then watch the election results," I said to my wife Tuesday night.

"That's a good idea," she agreed. "It's going to be a long evening but we'll get a head start."

We finished dinner at 8:15 P.M. and then went into the living room to sit back and watch what the pollsters had predicted would be one of the closest elections in history. I flipped on the set and heard either Tom Brokaw or John Chancellor announce: "NBC has projected that Ronald Reagan has won the election and will be the next President of the United States."

"What the hell is going on?" I asked my wife. "I haven't even finished my yogurt yet."

"Look at the map. The Eastern part of it is all blue."

"It takes Archie Bunker longer to open a door than it does to decide a presidential election," I said.

"How do they know?" my wife asked.

"I think they use an exit poll. They ask a black man in Buffalo, a Jewish man in Virginia, a housewife in Florida, a med student in Ohio and a steelworker in Pennsylvania whom they voted for, and then they start making the map all blue for Reagan. Would you care to play a game of Scrabble?"

"If we had known what was going to happen," my wife said, "we could have had an early dinner after the election results."

"I can't believe it," she said. "The polls aren't even closed in three-quarters of the states."

Since I had nothing to do, I called my friend Bernheim in California. I got him at his office.

"Where are you going tonight to watch the election results?"

"To Phyllis and Don's," he said. "I have to go home and get cleaned up first, and then vote."

"I wouldn't do that if I were you, Alain."

"Why not?"

"Reagan won, and there isn't a thing anyone in California can do about it."

"What do you mean, he won? It's only 4:15 P.M. here. How could he have won?"

16

"He took Ohio, Michigan, New Jersey, Connecticut and Illinois."

"Where did you hear this?"

"It's all over television. NBC interviewed a senior citizen in Delaware and then gave the election to Reagan. Do you know what this means, Alain?"

"I'm not sure."

"The network polling methods have become so sophisticated we don't need anyone west of the Mississippi to decide a presidential election anymore. You people are only wasting the nation's gasoline by going to the polls."

"But we're the most populous state in the union," Bernheim protested.

"Don't tell me your troubles. It's all over, Alain. As I talk to you, Barbara Walters is trying to get Nancy Reagan, and Walter Cronkite has just said, 'And that's the way it is November 4th, 1980.' Do you need any more evidence that you people are out of it?"

"Then you think I shouldn't vote?"

"Why not? It will kill some time when you get home. But if you think you're going to stop the landslide, you're out of your gourd."

"I guess I'll call Phyllis and Don. Maybe they can cancel the caterer. Where's Ann?"

"She went to bed with a headache. She said she's not going to spend any more election nights with me. As far as our political life is concerned, she claims the thrill is gone."

The Fashion Capital

You can say what you will about the Reagan administration, but you can't deny it has turned Washington into the fashion capital of the world. All it took was a rich First Lady from California, and her richer California friends, and suddenly this dusty, peanut-farming, Amaretto-drinking town turned into a land of lynx and sable.

The new California "laid-back look" has affected everyone. I went to buy a hot pretzel the other day from my favorite stand on K Street, when I noticed that Mary had a new look to her. Her frayed sweater had been patched up all over with ultra-suede, her muffler was thrown back across her shoulders, her wool Redskins hat was perched on top of her head like a pillbox, and she was wearing white gloves as she made change.

"Mary," I said, "you look absolutely smashing in that outfit."

"Bill Blass designed it for me," she said. "I adore his lunchtime things."

"May I have a pretzel, please?" I asked.

She handed me one wrapped in a page from last month's *Vogue* magazine and accepted my 50 cents. "Don't get me wrong. I don't have anything against Adolfo. As a matter of fact, I'll probably change into one of his suits when I move my cart over to Lafayette Park later this afternoon."

"I didn't know you were into fashion, Mary," I said.

"We all are," she replied. "Thank heavens we have somebody to set a standard in the White House. Let's hope the sidewalks of Washington will no longer be filled with un-combed hairdos, messy gold chains and raggedy jeans."

"People do look a lot more pulled together since the Reagans moved into Washington," I said as I ate my pretzel.

"Oscar de la Renta is supposed to stop by and show me some fabric for a coat I'm having designed when I sell pretzels outside the F Street Club."

"I like Oscar's things," I said.

18

"Myra said she prefers Jimmy Galanos, but I don't think he's right for pretzels."

"What does Myra sell?"

"Carnations at 18th and Pennsylvania Avenue. She found her first Galanos gown at Goodwill Industries and she's been loyal to him ever since."

"Isn't keeping up with the Reagans going to be quite expensive?" I asked her.

"I'll probably be criticized by some of the other pushcart dealers, but I think when you have money you should spend it any way you want to. It's been a long time since we women have been permitted to dress up, and I'm going to make the most of it."

"I don't blame you," I said. "I notice you're wearing a skirt. You always used to wear pants in the wintertime."

"Pants are out," Mary said. "Particularly at lunchtime. If *Women's Wear Daily* took a picture of me in pants, I'd never hear the end of it. The important thing is for clothes to match. Ruffles are replacing sequins. That's why my sweater is so ruffled."

"Who designed the Redskins wool hat for you?"

"Yves St. Laurent. He said he wanted me to have something that was not glitzy or show-off, and it's perfect if you miss your hairdresser's appointment."

I decided to have another pretzel.

"I don't want to be critical," I said, "but I notice you're still wearing crepe-soled boots."

"That was Halston's idea. He said it was the best way of showing the Californians that we in the East have a laid-back look too, and we intend to stick with it."

"He's right," I said. "There's no reason for the Californians to shove Gucci shoes down our throats."

A man came by with his hairbrush. Mary introduced him to me as Julius, her hairdresser. "He always comes by right after the lunch hour to give me a comb-out. If it weren't for darling Julius, I don't know when I'd find the time to sell pretzels."

Transition

The Republicans are in power and there are going to be tremendous changes in government. Right? No, wrong. It isn't that they are reluctant to make the changes—it's just that they can't. Thousands of patronage jobs are available, but no one can take them, and I'll tell you why. There is no available housing in Washington for the middle-management people who are supposed to take over the town.

The sad truth of the matter, as the GOP loyalists are starting to discover, is what the Democrats have learned in the last four years. Real estate rules the town and, although many people will be out in the streets, nobody is moving out of town.

The people on Reagan's team think this is very unfair. As one told me the other day, "How can we move in if they won't move out?"

"I guess the people you're firing have no place to go."

"But how can we increase military spending, cut taxes and balance the budget if our supporters have no place to live?"

"You should have thought of that during the campaign. Anyone who lives in this city would have told you that no one intended to pull out if Carter lost the election. Our $50,000 homes are now worth $350,000. If the Republicans want to come to Washington, they're going to have to pay through the nose."

"I'm aware of that," he said angrily. "I went out to see a Carter appointee yesterday and asked him if he would be willing to give up his house for his replacement. He just laughed at me and said, 'You can take my office away from me, but my home is my castle.' I told him he owed it to our American political system to move out of Washington when the other party came to power. He said he had no intention of leaving, that he was just joining a law firm and would be representing all the clients he had tried to throw into jail while he was in the government."

I said, "We in Washington call that the 'revolving door' system of government. When you're in, you represent the people; when you're out, you represent those who are trying to

20

shaft the people. That's why there is no turnover in real estate."

"I'm beginning to learn that," he said. "I went to see another high official in Carter's administration and asked him when he was moving back home. He told me he planned to stay through Reagan's entire first term, because with all the changes that would take place he'd be in heavy demand as a 'consultant.' He said he had messed things up so badly in his department that he was the only one in Washington who understood it."

"That's usually the case when someone leaves the government. He is then in great demand as a consultant."

"What am I supposed to do?" he said. "How can we ask our people to come to Washington if they have no place to live?"

"You could build Quonset huts on the Mall. They did it during the war. Or maybe you could put mobile homes on the back lawn of the White House. You could hook up water and electricity and set up a laundromat in the East Room. Of course you wouldn't want to put a trailer in the Rose Garden because that's a national treasure."

"You're not being very helpful."

"I really don't have any great ideas for you," I told him. "Reagan won because he attacked Carter's inflationary policies. The biggest inflationary problem is the housing in this town."

"But how can Reagan do anything if his own people aren't here in town?"

"He can't. That's why so many Democrats have taken his landslide victory in stride."

Jackie Is Coming!

MARTHA'S VINEYARD, Mass.—Ever since the rumor was announced that Mrs. Jacqueline Kennedy Onassis had purchased 375 acres of one of the most important tracts of land on this island, no one has talked about anything else. Reactions have ranged from fear and apprehension to excitement and envy that one of the world's most famous women had decided to make the Vineyard her summer retreat.

My phone hasn't stopped ringing since the story was published.

One lady who knows everything called and said, "Did you hear that Bergdorf Goodman is breaking ground for a new store next to Jackie's land?"

"I hadn't heard that," I said.

"Yes, it will be in the same complex with Gucci, Van Cleef and Arpels and Halston's, who have all decided to build next to her."

"That's fantastic. What about Yves St. Laurent?"

"He's building in Apelier down the road with Saks Fifth Avenue in the same mall. It will be just behind the New York Museum of Modern Art annex."

"The Museum of Modern Art is going to have an annex on the Vineyard?"

"Of course. Jackie loves art."

"Gosh," I said, "this is exciting. Keep me posted in case you hear any more."

The next morning my informant was on the phone again.

"*The National Enquirer* has decided to set up a five-man Martha's Vineyard bureau. *People* magazine is thinking of moving its entire staff up here. Three hundred free-lance writers from movie magazines have already applied for press credentials. And Eastman Kodak is going to construct a photo lab on the beach to develop all the paparazzi films, so the photographers won't have to send their stuff to Rochester."

"Where on earth are they going to put all these people?" I asked.

"You didn't hear about the Sheraton Vineyard hotel?"

"No, I haven't been out this morning."

"They bought a tract three miles away, and they're going to put up a 33-story hotel to house all the journalists who will be staying here in the summer. It will have a rooftop restaurant and 15 coin-operated telescopes, all aimed at where Jackie will be sunbathing. For 50 cents you can look at her for two minutes."

"That roof is gonna be a crowded place."

"I got this from a travel agent, so I can't confirm it, but the *QE 2* is thinking of anchoring offshore on its way to and from Europe."

"It won't be the same Vineyard that we used to know," I said.

"I heard at the post office that everyone in East Hampton is selling his home and moving up here."

"What on earth for?"

"To be where the action is. East Hampton is out now and the Vineyard is the place to be."

"But Jackie hasn't even built a house yet. Maybe she won't."

"Then what are the French interior decorators doing on the island?"

"You mean there are French decorators on the island?"

"All I can tell you is that Air France has asked for permission to land the SST five times a week at the Vineyard airport."

"How are all the people on the island taking this?" I asked her.

"At the moment there is a lot of grousing. But when the new Cultural Center is built at Menemsha they'll change their tune."

"Are we going to have a new Cultural Center?"

"Of course. You don't expect Nureyev and the New York City Ballet to dance in a tent."

Half-Fare Phobia

There are many people who are afraid to fly, and psychiatrists and hypnotists are now holding courses to rid these men and women of their fears.

While a great deal of attention is being paid to the problem, there are still other people who are *only* afraid to fly with children (not their own). Fear of flying with children has been named "half-fare phobia" by Prof. Heinrich Applebaum, who is the only one doing work in this field.

"Most of my patients are closet half-fare phobics," he told me. "They are afraid to admit they can't stand children on airplanes. These people don't hate children. They just freeze up when they have to sit next to one."

"How do you treat them?" I asked the professor.

He took me into a large room that looked exactly like the tourist-class cabin of a 727.

"We simulate the exact conditions of a flight," Applebaum said.

In the cabin were 33 men and women, all Applebaum's patients.

Most of them appeared to be very normal. Some were reading books, others were knitting, and a few were watching the stewardesses' hips as they swung up and down the aisles.

Suddenly Applebaum pushed a button and two dozen mothers and their children, ranging from babies to 12 years, rushed into the cabin from a door up in front.

The older children, carrying toys, ran down the aisles, climbing over the patients to "get the seat by the window." The mothers with their babies and their tote bags full of formulas and diapers sat down next to the patients.

"Where do you get the mothers and children?" I asked Applebaum.

"I pay them $4 an hour," the professor said. "They love it because it gives them a chance to get out of the house."

I noticed a remarkable change taking place among Applebaum's patients. Some were gripping the armrests for dear life.

Others were perspiring, a few were hyperventilating and three were upchucking.

Applebaum went to the front of the cabin. He held a pocket watch and chain in front of him and swung it back and forth.

"Keep looking at this watch," he said. "Relax. Let your mind pay attention only to what I am saying. You have nothing to fear from the child sitting in back of you. If he hits you on the head it will not hurt you. If the little girl in front of you sticks her tongue out at you, do not stick your tongue out at her. You will only encourage her.

"If the mother next to you starts to change her baby's diaper on the floor, stare at the FASTEN SEAT BELT sign. Do not notice what is going on around you. Think beautiful thoughts—you are on a singles' cruise or you are sitting in an R-rated movie where no children are allowed. Relax. Lift your hands off the armrests. Do not look to the right or left. In a few hours you will be safe in your office or home."

Some patients were responding while others were fighting to get out of the cabin.

"How many treatments do they have to have before they overcome their fear of flying with children?" I asked.

"Thirty."

The Answering Service

MARTHA'S VINEYARD, Mass.—What I did on my summer vacation:

I was a telephone answering service. Only people who have children between the ages of 14 and 30 will appreciate what an important function I performed.

I always started after dinner as soon as my daughter Jennifer asked, "Can I use the car?"

"What time will you be back?" I asked.

"Not late. If Debbie calls tell her I went with Tony over to Mike's, and if she doesn't get us there we'll be at David Crohan's Bar in Oak Bluffs."

"I gotcha," I said, writing it down.

Half an hour later the phone rang. "Is Jenny there?"

"Is this Debbie?" I asked.

"No, it's Sarah. And she was supposed to meet me at the Cafe du Port in Vineyard Haven," she said.

"Well, she went with Tony over to Mike's."

"Which Mike?"

"She didn't say which Mike. Is there more than one?"

"There are three. If she calls back tell her I went to the party at Ben's."

"The party at Ben's. I've got it."

Fifteen minutes later the phone rang again. It was Ben, who wanted to tell Jenny about the party.

I explained that she was with Tony at Mike's, but was going to David Crohan's Bar.

"Well, if Angel calls," Ben said, "tell him I need ice and wine."

"Why would Angel call?" I asked.

"To find out where Tony went."

"I gotcha," I said, writing it down. "Tell Jenny about your party and Angel about bringing ice and wine. Do you have any message for Debbie?"

"Who's Debbie?" Ben said.

"I don't know, but she's supposed to call Jenny and I'm to

26

tell her she's with Tony and they went over to Mike's and then they're going to David Crohan's Bar."

"Well, don't tell Debbie about the party because I don't know how many people will be with her."

"My lips are sealed," I promised.

I got into a hot tub when the phone rang again.

The party on the other end asked for Jenny.

"Who's calling?"

"Gordon Manning."

"You can find her at Mike's, David Crohan's Bar or Ben's party, depending how lucky you are."

"I'm calling from New Hampshire."

"That's too bad. There're lots of great things going on here," I told him.

"Well, will you tell Jenny I'm coming down on Tuesday and ask her to leave my beach pass with Ellen in Edgartown? But tell her not to tell Betsy I'm coming. You got that?"

"Of course I've got it. You think I'm a dummy? Listen, I have to get off the phone because I'm expecting a call from either Debbie or Angel or the police in Chilmark depending how lucky *I* am."

I started to worry about why Debbie or Angel hadn't called. I was watching Johnny Carson when the phone rang again.

It was Jenny. "We didn't go to David Crohan's. We're at the Phillips' in Lambert's Cove."

"*Now* you tell me," I said angrily. "Everybody's trying to find you with the exception of Debbie, who never called."

"She's with us," Jenny replied.

"And where the hell's Angel?" I wanted to know.

"He went back to Boston."

"Do you realize Ben was counting on him to bring the ice and wine to his party? Why didn't you call me?"

"I couldn't get to a phone. Who else called?"

"Naval headquarters. They told me to tell you to report back to your ship immediately."

"Dad, are you drunk?"

"Not yet, but by the time you get home I will be."

Double Indemnity

We see the advertisements in newspapers and magazines. Paid for by the insurance companies, the ads appeal to all members of the public who may someday serve on juries: Every time we award a plaintiff a settlement in an accident case, we are only hurting ourselves. It isn't the insurance companies who will suffer, we are told, but the public, because when we decide in favor of the plaintiff the companies have no choice but to raise our rates.

I don't know about you, but the advertisements have persuaded me.

I have this fantasy that I'm on the jury of a giant negligence case. We've heard all the evidence and we are now back in the jury room trying to arrive at a verdict.

The foreman of the jury speaks first. "All right. This is an open-and-shut case. The truck driver rammed into the victims' car, killing both parents and leaving four orphans. The evidence indicated the brakes on the truck were faulty and the trucking company sent it out on the road anyway. How much money do we award the children?"

"Wait," I cry. "There's more at stake than that. What about the trucking company's insurance people? What will happen to them if we award a sizable sum of money to the children?"

"They'll have to pay it," a juror says.

"But it will eventually come out of our pockets—yours and mine."

"What the hell are you talking about?"

"Don't you read the ads?" I said. "Every time a jury awards a large sum of money to the victims of an accident, we, the public, have to eventually pay for it. The insurance companies aren't in business for their health."

"What are they in business for?" another juror wants to know.

"To serve the public. They collect premiums from all of us to protect our lives and property. As long as they don't have to pay off, they can build skyscrapers, invest in the stock market, float real estate loans and sponsor some of the best programs on television. But if they have to start paying off on their policies they can get in serious financial difficulties, and then we, the policyholders, have to bail them out."

"Are you saying we shouldn't award the plaintiffs in this case any money because the insurance company will get hurt?"

I reply, "All I'm saying is we should think about it carefully. Why should we punish a poor insurance company, which, if it loses the case, will only punish us?"

"That's what insurance companies are for," a juror retorts. "They're supposed to take risks. The insurance business is nothing more than a giant crap game, and it's their job to pay off when they lose."

"That is exactly the attitude that is driving insurance rates up all over the country. Every time a case gets to court we say, 'Let the insurance company pay through the nose.' Why can't we be the first jury to say, 'Enough is enough. We will not reward people for negligence committed by another party'? Don't you see? We have it in our power to stop spiraling insurance costs once and for all."

"What have you been smoking?" one of the jurors asks.

"All right!" I shout. "I'll go along with whatever award you want to make. But when the insurance company has to sell its employees' golf course to pay for this case, it will be on the conscience of every person in this room."

Christina in Moscow

I guess the biggest thing that happened in the news this summer is the fact that Christina Onassis married a Soviet citizen and planned to live in Moscow. Since then Miss Onassis has returned to Athens and is not sure whether she will go back to Moscow.

I can tell you what happened.

Christina was in her two-room apartment in Moscow when there was a knock at the door. "Hallo, I am Mrs. Federov from across the way in 2-A. Welcome to the neighborhood. Why don't you invite me in for a cup of tea?"

"Won't you come in for a cup of tea?"

"Thank you, if it's not too much of a bother. My, what a lovely apartment. How many people you have living here?"

"There are three of us. My husband, my mother-in-law and myself."

"What a lucky girl to have such a big apartment with such few people. We have five in 2-A, not including myself. You wouldn't be interested in renting your daybed to my grandfather, would you?"

"No, thank you. We're not taking in boarders."

"It seems a pity to let so much space go to waste. You must be big with the housing commissar. So tell me, how does it feel to be a Russian housewife?"

"I love it. We're so happy. The only thing is, Mrs. Federov, I can't seem to get my husband's collars clean with this Red Star soap."

"Comrade newlywed, that is called in Soviet, ring-around-the-collar. All our men have it. If you don't have ring-around-the-collar the government knows you're not working hard enough, and they give you worse job."

"Then you don't think I should change detergents?"

"To what? How many soap companies you think we have in this country?"

"There was something else, Mrs. Federov. I can't seem to get the cabbage smells out of my kitchen. Do you know of a deodorizer that will do the trick?"

30

"Lenin's Airwick. Just four sprays and your kitchen will smell fresh and beautiful."

"Where can I buy some?"

"You can't buy it. They haven't made it for three years. And don't worry about clean linoleum either. I haven't seen a can of wax in the store since my brother and sister-in-law moved in with us. I'll give you 100 rubles a month if you take my grandfather. He'll just sit in the chair and won't be any bother."

"Mrs. Federov, we really don't need the money. My main concern is getting dinner for my husband."

"You want meat?"

"Of course, I want to serve him meat."

"It's too late today. All the good meat is gone by 10 o'clock in the morning. You have to get in line at 7 A.M. at the People's Butcher Store if you want something for dinner."

"What will I do? Sergei will come home and his dinner won't be ready."

"What about giving him a TV dinner?"

"Do you have TV dinners in the Soviet Union?"

"No, but we will someday. It's in our next five-year plan."

"Well, thank you, Mrs. Federov, you've been a big help. There's a lot more to living in Moscow than I thought. I didn't realize there were so many consumer shortages."

"Bite your tongue. If you complain about shortages Orlov will have to report you."

"Who is Orlov?"

"He's the block warden. He reports on all of us to the KGB. Three reports on you by Orlov, and you're going to have to take my grandfather in whether you want to or not."

No Divorce for Singles

Being a married man, I always believed that single people living together had the best of both worlds. Whenever I met someone in a leisure suit with a gold chain around his neck and a beautiful blonde on his arm, whom he introduced to everyone as his "roommate," I must admit I was wild with envy.

But things are tough even for unmarried couples—tougher in some ways. I discovered this the other day when Harlequin came to see me without an appointment. Harlequin is 30 years old and until his visit I always believed he had the perfect setup. His "roomie" was a sweet thing named Saralee, and they shared a lovely apartment overlooking the Potomac. They had a pet dog named "Pothead," and the thing they both used to brag to me about was that they had all the benefits of being married, without any of the hassles. That's the part I envied the most.

Therefore, when Harlequin told me what he came to see me about I was truly shocked.

"I want to break up with Saralee," he said.

"That's too bad. But what's the problem?"

"I don't know how to go about it."

"You just tell her, I guess."

"That's easy for you to say," Harlequin said. "But you're married and if you want to break up with your wife you ask her for a divorce. Since we're not man and wife what do I ask for?"

"I guess a separation," I suggested.

"Easier said than done," Harlequin whimpered. "If I do that she'll want to keep the apartment."

"Whose apartment is it?"

"It was originally my apartment, but as far as she's concerned it's ours. Why should I give up the apartment just because I don't want to live with her anymore?"

"I know apartments are hard to find, Harlequin, but I'm not a lawyer. When you start talking about property settlements you should seek legal counsel."

"It won't work. When you married people want a divorce, each of you hires a lawyer to thrash things out. Lawyers don't

want to have anything to do with single people who are
breaking up."

"Why don't you just tell Saralee that you don't want to live
with her anymore and you want her to get out?"

"You don't know Saralee. She looks like a lamb, but she
fights like a tiger. She'd throw all my stuff out the window."

"But didn't you have some understanding when you moved
in together? That if either party wanted to call it quits there
would be no hard feelings?"

"Of course we did. All singles say the same thing. But after
you live together for three or four years the vows don't mean
anything. The one who is rejected acts worse than the victim of
a divorce."

"It's funny," I said, "I thought the singles life was all cream
and strawberries."

"Boy, you are dumb," Harlequin said. "I've put up with fits
of jealousy that no married man would stand for. When you're
married you can at least flirt around with somebody and the
other partner doesn't get too shaken up if you don't make a big
deal of it. But when you're living with somebody, if you so
much as dance with another person, your roomie makes your
life miserable. I'm too young to be stuck with one woman," he
said, practically in tears.

I didn't know how to console him. "Look, this is a crazy
idea, but why don't you marry Saralee?"

"What would that accomplish?" he screamed at me.

"Once you're married you can ask her for a divorce and then
turn the whole problem over to your lawyer."

He kissed me on the head and said, "I knew you'd come up
with a solution. I'll go out and buy the wedding bands today."

It's All in the Image

On the question of human rights we must not overlook the highly respected Americans who receive large retainers from some of the most repressive regimes in the world. Some are Washington lawyers whose names are household words, and others are American public relations firms who will do and have done anything for a buck.

The other day, at his behest, I met with Fish, president of a Washington PR firm.

Fish was in a fine mood. "We just got the South American country of Tuna as an account," he told me.

"But isn't Tuna ruled by a ruthless junta that has tortured and jailed thousands of opposition leaders?" I asked.

"That's the image they have now. But after we get our campaign under way it will be known as the bulwark of anti-Communism in South America."

"How did you get the account?" I asked.

"I went down and made a presentation to Gen. Barracuda myself. I told him his country has a bad image in the United States, mainly because he keeps shooting all the opposition leaders. He said it was an internal matter. But I pointed out to him that the Carter regime is trying to cut off foreign aid to countries that do not respect human rights."

"Did you suggest in your presentation that the junta stop jailing and killing the opposition?"

"Of course not. I would never have gotten the account. What I told him was that he could still do it as long as he has a good public relations firm in the United States to see that his side of the story is told."

"Did you explain how you'd do that?"

"By taking out ads in *The Washington Post, The Washington Star, The New York Times* and *The Wall Street Journal* announcing that the junta was only torturing and shooting the opposition until it could hold free elections."

"He liked that?"

"He thought it was a great idea. I also proposed that we bring senators and congressmen down to Tuna and put them up at the Hotel Trocadero and entertain them for a week at the junta's expense. We'd arrange sightseeing tours for them and military parades, and have them talk to 'peasants' who think that Gen. Barracuda's government is the greatest thing since the invention of white bread."

"You really put a lot of work into your presentation."

"I also suggested that Tuna give scholarships to the leading American universities for the study of South American military coups."

"American universities will take money from anybody," I agreed. "Was Gen. Barracuda concerned about how much your PR campaign would cost him?"

"No, because he figured he could get American companies that do business with him to ante up most of it. And what he didn't get from them he could just confiscate from the people he was planning to throw into jail."

"Does your conscience bother you for taking on this account?"

"You have to be kidding. This is a real challenge for an American public relations firm. If we can change Gen. Barracuda's image in the United States, we might even get Idi Amin for a client."

"I never thought of that," I admitted. "One more question. Why did you want to see me?"

"Well, one of the things I promised in our presentation was that we'd bring American newspapermen down to Tuna, on the cuff, of course, and have them write about what a great tourist spot it is."

"I'd love to go," I told him, "but I've already promised the Herring public relations firm I'd do some puff pieces for them on Cambodia."

A 25th Anniversary Gift

A lady in Virginia was arrested and found guilty of eating two strawberries in a supermarket. It was a national story, and many people thought the arrest was outrageous. That is because they didn't know what the stores are getting for strawberries this summer.

The price of fruit is out of sight. I discovered this the other day when I took my wife to Neam's Market to buy her an anniversary present. We went to the fruit and vegetable department. But first we had to ring the bell before the guard opened the steel door.

"We're interested in fruit," we told him.

We were ushered into a carpeted room where Mr. Neam himself came out and sat behind his Louis XIV desk. We were asked to be seated across from him.

"Can I be of service?" he asked.

"We were looking for something in fruit for our 25th anniversary," I said.

Mr. Neam snapped his fingers and an assistant brought out a tray of strawberries.

"I have a matched pair that just arrived," he said, holding two of the most beautiful strawberries I have ever seen.

My wife's eyes glowed.

"How much are they?"

"With or without the sugar?" he wanted to know.

"With the sugar."

He wrote down the price on a piece of paper.

I gulped. "Do you have anything else?"

He snapped his fingers again and the assistant brought out another tray.

"These are pears shaped like diamonds," he said. "Note the luster of the skin when I hold it up to the light. Elizabeth Taylor had one of these for breakfast when her husband John Warner was running in the primary."

I could see my wife's mouth watering. "I don't think we're in Elizabeth Taylor's class," she said.

"Consider this diamond-shape pear an investment. In three

days when it's ripe it will be worth three times what you paid for it."

We both shook our heads. Mr. Neam, who is to fresh fruit what Bulgari's is to jewelry, was very polite.

He snapped his fingers and the assistant took away the tray of pears and brought a tray of peaches, each sitting on its own piece of cotton.

"One of these would go lovely with your wife's complexion," he said. "There are only 11 on this tray. Sophia Loren bought one when she was in town a few weeks ago. When these are gone, there won't be any more. As you can see, our designer has made it possible to either eat one as is, or cut it up into small pieces and add sweet cream."

He wrote down the price on a slip of paper.

There was no way I could afford it.

"We were hoping," I said, "for something that would take up more room in our Waterford fruit bowl."

"I have just the thing," said Mr. Neam, still smiling. He snapped his fingers and the assistant brought out a tray of bananas.

They were still green, but Mr. Neam explained the green ones had the most value because in time they would turn yellow.

My wife picked one up, and I knew from the way she held it that this was what she wanted. "What the heck," I thought. "A 25th anniversary only comes once in a lifetime."

I wrote out the check and they put the banana in a lined box.

Mr. Neam locked the safe and then escorted us to the door. "Come back next week," he said. "We're having an exhibition of rare raspberries loaned to us by the Mellon family who grow them on their farm in Middleburg."

The Junk Phone Call

When the history of the 20th century is written a special place must be set aside for the invention of the junk telephone call. Many people have claimed credit for this great boon to mankind, including Vladamir Gluck, with whom I visited in his spacious offices.

Gluck, who likes to call himself the "King of Junk Telephone Calls," believes that as the postal service gets worse the telephone will replace the junk letter as a means of reaching every reluctant consumer in the country.

"I'm not knocking junk mail," Gluck told me. "It served its purpose for a long time and we're all grateful to it. But you have to keep up with the times. If anyone is to blame for us going to junk telephone calls it's the consumer."

"How's that?" I asked.

"The consumer did not treat our junk mail with enough respect. Many threw it in the wastepaper basket without even reading it. It was an outrage. We put on the envelopes that if they opened our letters they could win $1 million in prizes, trips to Europe and Hawaii, $150,000 homes, but people still kept throwing away our sales pitches. They treated us very shabbily considering all the time and effort we put into attracting their attention. We had to figure out a way of getting into people's homes without being ignored."

"And so you came up with the junk telephone call?"

"The consumer left us no choice. The direct mail people decided that if people were going to throw away junk mail, our only option was to call them on the phone and speak to them directly."

"That was good thinking," I said.

"We used to have 100 people manning phones out there in the main room, but it was too expensive and many of us were getting discouraged about it. But then someone invented a telephone-calling computer. It was programmed to talk to a consumer just like a human being, and many people thought they were talking to a live person. The beauty of it was that the computer could work day and night and had the ability to call back the person when his line was busy or he was out.

"With the breakthrough of the computer the telephone junk call was no longer a cottage industry."

"I'll bet Alexander Graham Bell had no idea when he invented the telephone that it would save the junk mail business."

"The beauty of the junk telephone call is that you can now get into somebody's home and he or she can't ignore you. People have to answer their telephone ring because they have no idea who is on the other end."

"Don't they get mad when the phone rings and some computer on the other end is trying to sell them an encyclopedia?"

"Some do, but the computer is programmed to expect rejection. It never loses its cool. It's even programmed to calm down those people who tell it off. But our research has revealed that many people with children, particularly teenagers, have a great fear that when the phone rings it's going to bring bad news. So when they anxiously pick it up and discover it is only a company trying to sell them life insurance, they are so relieved that they'll order the policy without thinking twice about it. One survey we took showed that 87 percent of all telephone owners would rather get a junk telephone message than a call from one of their children after 10 o'clock at night."

"There are people who are trying to outlaw junk telephone calls by claiming they are an invasion of privacy."

Gluck said angrily, "If the Avon lady can knock on your door, there is no reason why a junk telephone call can't get you out of the bathtub."

Confessions of a Klutz

I stepped on a tennis ball this summer while running for another ball. I wouldn't mention it except that *Time* magazine did a piece on people over 40 who still think they are youngsters when it comes to sports. They ran a picture of me in a leg cast (I had a badly sprained ankle) and they called me a "klutz," which means a klunk who doesn't know what he's doing.

Naturally, I was offended, because Howard Cosell has said on many occasions that my performance on a tennis court could only be compared to Nureyev's on a ballet stage.

The problem with having any kind of sports injury when you're over 40 is not what it does to your body or even to your pride. It's the flak you have to take from well-meaning people who keep asking you what happened.

Since I was in the cast for six weeks, I was able to break these people down into categories.

In the first category were those who demanded to know WHY I stepped on the tennis ball. My stock answer for them was: "I always wanted to do it but I never had the nerve. It beats the hell out of ballooning, because when you're flying through the air you have a complete sense of weightlessness."

The second category of sympathizers I ran into would ask, "Why didn't you move the extra tennis ball off the court before you started playing?"

"Because that would have taken the fun out of the game," I would reply. "The thrill of tennis is to get the ball back without stepping on the one you left on the court."

I said this with so much conviction that most people would reply, "I didn't know that."

"Of course. Why do you think you play with three tennis balls? You need two to serve with, and one to leave on the court so you can trip over it."

The real agony of being in a cast is that you have to listen to everyone else's cast story. I don't believe I ran into one person who hadn't been in a cast at one time or another. And when you're on crutches, it's very hard to move away when someone starts telling you his or her own tale.

They were all horror stories and ranged from the fact that their bones hadn't been set right and had to be set again to how they were driven up the wall when their injured leg started itching and they had to poke knitting needles down the cast to get relief.

"The worst thing," one lady told me, "is that when they take the cast off and you see what your leg looks like, most people faint."

After a while I realized that people were not impressed with how I was injured, so I devised a story which would get their attention.

When asked what happened, I would say, "It's very boring, but if you're really interested—I was on a tennis court, and suddenly this flying saucer landed by the net and a little green man got out wielding a laser pistol. He said, 'Take me to your leader.' I didn't know who to take him to—so he shot me in the leg."

You would think that your own orthopedic surgeon would have sympathy for someone over 40 who had suffered a sports injury. But when I returned to Washington and went to my doctor to have the cast removed, he took one look at my leg and all he said was, "Did you have a nice summer?"

Cheers!!!!

A new element has been added to pro football. Thanks to the showmanship of the Dallas Cowboys, female cheerleaders have become as important as the teams, and every pro football club owner is determined to present the sexiest girls that money can buy.

The competition is so fierce that there is now talk of the NFL holding a draft for college cheerleaders similar to the ones they hold for players. The team with the worst cheerleading records would have the first picks of the new crop. There are trades now going on between the cheerleader coaches in the NFL, and every pro organization is looking for someone to bolster its line.

I was in the office of the coach of the Washington Redskinettes, and there was a great flurry of activity.

The coach was on the phone to the Los Angeles Rams. I heard her say, "Harriet, we need an offensive pompon girl. We'll give you two baton twirlers and a 1979 draft pick in exchange for a six-foot blonde with a 40-inch bust . . . No, we don't want her. Our scouts say she uses silicone. What about Genevieve? We hear she's fighting with the other girls and wants to move to Washington. I'll trade you Candy and Susie for her . . . What do you mean they're too old? Candy and Susie are in their prime. They haven't dropped a baton in six games. If they don't get injured, they're good for four more seasons. Get back to me because I may make a deal with the New England Patriots."

The Redskinette coach told her secretary to get the St. Louis Cardinals cheerleader coach on the phone. "Mabel, how would you like a defensive redhead who can do handstands? Joe Namath says she has the best legs in pro football. She can do 'Saturday Night Fever' in four minutes flat, and the ABC cameras had her on for 30 seconds while Howard Cosell was talking about Muhammed Ali . . . What do I want in exchange? Do you have a brunette who can do cartwheels and splits? . . . No, I'm not selling you a dog. We have too many redheads on the squad now, but we're weak on brunettes who

can do cartwheels . . . Honest to Pete, Mabel, I hate to trade
her, but I can only use her at halftime, and she says if she can't
dance during the entire game she doesn't want to sit on the
bench . . . No, I can't offer you our first draft choice for 1980.
We gave her away to Baltimore for Miss Maryland of 1971.
We needed some depth during the TV commercial breaks. Will
you get back to me?"

One of the Redskinettes' assistants came in. "Mary, Helen
wants to be put on waivers. She just broke up with one of the
Redskins, and she says she doesn't have the heart to cheer for
our team any more."

"Oh, God," the coach said. "We built Sousa's entire
'Washington Post March' number around her. Can't we find
her another player?"

"I spoke to Coach Jack Pardee, and he said he can't spare
any more players for the cheerleading team. He's having
enough trouble with bed checks now."

"Where does she want to go?"

"She said she'd like to cheer for Cleveland."

"Does Cleveland have anybody we want?"

"They have a kicker who's out of this world."

"How are her hips?"

"Terrific. She gets more applause when her back is to the
crowd than when she's facing it. And she can wiggle her fanny
to the 'Marine Corps Hymn.' "

"Why would Cleveland want to trade her?"

"She fumbles a lot."

"All right. I'll call Cleveland. Is there anything else?"

"The Women's Lib delegation is still sitting out in the hall
on the floor waiting to see you."

"What on earth do they want to talk to me about?"

"Beats me."

Part II

Somoza or Else

A well-known columnist came into my office the other day and asked, "Who are you for, Somoza or the commies in Nicaragua?"

"Why do I only have a choice between a dictator and the Communists? Why can't I be for Lopez?"

"Who's Lopez?"

"I don't know who Lopez is. Let's say he's the guy in the middle who hates Somoza and can't stand the Communists."

"Because Lopez would get eaten up by the commies. If you're for the American interests in Central America you have to be for Somoza."

"I don't want to be for Somoza. He's a tyrant and, from what I read, a crook. He's milked the country dry for 40 years. I hope he gets bounced out on his ear."

"What he is and what he does is not our concern. Do you realize if the other side kicks Somoza out, the commies will have a dagger pointing right at the Panama Canal?"

"Maybe so. But it's obvious Somoza can't hold on much longer, and we should see to it that Lopez is pro-American too. We're not going to do it if we keep training Somoza's national guard officers to shoot the Nicaraguan people."

"So what you're saying is that we should get in bed with Castro?"

"I'm saying no such thing. All I'm saying is that I don't see why we always have to support a military junta when the people want to throw the rascals out."

"It's quite simple. Most of the generals in South America have been trained at West Point, including Somoza. They speak good English and you can do business with them. You let the people take over and you'll have another Cuba in six months."

"Not if we support Lopez," I said. "The reason the commies have a chance of taking over is because the people know we're on Somoza's side."

"You're living in a dream world," the columnist said. "Lopez doesn't have the strength to run a middle-of-the-road government."

"He would if we gave him as much military hardware as we've given Somoza. The only thing that's keeping Somoza in power is the stuff we've sold him. Why can't we give it to Lopez?"

"Because if we give the stuff to Lopez it will eventually fall into the hands of the commies when they topple him. The only way Lopez can stay in power is by being anti-American."

"The people of Nicaragua are only anti-American because they know we support Somoza. If we said we were supporting Lopez we wouldn't get ourselves in a Marxist box."

"How can you be so sure of Lopez? We know what we've got with Somoza. He may be an s.o.b. but he's OUR s.o.b."

"So that means we have to support s.o.b.'s all over the world because it's in our best interests?"

"Every time we don't we get another Allende."

"But he was elected by the people and we knocked him off."

"With good reason. We haven't had to worry about Chile since."

"I'm not going to support Somoza no matter what you say."

"Okay, but when Lopez nationalizes the United Fruit Co.," my friend said, "don't come crying to me."

It's All in the Paint

It is not generally known, but one of the things the General Services Administration (GSA) does is train foreign bureaucrats in how to administer the housekeeping chores of their own governments. Now that the multimillion-dollar scandal is breaking in the agency, I keep wondering what some of these foreign government workers learned.

I take you to a GSA office where Amu Tiki has been assigned to study the latest methods used in servicing the U.S. government.

"Now Mr. Tiki, when you take charge of running the housekeeping of your government you will have to lease buildings, see that they are kept up through paint and repairs, purchase and dispense millions of dollars' worth of office equipment, run hundreds of supply stores, handle government transportation, and provide all the services that will keep the bureaucracy running smoothly and efficiently."

"It sounds like a lot of work."

"But it pays well."

"It does?"

"Yes, if you learn it right. Now let me give you an example. You walked through the halls of this building before you came here. Right? What did you notice?"

"They needed paint."

"Of course they did. Now your job would be to paint those walls. How many coats of paint would you say they needed?"

"At least three."

"Good. Now what you would do is give out a contract to paint the halls three times, but the contractor would only paint them once."

"What about the other two coats of paint?"

"They would go into the pockets of you and your contractor."

"I don't want paint in my pockets."

"Not paint, Mr. Tiki, the cost of the other two coats of paint."

"I see. One coat for the walls, one coat for the contractor and one coat for me."

"You learn fast. Now let's talk about furniture. You don't happen to have a brother-in-law in the office furniture business, do you?"

"No, he grows rice in his paddy."

"Well, put him in the furniture business fast."

"But where would I get the money?"

"From your coat of paint, dummy."

"Hee hee. I forgot about that."

"Now, once he's in the furniture business you will contract him for all your desks and chairs."

"My brother-in-law doesn't know how to make furniture."

"All the better. When it falls apart you'll have to order more."

"Why should I make my brother-in-law rich?"

"Because you'll be a silent partner in the furniture company."

"Hee hee. I'm going to like this job."

"All right, Tiki. The next thing you have to do is open office-supply stores in your government buildings. If your government is like ours, nobody knows how much paper it uses. You order twice the amount of paper that you think you'll need. Then you sell what isn't used to the private sector."

"Wait, suppose somebody finds out?"

"Then you give him some money from your furniture company to keep his mouth shut."

"This is getting complicated. Can I take notes?"

"NO NOTES! Never take any notes. If you want to be in your government's GSA you have to keep everything in your head."

"Please forgive me for wanting to take notes."

"Okay, that's enough for today. We'll talk about leasing space from private landlords tomorrow. Are there any questions?"

"If my President wants his palace painted, do I only use one coat?"

"No, dammit. Presidential palaces always get three coats of paint. The one thing you have to learn in this business is not to be greedy."

A Pea and Three Walnuts

In case you don't keep up with these things, the latest Pentagon toy being developed by the U.S. Air Force is the MX, which is a method of moving Minuteman missiles through miles of underground tunnels so that the Soviets won't know where they are. We're talking about $30 or $40 billion if the Air Force gets to build the system, which the general in charge describes as being like the "shell game where you have one pea and three walnuts."

Nobody wants to fool the Soviets more than I do when it comes to pinpointing our missiles. But the cost of the project seems so great that I think we should seek out alternate ways of accomplishing the same thing.

At the moment the contracts for developing the "MX shell game" have been awarded to the Boeing and the Martin Marietta companies. I believe the Air Force made a mistake in turning over the problem to them.

The company which should have gotten it is Amtrak, which runs most of the passenger railroads in the United States. The beauty of turning it over to the Amtrak people is that they already have the equipment and the know-how to fool anyone when it comes to figuring out where one of their trains is at any given time.

Let us say you put a missile on an Amtrak train in one of the underground tunnels. Then the Air Force puts out a schedule at which site the train will be, on what day, at what time. They would make sure that the Soviets got a copy of the schedule as part of the SALT agreement.

Obviously the train would never be where the schedule said it would be, and the Soviets would go nuts trying to figure out where the missile train was. It would accomplish the same goal as the MX program at half the cost.

If the Soviets protested that we were not living up to the SALT agreement, the Pentagon could invite them to send over their top generals and have them ride on an Amtrak train to prove the Air Force has no control over how the United States runs its railroads.

Once the Soviet command realizes that it could never depend on knowing where a missile train is going to be, it would be deterred from launching a first strike on our Minuteman sites.

The advantage of the plan is that the money Amtrak received for this defense contract could be spent on new equipment and rails for its civilian passenger service above ground and we would no longer have to subsidize this mode of transportation.

When I made this suggestion to an Air Force general, he had one major objection to it. "The trouble is that if we gave the contract to Amtrak, not only would the Soviets be fooled, but we ourselves would have no idea where the missiles were."

"I thought of that," I said. "What you could do is set up a hotline between Amtrak and Air Force missile headquarters. It could be attached to a loudspeaker and an Amtrak announcer would man it 24 hours a day. He could say, 'Missile launcher 104 scheduled to arrive in Cheyenne, Wyoming, at 11 A.M. will now be arriving on track 9 at 4 P.M. this afternoon.' Or 'Due to a derailment outside of Philadelphia, the Minuteman Limited, scheduled to leave tonight for Amarillo, Texas, has been canceled until further notice." Or 'Amtrak is sorry to announce that its Nuclear Comet, which was to stop in Baton Rouge, has now been diverted to Denver because of inclement weather.' Amtrak would keep you up to date on every change in its schedule."

"It might work," the general said. "It certainly fits our one pea and three walnut strategy. The only thing that bothers me is that we've told Congress the MX system will cost $30 billion. If we now go back and say we only need $15 billion for it, the Air Force will lose all its credibility on the Hill."

Cutting Taxes

Every politician running for office this year seems to have the "Jarvis Flu." The name of the game in this November's election is: how much each candidate can promise to cut the voters' taxes.

In New Jersey, Bill Bradley, running for the Senate, is calling for a $25 billion tax cut; and in Minnesota, Robert Short, the Senate hopeful, is promising a $100 billion cut. No one knows where the political tax-cut rhetoric will end.

At Finchley for Senate headquarters, I found the candidate sitting behind his desk in his shirt sleeves, looking more like a pork-belly commodity dealer than a man seeking to represent the people of his state.

There was a large blackboard on a raised platform at the end of the room where a volunteer was erasing numbers and writing new ones. Forty people were manning telephones in the other room.

"What's going on?" I asked Finchley.

"We're dealing in tax-cut futures," he said. "We're monitoring what all the candidates around the country are promising the voters in cuts, and then we intend to top them."

One of the people on the phone yelled out, "Bob Short has upped his tax-cut promise by $5 billion."

The man at the blackboard erased $100 billion and wrote in "$105 billion."

Finchley yelled out, "We'll go $110 billion."

The blackboard-keeper wrote in the figure for Finchley.

"Gluckstern from Ohio has gone to $130 billion."

Finchley shouted, "Make our cut $150 billion."

"You people are spending money like water," I said.

"No, we're not. Those billions are all cuts. We're saving the voter money. Every billion dollars we promise the taxpayer we're going to cut is money in his pocket."

Another volunteer on the phone shouted, "Thyroid in California has just vowed if he is elected he'll cut taxes by $180 billion."

Finchley shouted, "Put us down for $190 billion."

The man at the blackboard was erasing and writing as fast as he could.

"You got a lot of guts, Finchley," I said with admiration. "There aren't many people in this country who would promise the voters a $190 billion tax cut."

"Stick around," he said, studying the board. "You haven't seen anything yet. This whole election has to do with taxes. The guy who promises to cut them the most has to win."

A volunteer on a phone screamed, "An Arizona congressman has told a Rotary Club he will cut $200 billion out of the federal budget."

"I'll raise him 25," Finchley called out.

"You sure are cool. I've never seen a politician promise to give the taxpayers a $225 billion rebate."

"You have to be cool in this business," he said as he swallowed a tranquilizer. "When you're dealing in tax-cut futures you can't think of it as money. You have to think of it as votes. I'm prepared to match and raise any tax-relief promise made by any politician in this country."

"It seems to me you're trying to corner the tax-cut market. Isn't that illegal?"

"Not under Proposition 14. There is no limit on how much you can promise to cut taxes. Don't forget we're dealing in futures. No candidate has to deliver on his promises until after November."

A phone handler yelled out, "A Texas Democrat has just promised the Dallas Garden Club to cut taxes by $240 billion."

Everyone in the room looked at Finchley. He lit a cigarette and said calmly, "Put me down for 250."

We all stood on our chairs and cheered. It was the biggest tax-cut promise made by a candidate in American political history.

"Casey at the Bat"

NEWS ITEM—Judge rules that women reporters must be permitted in baseball locker rooms.

It seemed extremely rocky for the Mudville Nine that
    day;
They blew the game in Springfield on a stupid double
    play.
So when a girl reporter walked in their locker room
They decided to play ball with her to take away the
    gloom.

Cooney made the first pass, and he fell upon his face;
Burrows tried to sacrifice, but couldn't get to base.
Flynn was left in right field, and never got her name;
It looked as though poor Mudville would lose another
    game.

Then from the locker players went up a joyous yell;
It rumbled in the showers, it rattled in the dell.
It struck upon the saunas, and rebounded on the flat;
For Casey, Mighty Casey, was advancing to the bat.

There was ease in Casey's manner, a smile on Casey's
    face,
As he whispered to the lady, "Would you like to see my
    place?"
"Pas ce soir," the lady said, "and please take off your
    hat."
"That's no way to talk," Flynn said, "when Casey's up to
    bat."

She frowned in great displeasure, a hand upon her hip.
She stuck a mike in Casey's face and almost cut his lip.
"Strike One," the shortstop called out, as he doubled up and
    roared.
"Casey's swinging wildly and he hasn't even scored."

Casey dug his feet in as he made another pitch:
"Let's have a drink at your place and take away this itch."
"I have a date," the lady said, "so knock off all the chatter;
Tell me why you blew the game as Mudville's greatest
batter."

"Strike Two," the catcher shouted as he rolled upon the
floor.
Casey blushed with anger for he could not take much
more.
"I have a brand-new Caddy sitting in the parking lot."
The news hen shrugged her shoulders, "I guess that's all
you've got."

"Fraud!" cried Casey's teammates and the echo answered,
"Fraud!"
But a scornful look from Casey and the locker room was
awed.
They saw his face grow stern and cold, they saw his muscles
strain,
And they knew that Mighty Casey would not foul out
again.

"Look, honey," he said plaintively, "I'll talk about my
pain.
"Let's do it over pizzas and a bottle of champagne."
"I haven't time to mess around," the lovely girl cried
out.
"I've got to meet a deadline; that's what news is all
about."

The sneer was gone from Casey's lips, his teeth were
clenched in fear.
He put his arm around the girl—she socked him in the ear.
She took her mike and hit his hand, and kicked him in the
shin.
"Now tell me, when you get your breath, just why you
didn't win!"

Oh, somewhere in this favored land, the moon is shining
bright,

And girls are doing disco in pants that are too tight;
And somewhere men are laughing and drinking Guinness
   stout,
But there's no joy in Mudville—Mighty Casey just struck
   out.

When Not to Call the Doctor

Because medical costs are rising so fast, more and more people are diagnosing their own illnesses or, worse still, those of their friends. The government would do well to make a study of how these nonprofessional diagnoses are affecting the nation's health picture.

The other day I had a cold. It was just like the ones you see on television. I was sneezing, coughing and looking mournfully at my wife. I called my secretary at the office and said I wouldn't be in because I felt lousy.

"You must have one of those 'eight-hour things' that's going all around town," she said. "You'll feel perfectly well tomorrow."

Eight hours seemed to be a reasonable time to have a cold, and I was looking forward to staying in bed, particularly since the Yankees and Red Sox were playing a crucial game to get in the American League playoffs.

My sister called, and I told her I had one of those "eight-hour things that's been going all around."

"Are you sure it's only an 'eight-hour thing'?" she asked. "It could be the '24-hour bug.' Harold had it last week. Do you have any fever?"

"A little—maybe 100."

"That's the '24-hour bug' for sure. Drink lots of fluids and take aspirin, and you'll be able to shake it off."

I really hadn't counted on staying in bed for 24 hours, but it's stupid to fight a bug.

My other sister called up 10 minutes later. "Edith says you've got a '24-hour bug.'"

"I don't know if it's a bug or just a cold."

"Is your nose red from blowing it?"

"Yah, sure it is. Why do you ask?"

"Then you don't have a '24-hour bug.' You have a '48-hour virus.'"

"My secretary said all I had was an 'eight-hour thing.' How come you moved it up to 48 hours?"

"The 'eight-hour thing' is entirely different. You feel funny

58

but your nose doesn't get red when you blow it. The '24-hour bug' has all the symptoms of the 'eight-hour one,' except that you cough a lot. The '48-hour virus' makes you sneeze, cough and perspire while you're sleeping. You have to stay in bed for two days."

"But I can't stay in bed for two days!"

"Look," my sister said. "If you don't want medical advice, don't ask me."

I think I might have been all right except that my secretary told Healy I was home with the flu.

He called, of course, "I feel for you," he said. "You won't be able to shake it for two weeks. If it were a winter cold I'd say you'd be better in five, maybe six days. But you have an October cold. It's almost impossible to get rid of. You hear my voice? It's been like this since August."

"But suppose my cold goes away in 24 hours?"

"That's when it can become the most dangerous. You think it's gone away and then a week later you wake up and it's back with a vengeance. I'd rather have a two-week bout with a chest cold than a '24-hour bug' which sneaks up on you like a thief in the night."

Word travels fast in Washington, and Elfin of *Newsweek* was terse and to the point. "Healy tells me you have an incurable form of pneumonia."

"Either that," I said, "or an 'eight-hour thing' or a '24-hour bug' or a '48-hour virus' or a two-week bout with the flu or a simple cold. I'm waiting on another opinion right now."

"From whom?"

"My druggist. He says there's a lot of it going around."

"What's going around?"

"You name it, and he says he's never seen so much of it going around."

A Man for All Seasons

When it comes to watching TV sports, the last two weeks have been as tough as I can remember. Between college football on Saturday, the American and National League baseball playoffs, as well as the World Series, not to mention double-header pro games on Sunday, and *Monday Night Football,* the American sports fan has been glued in his chair for days on end.

The other night I dropped over to see McCloskey to watch a football game with him. He didn't recognize me when I walked in. His eyes were red and bulging out.

"McCloskey," I cried. "It's me. Are you all right?"

Mrs. McCloskey took me by the arm, out of earshot. "Don't worry, he doesn't recognize me either. He just sits there for hours staring at the set."

"Uhhhhhhhhhhhhhh," McCloskey groaned, waving his hand back and forth.

Mrs. McCloskey rushed to his side. "What is it, Phil? Do you want water? Is that what you want?"

"Uhhhhh," McCloskey said, nodding his head in the affirmative. Mrs. McCloskey rushed out to get him a glass of water. I sat down next to him. When the quarter was over and there was a commercial break, I said, "Well, Phil, how's it going?"

He looked annoyed that I had spoken.

Mrs. McCloskey returned with the glass of water.

"Don't be upset if he pretends he doesn't hear you. He hears what he wants to."

"When did he get this way?"

"I think it was during the third Yankee-Kansas City game. He just went into a TV coma and hasn't come out of it. I called the doctor, but he wouldn't come over because he said he didn't want to miss Oklahoma playing Texas. He told me to turn off the set and give him two aspirin. I tried to turn off the set but Phil became so violent, I had no choice but to turn it on again."

"Uhhhhhhhhhhhhhhhh," McCloskey said.

"What is it, Phil? What do you want?"

McCloskey. put his arms around his shoulders.

"You're cold, is that it? Here's a blanket. See, I'm wrapping it around you. Now isn't that better?"

McCloskey's head just drooped.

"He dozes off every once in a while," she told me. "But he never fails to wake up when something exciting is about to happen."

"This must be pretty tough on you," I said.

"The children and I take turns sitting with him. The doctor says once the World Series is over, he'll have only football to watch and he'll get better."

"Do you want me to go?" I asked.

"No, the doctor said it's good for him to be around people even if he refuses to speak to them."

"Uhhhhhhhhhhhhhhhh," McCloskey said.

"What's he saying?" I asked.

"He wants something to eat," Mrs. McCloskey said. "He always gets hungry when he sees a McDonald's commercial. Phil, don't go away. I'm bringing you a nice bowl of soup."

"Uhhhhhh."

"You want potato chips, too? It's coming right up. Keep an eye on him," Mrs. McCloskey said. "If he gets out of his chair, grab him. He hasn't been on his legs in two weeks."

Suddenly McCloskey turned to me and tried to say something. "What is it, Phil? Spit it out. What is it?"

He made a gesture for me to lean over so he could whisper in my ear. The words came out slowly, almost as a grunt, but they were clear. He said, "Cosell . . . talks . . . too . . . much."

No Time for the Godfather

The Godfather was in a very good mood when I kissed his ring. He invited me to sit down in his office and offered me a cigar.

"What can I do for you?" he asked. "You have any enemies you want me to take care of? Does your son need a job in Las Vegas? Would you like me to fix a horse race for you?"

"No, Godfather. You asked to see me."

"That's right," he said. "I don't remember as well as I used to. Let's see now. Oh, yeh. Tell me about Washington."

"It's okay, Godfather. No better or worse than usual."

"There's lots of crime down there now, huh?"

"Well, there seems to be more than usual. White-collar stuff. You know, federal employees ripping off the government; congressmen and senators taking money they shouldn't; contractors being accused of payoffs; not to mention the usual stuff of legitimate companies being indicted for violating every law in the book."

The Godfather said, "I imagine the FBI must be working day and night finding out who is doing what to whom down there."

"They're pretty busy, because every time a scandal breaks, the President or Congress asks the FBI to investigate. It gets them off the hook."

"That's what I figured," he said. "I was wondering why it was so quiet around here. My people said it was too quiet and something was up. But I said, 'Just read the papers. The Feds don't have time to fight organized crime. They got too much to do in Washington investigating their own people. They got nobody left to find out what we're up to.' "

"I think you're right, Godfather. I haven't heard one FBI man or Justice Department lawyer mention the mob since the Watergate scandal broke."

"I know I'm right. I used to have round-the-clock surveillance in front of my house. Four guys in a car at one time, and they took movies of everyone going in and out. Now there's one gumshoe comes on Thursdays and takes three Polaroid pictures, and you don't see him again for a month."

"Does it bother you, Godfather?"

"When you're in the big-time rackets you like to be taken seriously. The soldiers in the family are losing respect for me. They figure if the Feds aren't interested in what I'm up to, I can't be that important. How can I keep everyone in line if the Justice Department acts like I'm not a threat?"

"You have a good point," I said. "What can I do, God-father?"

"I want you to tell my boys—they only read the sports pages —why the Justice Department doesn't have time for people like us anymore. I want you to explain that there's so much stealing going on in Washington, all the resources of the FBI have been mobilized to root out corruption in the government. That's why they've put people like me on the back burner. Tell 'em that the Justice Department still considers me a menace to society, but they just don't have the legal talent to find out what I'm up to."

"I'll do it, Godfather. After all, it's the truth. There's just so many FBI agents to go around and they have to clean up their own backyard before they go picking on strangers."

"I want you to know I appreciate you doing this," the Godfather said. "I never forget a favor. Can I hijack a truckload of cigarettes for your wife?"

"Thank you, Godfather. But she just gave up smoking."

The Big Talk in Washington

Most people who live outside Washington are under the impression that the only two topics of conversation in this town are politics and government. This may have been true at one time, but it isn't anymore.

For a while the main topic was sex. But recently this subject has waned, and now all people talk about is the high cost of real estate.

I went to a party the other night and cornered an assistant secretary of state. "How did things go at Camp David?" I asked him.

"It was beautiful. My wife and I are thinking of buying a weekend retreat near Thurmont. It's 40 acres of farmland and they want $3,500 an acre."

"What about the talks? Do you think anything will come of them?"

"Oh, we talked to the bankers. They'll give us a mortgage at 10 percent, however we have to put 30 percent down. But it has a stream running right through it, and I'm told if I hold on to it for five years I'll double my money."

"Did you speak to Sadat and Begin?"

"What for? They don't know anything about real estate in Maryland."

I wandered over to a couple who were whispering and giggling. I thought there was some hanky-panky going on since he was a congressman and she was from the typing pool in HEW.

I strained my ears to hear what they were saying.

"So I figured after my divorce, I'd keep the home in Washington and give my wife the house in Georgia. She agreed. I didn't want the house in Washington so I put it up on the market, thinking I'd get $90,000. The first offer came in and it was $120,000. I was about to agree when I got the second offer for $145,000. Do you know what I finally sold the house for? One hundred and sixty thousand dollars."

You could tell the secretary was impressed. "Now I know why the people from your district elected you."

"Why don't we go to your place for a drink after the party?" the congressman said.

"I'd love to, but I live with four other girls. We pay $250 each a month and that doesn't include utilities."

"Well, my kids are staying with me at the Watergate in a two-bedroom flat which costs me $1,000 a month. As soon as I buy a condominium for $90,000 plus $450 maintenance, I'll give you a call."

I tried to get in on the conversation. "The house next to me just went on the market for $250,000 and it doesn't even have a finished basement."

The congressman took the girl by the arm and started to walk away. "I'm sorry," he said, "this is a private conversation."

I looked around the room and saw a Treasury official. "How far do you think the dollar will fall against the Japanese yen?" I asked him.

"It's hard to say. Frankly, I think it's bottomed out. A Japanese official with the World Bank looked at a house on our block in Cleveland Park, which was selling for $180,000, and he told the owner he couldn't afford it. When the Japanese start talking like that you know the yen is in trouble."

Driving home that night my wife said, "I sat next to the most fascinating man at dinner tonight and we had a marvelous talk."

"You were sitting next to Henry Kissinger."

"Not him; the man who was sitting on my left. He's a contractor and he's building 20 new townhouses on Chain Bridge Road."

Defectors Need Love, Too

As the conscience of America, I have been giving a lot of time and thought to recent events surrounding the Soviet defector Arkady Shevchenko and his paramour Judy Chavez.

While all the facts in the case have not been disclosed (we have to wait for Judy's and Arkady's books to get the rest of them), this much is agreed upon by everybody.

Shevchenko had a high position in the U.N. when he came over to our side. He met, or was given, as a reward, Miss Chavez, who worked for an "escort" service in Washington. He paid Miss Chavez $500 a night for her friendship, and spent between $35,000 and $40,000 on her for gifts and a trip to the Virgin Islands. He was known in the CIA as "the spy who was never cold."

The facts that are in dispute are whether Mr. Shevchenko paid for Miss Chavez' services out of his own pocket or whether they were paid for by the CIA to keep him happy and talking. If Arkady spent his own money, he was taken advantage of for being a foreigner. But if the CIA paid for the undercover operation, then the taxpayers have a right to ask some questions.

The first is: Why on earth was the CIA paying Miss Chavez $500 a night when the going rate in the intelligence business for this sort of thing is $100? If Arkady was paying for it, why didn't someone in the FBI or CIA warn him that he was being overcharged for Miss Chavez's nightly companionship?

If the CIA is footing the bill, as Miss Chavez claims, it means there is a serious lack of cost control in the agency when it comes to providing escorts for Soviet defectors.

No loyal American would take issue with the fact that a high-ranking Soviet official who wants to come over should get anything he wants from the CIA in exchange for intelligence secrets.

But when you start paying outrageous prices for close encounters of this kind, you are not only contributing, as President Carter said at his press conference, to inflation but you are setting a precedent for other Soviet defectors which the United States can ill afford.

The next defector will also expect a $500-a-night female companion, and if she is paid less he will feel that the CIA is not treating him with the same respect they did Arkady. How many "escorts" can our intelligence agency supply at these rates before it starts shortchanging our other spy operations?

Even if the CIA can afford it, other friendly intelligence organizations are furious about the publicity given to the Shevchenko-Chavez affairs.

"We've never paid our girls more than $50 a night," a French intelligence agent told me. "This puts every Western intelligence agency on the spot. The CIA has made the price of sex so high, we may not be able to use it any more as the ultimate weapon."

An Israeli agent thought Arkady was a KGB plant. "What better way to break the CIA budget than to have a defector demand a woman with expensive tastes, a yen for beautiful cars and a desire to make love in beautiful resorts. We could have put up a spy satellite for what it cost the Americans to keep Arkady talking."

Because of all the publicity, the CIA must now give Shevchenko a new cover and move him to a safer city than Washington.

I suggest Cleveland. It is not only a nice place to live, but the going rate there for an "escort" is $35 a night including taxi fare. Making Arkady live in Cleveland while they debriefed him would certainly save the CIA a lot of money.

Consumers Beware

The Washington Gas Light Co. just announced that it was seeking permission to impose new charges ranging from $7.80 to $14 a month on customers who cut their gas consumption significantly by substituting for it electricity or some other form of energy.

Companies around the country that supply electricity have warned people that if they conserve too much electricity their rates will also have to go up; and during California's drought last year the water companies raised rates on customers because they were not using enough water.

What is dawning on people of this country is that conservation may not guarantee anyone cheaper utility bills.

* * *

The Antrobus family was sitting around the living room during a freeze in 1989. They had all their clothes on but were still frozen. Mr. Antrobus had thrown most of the dining room furniture into the fireplace when there was a ring at the door.

It was the man from the gas company:

"Mr. Antrobus, I see you're heating your house by furniture instead of gas. We'll have to add an additional $50 to your bill."

"But we can't afford to heat with gas ever since they took the controls off. We have to conserve every cubic inch we can."

"That is not our problem, Mr. Antrobus. We're willing to provide you with gas at a price. If you don't buy it, it costs us money. We're not in the energy business for our health."

Mr. Antrobus threw a table into the fireplace.

"But we need gas for cooking, not for heating our home. We can't afford both."

"Then you'll have to pay for it. We don't like consumers who just want to cook with gas, but prefer to heat by burning their tables in the fireplace. I'm sure an extra $50 surcharge is not out of line."

"I guess not," said Mr. Antrobus wearily. "Would you give

me a hand with this dresser? The top is Formica and won't burn."

The gas man left by the front door. A few minutes later the man from the electricity company came in the back one.

"Why is everyone reading by candles?" he wanted to know.

"We're trying to save on electricity," Mrs. Antrobus said. "This is supposed to be the worst winter in years, and we need what little electricity we can afford for the television set."

"Our reports indicate you've only used a third of the amount of electricity you used three years ago."

"Yes, sir. We've been very careful. We never put on a light unless we have to."

"We'll have to charge you an extra $100 a month."

"Is that a surcharge?"

"No, that's a fine. Anyone who uses less than half the amount of electricity he used in a previous year is subject to a $100 fine and six months in prison. In your case the fine will be sufficient warning. But watch yourselves because we're keeping files on you." He exited.

"This conservation is really costing us," Mrs. Antrobus said.

"It's still cheaper to burn the furniture than to pay the gas bills," Mr. Antrobus told her.

There was a knock on the door. It was a man from the Washington Furniture Energy Co. He said, "I regret to inform you that we will have to raise the price of furniture you are burning by $18 a chair."

"But why? We're using everything we can burn."

"So is everybody else. At this rate, all the furniture in the country will be used up by 1995 and we will be unable to supply our customers. We hope that by raising our rates, people like you will give some thought to conserving furniture, which is the country's last valuable energy source."

"The hell with it," Mr. Antrobus said to his wife. "Let's go back to gas."

"If you do," warned the furniture man, "we'll have to charge you extra for it."

The Liberated Woman

This is the story of a liberated woman who is sorry she became liberated. Her name for this article will be Ghiselda Manifesto.

She is a friend of mine and as far as I know she is as happily married as most people are these days. She doesn't have to work but decided that when her children went off into the world to find themselves she would get her degree and become a lawyer.

She did. She was accepted by a law firm and is now working for Blah, Blah, Objection & Sustained.

I saw her the other day at lunch.

"How's your tennis?" I asked her.

"I don't have time for tennis anymore. In fact I don't have time for anything."

"But you loved tennis," I said.

"I loved drinking coffee and watching soap operas, too. But now that I'm a liberated woman I can't do that either."

"I don't understand it. It seems like only yesterday you were telling me how wonderful it would be to get out in the give-and-take of the real world. You dreamed of becoming a lawyer and being somebody in your own right."

"Yes," she said, "but I didn't think it would mean giving up the King Tut exhibit at the National Gallery."

"You missed the King Tut exhibit?" I tried to keep the shock out of my voice.

"I was in court every day trying to keep the FCC from taking a radio station away from somebody in Hoboken, New Jersey."

"I guess the thrill of being a lawyer wears off very fast."

"Do you know what my dream in life is now that I'm a liberated woman?" she asked.

"I can't guess."

"To see a matinee of *Hello, Dolly* with Carol Channing."

"Why can't you go in the evening to see it with Charlie? Is he too tired?"

"I'm too tired. When I get home I just want to sit in a chair and drink a glass of white wine and watch the evening news."

"Why can't you?"

"I have to do the shopping at the supermarket on my way home, and then make dinner, and then do the dishes and clean up the house. I may be a liberated woman to the world, but I'm still 'good old Ghiselda' to Charlie, 'the best little woman a man could have.' "

"But isn't Charlie proud of the fact that you're a lawyer and a person in your own right?"

"Oh sure. He tells everyone: 'Meet my wife, she's a lawyer and makes $40,000 a year and she still has time to cook, clean, do exercises, take vitamins and Geritol every day.' Then he kisses me on the cheek and says just as they do in the commercials, 'My wife, I think I'll keep her.' "

"That's tender," I said.

"You want to hear of another fantasy I have?" she said.

"Sure."

"I pretend it's 10 o'clock in the morning and Gloria calls me up and says, 'Let's go over to Neiman-Marcus and try on every suit they have hanging in the store. And then let's go to lunch and tell terrible things about everyone we know.' "

"That's a nice fantasy," I admitted. "I guess it will never be, but at least you're not bored now."

"Have you ever tried to write a brief defending a gas line company in an anti-trust suit? If you think waxing floors is drudgery, spend a day in a law library sometimes."

"Gosh, I thought liberated women had the best of both worlds—ego-massaged all day long and cuddled at night."

"You've got it all wrong. No one massages a liberated woman in the daytime because he thinks he'll be patronizing her. And when she comes home at night the husband figures he's doing such a nice thing by letting her work that he doesn't have to cuddle her."

"What about joining a women's bowling league on Thursday?" I finally suggested.

She paid her half of the check and left in a huff.

To Have or Have Not

The meanest thing about inflation is that it is making so many HAVES into HAVE NOTS. How does one distinguish between a HAVE and a HAVE NOT? It's done by a federal bureau in Washington, which sends you a registered letter when your standard of living falls below that of everyone else around you. If you are officially designated a HAVE NOT you are eligible for all sorts of government benefits, though your credit rating in the private sector is marked "deadbeat."

I went to the Bureau of Haves and Have Nots to talk to an official who was keeping score.

He was at his desk, with a large stack of files, stamping HAVE or HAVE NOT on the top of each folder.

"This must be tough work. It can't be much fun making a HAVE into a HAVE NOT."

"I don't make them into HAVE NOTS. Inflation does that. For example, look at this file. This family makes $18,000 a year; they have a small house and a car. A few years ago there was no question that they belonged to the HAVES in the country. But now they must be considered part of the HAVE NOTS. They're just not making it anymore."

"But why?" I asked.

"They're living over their heads to keep up with the Joneses. The ironic part of it is that the Joneses are living over their heads to keep ahead of these people, and therefore we had to put the Joneses in the HAVE NOT pile as well."

"The Joneses are also HAVE NOTS?" I said, shocked.

"That is correct. When you get into double-digit inflation you'd be surprised how fast HAVES become HAVE NOTS.

"This fellow here had all his money invested in the stock market. In one month he became a HAVE NOT—and so, by the way, did his broker."

"How long has your bureau been in existence?"

"It started during the Roosevelt era when a majority of the people were HAVE NOTS, and the HAVES could be counted on your fingers. Then World War II came, and the HAVE NOTS were determined to come back from the armed forces and become HAVES. They did, by going to school and working their tails off. Many moved to the suburbs where they thought they had found The American Dream. But although they were HAVES in other people's eyes, in their hearts they were HAVE NOTS, because they were always afraid someone would take everything they had away from them.

"The post-World War II HAVES decided that because they were originally HAVE NOTS, their children would lack nothing. So the kids were raised as first generation HAVES, and didn't know what it was like to do without. It ruined a lot of them, and I've heard many HAVE parents say that if they had to do it all over again they would raise their children as HAVE NOTS."

"Apparently, from your HAVE NOT pile of folders, many of them will soon have the opportunity."

The official said, "The problem is that a lot of HAVES could remain HAVES if they just weren't so worried about what other HAVES think about how they live."

"Do you find many HAVE NOTS becoming HAVES?"

"All the time. I would say more than 50 percent of the children of HAVE NOTS in this country eventually wind up as HAVES."

"What do you do with all the folders after you mark them?"

"We tally them and send the figures out to every politician in the country. At the moment the pols are still aiming all their rhetoric at the HAVES—but if inflation keeps making many more HAVE NOTS, you'll be surprised how fast the politicians change their tune."

Cheap Fares

The airlines are trying to make it up to people who have to pay more for flying in coach than those who fly on special thrift rates.

A barrage of newspaper, magazine and TV commercials are now informing us that the airlines really "revere" their "full-fare" passengers, and are making sure they get treated better than those on discount fares.

For one thing, the people who pay full coach fare will be seated in the middle of the plane just behind those in first class. The discount passengers will be placed in the rear of the craft where no one can see them.

Coach passengers will have their own check-in lines and presumably first crack at the plane's free magazines.

The reason for the sudden decision to advertise the advantages of full fare, as opposed to discount, is that the airlines have had a backlash from businessmen who travel all the time and feel they're being taken for a ride. No one likes to sit next to a person who has paid 30 to 40 percent less to go to the same place and arrive at the same time.

I believe the airlines will have to do more than just seat the discount people in the back of the plane to placate the people who pay full fare. Stronger measures must be taken.

I foresee in the not too distant future that, after the coach passenger has been seated in the middle of the plane, the discount passengers will be loaded on board in leg irons. They will be driven to the back of the aircraft by a giant black-bearded man who is stripped to the waist and cracking a long whip.

Once in the back, they will be shoved down on wooden slats and chained to the bulkhead. The man with the beard will be their steward. He will walk up and down the thrift section aisle shouting, "All right, you scurvy. There will be absolute silence in this section of the plane. Anyone who opens his mouth will get a taste of the whip on his worthless tourist back.

"Now this is the drill. Because we are flying over water part of the time, pay attention to these safety precautions. In case of the unlikely event of an emergency, a saw will be lowered from above you so that you can file off your leg irons and the chains on your wrists. There are emergency exits in the front of the plane. They may not be used until you pay a surcharge of $40.

"Once we are in the air we will be serving a delicious meal to passengers up front, consisting of vichyssoise, roast duckling with orange sauce, wild rice with raisins, and a Château Mouton Rothschild, 1969. As for you riffraff back here, we will pass around this wooden bucket of watery gruel, which the trusty will put in your slop bowls.

"Each passenger will be offered a choice of coffee, tea or milk. If he doesn't guess the right one, he will be hung by his thumbs from the luggage rack. One more thing, if any of you are planning to escape into coach class—forget it.

"This 747 has a snake-filled moat separating the cabins.

"All right, you miserable wretches. We're ready for takeoff. Are there any questions?"

"Sir, what is the movie playing today?"

CRACKKKKKKK!!!!!!!! "Take that, you penny-pinching cur. No one is entitled to a movie in discount class. Where the hell do you think you are—on some kind of vacation?"

Anyone for Civil Defense?

I have good news for all of you who were wondering how you were going to survive World War III. President Carter has a plan. At last he's given the go-ahead to the civil defense people in the government to come up with a plan, which would protect 140 million Americans in the event of a Soviet nuclear attack.

The cost of *designing* the plan (as opposed to the plan itself) is $2 billion, and unlike previous civil defense ideas, this one does not include building bomb shelters. Instead the emphasis will be on evacuating people from the large cities to the countryside as soon as hostilities begin.

This is not a joke—this is not a drill—this is a real, bona fide plan which the President is asking Congress to finance.

According to Pentagon experts, all the U.S. would need is warning of a Soviet missile attack, and it would then put its evacuation plan into effect. The success of the program would depend, of course, on how fast we could move everybody out of the cities, presumably by automobile and bus. The Pentagon says we need the plan in the worst way because the Soviets are going ahead with their civil defense plans, and we must maintain a "crisis stability" with them. This means that if the Soviets *thought* we could survive an attack by them, they wouldn't dare to try to kill us.

Okay. But before we spend $2 billion on an evacuation feasibility study, I have one favor to ask of the President. And that is, the next time he decides to spend a weekend at Camp David in the Maryland mountains, he go by car instead of by helicopter.

As soon as the President nears the Beltway surrounding Washington, he will realize that there is absolutely no way of getting out of the city on a Friday night, much less if we have a real live nuclear alert.

The truth of the matter is the Soviets know that we could do more damage to ourselves through civil defense than they could ever do by starting a war.

This is the scenario that the Russians have planned for us:

They aim a series of dummy missiles, with condemned Pintos as warheads, at the major cities in the U.S. We go on red alert and the sirens start whining, ordering everybody to leave at once.

People pile into cars, taxis and trucks and head for the outskirts of town. The Pintos are pinpointed to land on the arteries to every major expressway, tying up traffic for miles.

The panic-stricken city dwellers jump out of their cars and start beating up the people in the vehicles in front of them. Other drivers attempt to push stalled autos off the road. Still others start running across the roofs of the cars to get away from what they believe are mushroom clouds, which are really autos that have overheated.

Under present American driving conditions, it is my belief that the Soviets could do more damage with 100 Pintos than they could with 100 nuclear warheads.

Therefore, before the President tells Congress that civil defense is the moral equivalent of war, I urge him to get behind the wheel of Billy's pickup truck, and drive from the White House to Alexandria, Virginia, during rush hour. If he can make it in less than an hour, I'll give him the $2 billion out of my own pocket.

Hyping the Shows

In case you haven't noticed, the networks are spending more and more time plugging their future shows and less time telling you what is going on at the moment. Anyone who has watched a televised football game is conscious of how sports announcers are forced to hype other network programs that have nothing to do with the game.

"Fourth down and a yard to go. Dallas has decided to try a 52-yard field goal. If they succeed they will tie the score."

"Fred, there's beautiful Rachel Carberry of the HYP network's smash series, *Ripoff from Star Wars*. I hear next Thursday's episode is a dilly of a show."

"You heard right, Harold. What time is it on?"

"Eight o'clock in the East and West, and seven Central time."

"The Redskins have called time out to give the Dallas kicker more time to think about the field goal."

"Well, if they want to think about something, I might remind the Cowboys that next Saturday HYP Sports will bring you live, on most of these stations, the Orange Bowl Demolition Derby, the Grand Prix grudge car racing match between Paul Newman and Dolly Parton."

"I wouldn't miss that, Dave. Now back to live action."

"There goes a penalty flag. Dallas has taken too long in the huddle."

"Speaking of huddles, Fred, on Friday evening, three weeks from tonight, Charlie's Angels get themselves into a huddle and have to be rescued by Bill Cosby. It's all in fun right here on HYP."

"I'm going to stay home that night, Harold."

"Where are we now, Fred?"

"I think Dallas is ready to try for a field goal from their own 43."

"While the holder of the ball is getting into position, Fred, let's go down on the field and talk to Sam Francisco, who plays the private eye in *Golden Gate, Don't Be Late*."

"Sam, I hear your next show has to do with a race horse who tries to jump off the bridge."

"That's right, Harold. He's despondent because his jockey is riding another horse in the Kentucky Derby, and he decides he has nothing to live for."

"Well, lots of luck, Sam. All of us will be watching *Golden Gate, Don't Be Late*. Now back to Fred."

"Harold, while you were talking to Sam, Dallas made the field goal and then kicked off to the Redskins' Tony Green, who ran 90 yards for a touchdown. Moseley got the extra point, and the Redskins then tried an onside kick which Dallas recovered. It's third down and four to go on the Skins' 12-yard line."

"Fred, before Dallas scores, or loses the ball, I think we should remind everyone that HYP network's presidential election coverage is only two years away, and we advise everyone to stay tuned to this station for complete up-to-the-minute results by the best political reporters in the business. We have spared no expense to bring you the most exciting election night ever."

"Back to you, Fred."

"There's an injured man on the field. Dave, you were telling me about a mini-series you're appearing on in 1981."

"It's sort of a white man's version of *Roots*. I play a slave owner who goes back to England to discover where my ancestors came from, and what got us into slavery in the first place. I find an old man, who lives in Yorkshire, who remembers my grandfather as the biggest bigot in the county."

"We won't miss that, will we, Harold?"

"It depends on whether we have a football game or not, Fred. And speaking of football, what's the score of this game?"

"I have no idea, but next week's contest between Oakland and Pittsburgh should be a beaut."

"Not to mention the show that precedes it, *King Tut Meets the Incredible Hulk*."

"So it's good night from all of us here in Dallas. See you in Pittsburgh next week, or if you can't make it then be sure to be with us on January 12, 1980, for the Lake Placid Winter Olympics."

Garage Sale

NEW YORK—It started off as a joke. What would happen if Europeans, Japanese and OPEC-rich zillionaires decided to buy up everything they could get their hands on in the United States? But no one is laughing anymore.

The United States is now holding a garage sale for the rest of the world. I hadn't realized how serious it was until I met a friend of mine from Paris named Alain at the Pierre Hotel. We embraced, kissed on both cheeks and headed for the bar. Alain owns a grocery store in Paris and I assumed he was in the United States to replenish his shelves with Kellogg's Corn Flakes.

But when I asked about it he was uncertain. "I don't know whether to buy Kellogg's Corn Flakes or Post Toasties."

"They're both very good," I said. "Of course I also like a bowl of shredded wheat once in a while."

"I don't want to buy a bowl. I want to buy the company."

"The company?"

"Of course," he chuckled. "Why do you think I am in the United States?"

He showed me the valise full of Eurodollars he was carrying.

"Don't they remind you of Kleenex?" he asked.

"What a thing to say about the American dollar, Alain!"

"That's what you Americans used to say about the French franc."

"It was a joke," I protested. "Can't you let bygones be bygones?"

"All right," Alain said agreeably. "You see those Japanese businessmen over there? I heard them talking in the elevator. The little fellow with the Nikon camera just bought some land in New York."

"How many feet?" I asked.

"I'm not sure. I think he said it was 60th Street to 83rd Street on Park Avenue. How many feet would that be?"

"Both sides of Park Avenue?" I asked.

"Of course. He had to protect himself from any Arabs moving across the street."

I ordered a rum and Coca-Cola.

"A Swiss friend of mine is thinking about buying the Coca-Cola Co. Do you think it's worth the trouble?" Alain asked.

"It's not a bad company if you like Atlanta. Of course, if he bought Pepsi-Cola he could live in Greenwich, Connecticut," I said.

"He doesn't want to live over here," Alain said. "He just wants to own something so that when he comes on a pleasure trip he can say it was a business trip and deduct his expenses."

"I see," I said. "Were you thinking of buying anything besides an American cereal company?"

"Well, I'm not going out looking, if that's what you mean. But if my wife takes a fancy to something, as she did the other day, I'm not going to tell her no."

"What did she want you to buy for her the other day?"

"Central Park," he said.

"I didn't know it was for sale."

"Neither did I. The negotiations were very tricky. First, I bought up the New York subway system, very quietly, through a Nassau Island bank. Then I went to Mayor Koch and offered to give him back the subway system in exchange for the World Trade Center. He made the deal. I then went to the World Trade Center people and threatened to tear down both buildings and make a park out of it unless they could find something decent for me. They finally came up with Central Park."

"But Central Park doesn't produce any income," I said.

"Who needs income? The only reason we're buying over here is to get our money out of Europe."

"Now wait a minute, Alain. I don't understand this. You Europeans have been attacking the U.S. dollar for several years because you say you have no faith in it. Why put funds into America if you don't believe in our economy?"

"Because, dummy, the only safe country in the world for a foreigner to invest his money in is the United States," he replied.

Alain called for the check in the bar. As he signed it, he asked, "What's a decent tip for the waiter when you own the hotel?"

What Would You Do?

I believe it's time to do my Woody Hayes' think piece. For a week now, sports pundits, editorial writers and television commentators have been discussing one of the major issues of our time; that is whether Woody Hayes, coach of the Ohio State football team, should have been fired for slugging a Clemson University player in the Gator Bowl last week.

The incident, which is now considered comparable to Gen. Patton hitting a GI in the face during a tour of a hospital in World War II, has ramifications far greater than football. It makes us all ask ourselves, "Whither America's will to win?"

First, the undisputed facts. Ohio State was playing Clemson in the Gator Bowl at Jacksonville, Florida. The Ohio team was losing with 15 points to Clemson's 17. There was one minute and 58 seconds to play. Ohio State had a chance to score. Its quarterback threw a pass, which was intercepted by the Clemson guard, Charley Bauman, who was knocked out of bounds a few feet from coach Hayes on the sidelines. Woody was so furious at the interception that he hit Bauman in the face. Woody wanted to continue the fight but was separated by his own players. The next morning Hayes was fired.

All right, now let's face the tough question. Did Hayes have the right to slug the Clemson guard?

I say the answer to the question is an unequivocal yes.

Let's put ourselves in Woody Hayes' shoes for just a moment. His team is playing in the Gator Bowl, which is in itself a comedown for the Buckeyes, who usually wind up in the Rose, Sugar or Cotton Bowls. The opposition, Clemson, a school with one-tenth the student body of Ohio State, is kicking the hip pads out of the Hayes-coached team. With less than two minutes to go, Hayes' boys have a chance to get in field goal range and win the game.

Then Clemson guard Bauman spoils everything. The Ohio State quarterback throws a pass, Bauman gets in the way and grabs it, thus ending the Buckeyes' chance of winning the game.

If you were the coach of Ohio State, and one of the

opposition players snatched victory from your team, would you just stand on the sidelines and do NOTHING? Of course you wouldn't. Your first instinct would be to hit the player who stole your ball. This is what Woody Hayes did.

He didn't do it for himself. He did it for everyone who loves the American game of football. He showed the country on nationwide television that law and order on the gridiron still prevail, and when a kid steals a pass, he's going to pay for it.

It's a coach's job to do everything in his power to win. If this means hitting a player on the other team—so be it. Some say Bauman, the Clemson guard, was the victim of the Hayes attack. I say he invited the slugging match. Bauman knew the pass wasn't for him. He knew it was thrown to an Ohio State receiver. He had no right to get in the way of it, and even less right to catch it and run in the opposite direction.

Unless we are willing to see college football go down the drain, all of us are going to have to speak up and reiterate what American coaches have been telling their players for years, WINNING IS EVERYTHING. If we don't allow coaches to slug players on the other team, then there is no sense suiting our kids up to play the game. Hayes' hit in the mouth might have been the best thing to happen to Bauman, who I am certain will think twice before he ever steals a pass again.

Nobody Knew

The question President Carter and everybody else in Washington keeps asking is, "How is it possible that no one knew the Shah of Iran was in trouble?"

It's hard to get an answer.

Over at the Pentagon, I spoke to someone in sales.

"What can I tell you?" the sales manager said. "We checked out his credit and it was good. He ordered more airplanes, tanks, guns and rockets than any shah in the world. He never haggled about price, and he bought everything in our catalogue, whether he needed it or not. When it came to American military hardware he was the last of the big spenders."

"So you had no idea he was in over his head?"

"Look, a guy comes into the Pentagon showroom and there's oil spilling out of every one of his pockets. No one asks any questions. The guy's eyes light up when he sees a helicopter, so you sell him all the helicopters he wants. He picks up an F-16 fighter plane and doesn't even ask for it to be gift-wrapped. He takes all the tanks we have in stock. He orders boats and submarines by the dozen. If someone came in your shop and did that, would you suspect he was having trouble at home?"

"Probably not," I said. "Let me ask you this. What happens if Iran won't pay for the stuff that the Shah ordered?"

"We're going to bill the CIA. They should have warned us there was something rotten in Tehran."

I went over to the CIA and spoke to one of the guards at the gate. "The military says the CIA is responsible for them having to hold a garage sale on all the stuff the Shah of Iran bought and can't pay for. What do you have to say to that?"

"It's not the CIA's job to butt into another country's business," he said indignantly. "The Shah has been our friend for 20 years, and when he told us everything was hunky-dory, we took his word for it."

"So you didn't do any cloak and dagger work in Iran?"

"That would have been violating the Shah's sovereignty. What kind of people do you think we have working here?"

"But I thought the CIA's main function was to keep the President informed on what was going on in every country of the world. Why weren't you watching Iran?"

"Because we had to cut back on personnel. Our director, Stansfield Turner, lopped off 800 heads when he took over so we can no longer keep track of every backwater place on the globe. We've only got one agent in all of Africa."

"Iran isn't in Africa," I said.

"It isn't? Well, then, that explains why we didn't know, doesn't it?"

My last stop was the State Department. I asked for the Iranian desk.

"He's out to lunch," the receptionist said.

"Perhaps you can help me," I said. "I was wondering if you could explain why the State Department had no idea that the Shah of Iran was on such thin ice with his people?"

"I don't think the State Department is the place to discuss personalities," she replied.

"I appreciate that. But wasn't State aware of the opposition in the streets?"

"Our people never went into the streets," she said.

"Why not?"

"Because it was a lot more fun going to the palace."

Putting Seattle on Hold

The telephone company has the image of being staid and old-fashioned. But Ma Bell can no longer be accused of sitting back and waiting for someone to deposit 20 cents into the phone box.

They're after business and, by gosh, they're getting it.

Here is a good example of how a giant company is creating new markets never dreamed of before.

Out in Seattle, Washington, the Pacific Northwest Bell Co. ran ads in both Seattle papers a few weeks before Christmas telling children they could speak to Santa Claus by dialing the number in the ad. It was a great idea and one that would warm the heart of any parent. The only trouble was the area code to be dialed was 212, which is New York City.

Many parents in the Seattle area thought this was dirty pool and that if the Pacific Northwest Bell really cared about Christmas they would have listed a local number where Santa could be reached.

But Jim Moznette, a PNB spokesman, said the telephone company was trying to encourage long-distance calls and that if Santa Claus could be reached in Seattle by Seattle children it would not be worth the phone company's time.

He was quoted as saying, "We're a commercial enterprise and one of our main sources of revenue is long-distance calls. The ad was run to see if people would make calls and to generate enough long-distance revenues to make some profit to boot."

According to reports, 15,000 to 20,000 children made the calls and heard a one-minute recording from Santa. But there was such a flap about it from Seattle parents that the FTC regional director suggested PNB refund the cost of the calls. The phone company thought this was a stupid idea, and said they were willing to discuss refunds with parents but only on a "case by case" basis.

As a stockholder in the telephone company I am delighted that it is finally putting some imagination into increasing the use of its equipment. The idea of having kids call Santa Claus long distance is just the beginning.

I can see the day when Boston children will be urged to telephone the Easter Bunny in Hawaii, and Atlanta tikes will be induced to dial Anchorage, Alaska, to hear a message from the tooth fairy.

Further possibilities are long-distance calls to *The Daily Planet*, Area Code 416 (Toronto, Canada), which would give a child in New Orleans a chance to chat with Superman, and Salt Lake City children could phone London, England, to listen to a recorded message from the Queen.

The beauty of encouraging children to call long distance is that, while the cost of the minute may be relatively cheap, most kids tend to hang on much longer in the hopes that Santa Claus or whoever is on the other end will have more to say. I've seen six- and seven-year-olds hold the phone to their ear for 10 minutes, utterly fascinated by whatever is being said at the other end of the line. While the idea of dialing New York from Seattle may not be a big deal for an adult, it's still a thrill for a little kid, and it means money in the bank for the phone company.

No one knows who the genius was at Pacific Northwest Bell who thought up the idea of getting kids to call Santa long distance, but I sincerely hope that the person involved gets the recognition he or she so richly deserves.

Alexander Graham Bell invented the telephone but he never appreciated the commercial potentiality of his device. It took someone from the cold reaches of the Northwest to plant Santa Claus in New York City, and then urge youngsters to get on the blower and call him from Seattle. If the phone people can get pre-school children into the habit of dialing long distance, they will generate a fantastic new market that has never been tapped before.

"He Didn't Watch the Game"

A bunch of us were standing around the bar on Monday talking about Super Bowl Sunday, and what a dandy day it had been. We all had that warm feeling you get when you have shared a great common experience. I was telling everyone how I had watched the game on a large super screen which my friend Stevens had bought just for the occasion. Next to being at the game itself, this gave me quite a bit of clout.

I noticed that the only one who wasn't enjoying the scene was Apple. With good humor I said, "Where did you see the Super Bowl, Apple?"

"I didn't," he replied.

There was a hush in the bar.

"Did someone die in your family?" Nelson asked.

"No," Apple said.

"I know," Bailey interjected, "you were on an airplane, flying back from a business trip."

Apple shook his head. "I wasn't on an airplane and no one died in my family and no one got sick. I was home."

"Your television set was broken?" someone suggested.

"My television set was perfect. As a matter of fact, my wife and I watched *To Kill a Mockingbird* with Gregory Peck. It was an excellent movie."

"What were you doing watching a movie instead of the Super Bowl?" I wanted to know.

"I don't believe in the Super Bowl," Apple replied, "and neither does my wife."

Ogilvy slammed down his beer. "What the hell do you mean —you don't believe in the Super Bowl? Are you some kind of atheist nut or something?"

Apple was really cool. "I believe in God, but I don't believe in football."

I thought Woodstock was going to slug him. "Super Bowl Sunday is the holiest day of the year. One hundred million Americans observe it, believe in it, live for it. And you're trying to say it don't do nothing to you?"

"It may have religious significance for some people. But it

doesn't have meaning for my family. I have no objection to other folks believing that the day has some super power as long as they don't try to inflict their beliefs on me."

The bar was tensing up. I tried to be the peacemaker.

"Apple may have a point," I said. "After all, what makes America the greatest country in the world is not that you have to watch 'The Game,' but that you DON'T have to watch it if you don't want to."

"If you don't like it here," Ogilvy spat out at Apple, "why don't you go back where you came from?"

"Ogilvy's right," Nelson said. "Millions of dollars were spent to give us the Super Bowl. The two greatest teams in American football played their hearts out, and many fell on the field of combat.

"They put on a half-time show that would put the Roman circuses to shame. American advertisers spent every nickel they had to bring us a day we will remember for the rest of our lives. Only a pervert would be tuned in to *To Kill a Mockingbird*."

"I'm sorry you all feel this way," Apple said, "but we do have separation of state and sports in this country. Besides, I believe the Super Bowl has been hyped up to the point where it has lost all sportsmanlike meaning. It is now nothing but junk food."

I wish Apple hadn't said that. But our lawyers tell us that, no matter how much Apple sues us for assaulting him, no jury of 12 just men is going to award him a dime when they find out he doesn't believe in Super Bowl Sunday.

"You're a Winner!"

It seems every time the mailman comes he delivers another large envelope addressed to me announcing that I have either won a GIANT SWEEPSTAKES, or have a CHANCE of winning one if I will just open the letter.

I want you to know that these are not pieces of impersonal junk mail. They are addressed "Dear Art and Ann," and go something like this: "We're happy to inform you that you have almost won a $150,000 solar home, $20,000 a year for life, a three-month cruise around the world or a Gillette double-edged razor. You do not have to do anything to win one of these prizes except subscribe to *Drowning* magazine, the new bimonthly publication devoted to people who can't swim. Even if you don't subscribe to our magazine you have an opportunity to participate in a drawing for an all-day trip up the Amazon (air fare not included) or a portable screwdriver with your initials on it.

"This is how you can win: Rub the blank white square below. If a buffalo appears in the space, then you are one of the really lucky ones who may be moving into your new solar-heated $150,000 house next month. If a turkey shows up your name automatically goes into a box for the $20,000-a-year for life annuity. If no animal appears in the white space YOU HAVE NOT LOST. You are eligible for an oil change at the gasoline station of your choice.

"Wait, there's more. Because we believe *Drowning* magazine will not only appeal to your desire to learn more about what happens when you sink to the bottom of the sea, we are offering the first one million subscribers a chance to win 1,000 gold-minted coins dredged up from a Spanish galleon which sank off the coast of Florida in 1665. These coins are practically yours if you act NOW.

"Art and Ann, I'll be very hurt if I don't hear from you this week.

"Love,

"Judy Hammer"

I must admit that even I get sucked in by this kind of mail, and my wife also gets very excited the day a sweepstakes letter arrives.

The other afternoon when I came home she couldn't contain herself. "We've just won a three-year-old race horse," she said hugging me, "and it will probably win the Kentucky Derby."

"What do we have to do for it?" I wanted to know.

"Nothing," she said, "but take out a health and accident policy which will guarantee us $10 a day for 12 days in any city-owned hospital in the country."

"And for that we get a race horse?"

"We do if our insurance policy number matches the winning number of the Irish Sweepstakes."

"I'm not sure I want a horse," I said. "If he wins the Kentucky Derby the sportswriters won't give us any peace."

She went through some other letters. "All right, then, how would you like a 707 Boeing jet with leather seats designed by Gucci?"

"That sounds more like it. How do we win that?"

"I'm not sure. All the letter says is 'Dear Art and Ann, You have won a 707 Boeing jet airplane. Please fill out this card and enclose $29.50 for luggage tags. These tags will be placed in a computer, and if your tag is selected the Boeing will be delivered to your hangar or any airline terminal gate that you specify. All cards with checks must be in no later than March 1st.'"

"I don't see how the sweepstakes mailers do it," I said. "They give so much and ask so little in return."

My wife agreed. "And people say there is no such thing as The American Dream."

The Soft Underbelly

There has been a great deal of recrimination over the change of governments in Iran. One of the biggest questions being asked is why no one in this town knew the Shah was in trouble. Some of the credit for this must go to Ambassador Ardeshir Zahedi, and Washington's unquenchable appetite for good caviar.

Before it is published by the new regime at the Iranian Embassy, I wish to confess that my wife and I were on Ambassador Zahedi's special caviar list, which meant that every Christmas Eve we would find a nice plump can of it on our doorstep when we went out to light the Christmas tree. The first time there was no message with the can except for a card attached, which said, LONG LIVE THE SHAH.

"I wonder who it's from?" my wife asked.

"It beats me," I said, salivating. "All it says on the can is GOLDEN PEARLS FROM THE CASPIAN SEA."

"Well, that rules out the Dominican Republic," my wife said as she started making toast.

"Wait a minute," I warned her. "This could be a bribe. People don't just leave caviar on your doorstep unless they want something in exchange."

"What could anyone want in exchange for a can of delicious caviar?"

"My Redskins tickets," I said. "But they're not going to get them —not for all the caviar in Zambia."

"I didn't know Zambia had any caviar," she said.

"That's just my code name for the country where I think it came from. I believe the first thing to do is call one of the editors at *The Washington Post* and ask him if it's all right to accept the gift."

I made the call.

"Is it ethical to accept a can of Golden Iranian caviar from an anonymous embassy in Washington?" I said.

"It all depends," the editor replied. "How much caviar is there?"

"Enough for four people," I said.

"My wife and I will be right over," he said.

"I knew I shouldn't have called. Now we have to share the stuff," I told my wife.

A half-hour later the phone rang. The editor said, "Never mind. We found a can of caviar on our doorstep with a peacock throne on it."

"Then that means it comes from Switzerland," I said.

"No, you dummy. The Swiss ambassador only sends chocolates."

On Christmas Day we went to visit friends who worked in the State Department on the Middle East desk. "Have some caviar," the former ambassador said.

"No, thanks," I said. "We're going over to Adm. Pinkerton's tonight for caviar and baked potato and we don't want to spoil our appetites."

The day after Christmas our son, who plays with a boy whose father is in the CIA, said, "If you think we have caviar you should see the Dinkhams' fridge. It's loaded with fish eggs."

"That's too bad. I thought we'd share ours with them since I figured by being government employees they probably never got to eat any."

"Mr. Dinkham says you're nothing if you don't have a caviar source at the CIA."

Whatever else you want to say about Ambassador Zahedi he certainly was lavish with his country's edibles. Almost everyone I knew of importance in the capital was up to his hips in sturgeon eggs. Zahedi had penetrated the soft underbelly of Washington, and as long as the stuff kept coming no one was really interested in how the Shah was doing.

I guess this should be a lesson to all of us. The next time we find a can of caviar on our doorsteps we're going to ask some tough questions about the regime's survival before we start chopping up eggs and onions and cutting up lemons.

Goodbye to Mr. Big

WASHINGTON—Something happened in Washington last week that has caused great consternation in the power structure of this town. Paul de Lisle, the maitre d'hotel at the Sans Souci Restaurant, resigned, leaving a vacuum in the luncheon scene that is hard to fill. There are better restaurants than the Sans Souci in the capital, and one would be hard pressed in recent years to give it even one star. But the Sans had other things going for it—the most important being Paul.

Paul was really the Mr. Big in this city—the man to whom all of us went to get our orders. He never took credit for it, but it was his idea to send Henry Kissinger to China during the Nixon administration.

He got the idea when he overheard the Soviet ambassador tell the Polish minister at Table 5 that the Russians would take a very dim view of the United States recognizing the People's Republic of China.

During the Cuban missile crisis, Paul was constantly on the phone to President Kennedy. "I heard an NKVD man," Paul told the President, "say that if you eyeballed it, the Russians would be the first to blink."

This is probably the first time it's appeared in print, but Paul came up with the idea for President Johnson's domestic program. Jack Valenti, who then worked for Johnson, was sitting at Table 12 with Bill Moyers. Paul stopped by the table and Jack said, "Paul, who are the people who eat here?" Paul replied, "To my knowledge, they are all members of a great society."

At that very moment Johnson called and said, "Where are you, Jack?"

"I'm eating with the great society," Jack replied.

"That's it," President Johnson said. "What would you think about calling my program 'The Great Society'?"

"It sounds great to me," Valenti said.

"Who asked you?" Johnson wanted to know.

There was some talk at the time of Watergate that Paul was "Deep Throat." My suspicions were aroused early in the scandal when Paul did not recognize Bob Woodward or Carl Bernstein when they came into the restaurant. He told Bernstein he couldn't seat him unless he wore a tie and a jacket. Bernstein said, as he left in a huff, "We'll talk about this in the garage tomorrow morning."

As for myself, it is no secret that I ate at the Sans Souci for lunch every day at the same table. The reason for this was that Paul was my main source of news for the column. We had our own code. When he said, "The roast lamb is very good today," that meant we were sending 50 more fighter planes to Saudi Arabia. Or if he handed me the wine list and remarked that the Beaujolais Villages was drinkable, it really meant that the Fed was going to raise interest rates by 2 percent.

It was no accident that I found 18½ minutes of Nixon's missing tape in my spaghetti one day. Paul had cleverly denied putting it there.

I've had a lot of calls since Paul's departure asking me where I planned to eat lunch, now that he is no longer at the Sans Souci.

Duke Zeibert has offered me a free baked potato with my steak. Paul Young says I can have all the after-dinner mints I can eat, and the Maison Blanche, a new restaurant in the Federal Home Loan Bank Building on 17th and G streets, has offered me the same interest rate on my house as the National Bank of Georgia gave Jimmy Carter on his farm.

But I'm keeping my options open. This is a very class-conscious town, and as Pierre Salinger told me when I first got here, "You are where you eat."

Part III

Saving Paper

They've been trying to keep it a secret, but there is a serious paper shortage in Washington. A strike of Western paper workers, which is expected to be taken up by workers on the East Coast, has caused a paper deficit in Washington. The reason the government has been keeping it a secret is it fears that if the word gets out, panic will set in and different departments and agencies will start hoarding paper, while others might resort to some very dirty tricks to ensure that its memo flow is not turned off.

One department, which shall remain anonymous, got wind of the shortage and has already held 27 meetings on the crisis.

At the last meeting it was decided to alert all employees to the situation.

In a memo, which was sent to the agency's 27,500 workers, a deputy director wrote: "It has been brought to my attention that we can expect a serious paper shortage in the next few months, which could affect productivity and the morale of this agency. Therefore, I am asking everyone to conserve every sheet of paper possible, even if it involves such dire emergencies as using both sides of the paper. I am also requesting all employees to submit to me in writing how the agency can conserve paper. These suggestions should be made out in triplicate with one copy for me, one for your supervisors and one to keep for yourself in case any action is taken.

"Supervisors are requested to submit weekly reports to the

Administrative Supply Office as to how many employees are following this directive, and if this memorandum has increased or decreased the use of present supplies. If an employee does not send in a suggestion, his or her supervisor must put in writing to the personnel director why he or she failed to do so. The personnel director will evaluate and report on Form 2-D to his superior whether or not the excuse is valid.

"What we plan to do with the suggestion is have the public affairs division compile a collection of the most interesting ones, which will then be distributed to all personnel—not only from this agency but from corresponding agencies, which find themselves in the same shortfall position.

"It is my hope that this compilation can be published by the General Printing Office and sold to the public. A steering committee has been appointed to study the best methods of distribution, as well as costs, and the report should be on my desk by the early part of next month. Each department head will receive a copy of the report comments as well as additional thoughts.

"To facilitate matters on the book project, it is suggested that all departmental correspondence concerning conservation be submitted on yellow 8 x 10 Memorandum Sheets (G-234 forms), while those regarding distribution be written on the blue double carbon pads (K-677). If you do not have these colors in stock, you can obtain them from the supply room by filling out Form 2323.

"It goes without saying that this agency will be out of business if it is unable to supply the documentation to justify the written decisions it makes. Therefore, everyone from the top agency officials to the mail-room personnel must comply with all regulations regarding the conservation of our paper supply.

"The first of these regulations is now being distributed. If you do not receive it in a week, please notify this office on Green Form 1456, using the White No. 10 envelope.

"Anyone who does not have a Green Form 1456 may apply for a written waiver by using the Manila Folder 1O-DC in which this memo is being distributed." —A. Clancy, Acting Chief Deputy Counsel, Paper Conservation Committee.

Breathe Deeply, Please

The Environmental Protection Agency relaxed the nation's smog standards last month by 50 percent because it believes the average American can breathe twice as much smog as was previously thought, without falling down on the sidewalk.

As soon as the news was announced I went over to see a friend at EPA, named Harbinger.

"How do you feel about relaxing the nation's smog standards?" I asked.

"Very relaxed," he admitted. "We've been able to thicken the air with pollutants without doing any damage to the human body, which during an inflationary period could save this country billions of dollars."

"How have you been able to do this?"

"Instead of demanding a standard of .08 per million, we will now allow .12. I know it doesn't sound like much on paper, but it really has a lot of significance for the little guy who produces automobiles and burns coal to produce electricity."

"How do you know it's safe?"

"Oh, it's safe for autos and electricity. They can take twice as much pollution as that."

"I wasn't talking about autos and industry. I was talking about people. If you up the permissible amount of pollution, aren't you endangering the lungs and life of the average person?"

"I believe you're getting into a sensitive area. You're now talking about someone's health."

"I guess that is the area I was talking about."

Harbinger continued, "EPA can do just so much to keep a person alive. When we set certain anti-pollution standards we expect Americans to live up to them. If they're going to get sick even after we've announced that these standards are perfectly safe, it's their fault not ours. We publicize these figures as much as possible and people should keep up with any changes we make in them.

"If I tell you on the basis of medical and scientific evidence you can breathe twice as much smog as we originally thought, it's up to you to get the word."

"But there are some people who say you're lowering the pollution standards at the behest of the auto industry and other large urban polluters, who will have to spend billions of dollars to meet the guidelines set by the EPA."

"Let the environmentalists say it. There's always someone who can't get enough clean air. But they're not the ones who ask how much this smog-free air is going to cost. Everyone has to make tradeoffs in this world. Before you throw your weight behind the clean-air enthusiasts, I would like to ask you a question: Would you rather spend $500 extra for a new car in 1982 or live a few more lousy years?"

"Is that my only choice?"

"Yes."

"I'd prefer to save the $500 on the car."

"And so would most people. To Americans a car is a necessity, and they don't wish to be penalized just because there are a few health nuts out there who want to go back to Walden Pond."

"Do you think there will be a fight over the lowering of the EPA standards for clean air?" I asked Harbinger.

"Isn't there always?" he sighed. "Every time we decide what's good for the American people, someone is going to contest us. Our job is not to prevent the air from being poisoned, but to make sure that the public can live with the poison in the air.

"The last thing to remember is that the American people can take a lot more pollution than they think they can. If, in the next few years, you start to cough, wheeze, or get headaches, I think you owe it to yourself to ask, 'Am I really sick, or is it the government?' "

The Hydrogen Bomb Lobby

As soon as it was revealed that a reporter for *Progressive* magazine had discovered how to make a hydrogen bomb, a group of firearm zealots formed the National Hydrogen Bomb Assn., and they are now lobbying against any legislation to stop Americans from owning one.

"The Constitution," said the association's spokesman, "gives everyone the right to own and bear arms. It doesn't spell out what kind of arms. But since anyone can now make a hydrogen bomb the public should be able to buy it to protect themselves."

"Don't you think it's dangerous to have one in the house, particularly where there are children around?"

"The National Hydrogen Bomb Assn. hopes to spend a good portion of its dues on educating people in the safe handling of this type of weapon. We are instructing owners to keep the bomb in a locked closet and the fuse separately in a drawer. We also will hold classes in how to fire the bomb. We believe that if a person knows how to take care of his bomb there is no danger to himself or his family."

"Some people consider the hydrogen bomb a very lethal weapon which could kill somebody."

The spokesman said, "Hydrogen bombs don't kill people —people kill people. The bomb is for self-protection and it also has a deterrent effect. If somebody knows you have a nuclear weapon in your house, they're going to think twice about breaking in."

"But those who want to ban the bomb for American citizens claim that if you have one locked in the closet, with the fuse in a drawer, you would never be able to assemble it in time to repulse an intruder."

"That's garbage put out by the anti-nuclear weapon people. We are only advocating ownership of hydrogen weapons by law-abiding citizens. If someone commits a crime with one, he should get a stiff jail sentence."

"Another argument against allowing people to own a bomb is that at the moment it is very expensive to build one. So what your association is backing is a program which would allow the middle and upper classes to acquire a bomb while poor people will be left defenseless with just handguns."

"That's pure propaganda put out by the bleeding hearts. In a year or two there will be Saturday Night Hydrogen Bomb Specials costing less than a hundred dollars. It's worth that to protect your family."

"Would your association be willing to permit the registration of bombs by their owners?"

"Absolutely not. If we ever go to war the Communists will have a list of everybody in this country who owns the bomb. They could disarm us overnight. The strength of this nation is still in a citizens' army, and our members are pledged to fight to the last man."

"Do you plan to use the bomb for hunting?"

"Only for big game. We're not going to use it on a rabbit or a duck because that would be overkill. But it's a perfect weapon for knocking down an elk or a bear."

"A recent Gallup survey has indicated that 78 percent of the people polled said they were in favor of banning the hydrogen bomb in private hands. What is your response to that?"

"Our recent survey indicates just the opposite," he replied. "People favor keeping the bomb out of the hands of criminal elements, and believe that if you carry one around in your pocket you should have a license. But it's nobody's damn business what you do with one at home."

Gas on Credit

As the price of gasoline keeps going up, people may have to resort to buying it on long-term credit.

The scene is a branch of Morgan Chemical Bank of America. Mr. Klingle is ushered toward the loan officer's desk.

"Can I help you, Mr. Klingle?"

"Yes, sir. I would like to make a gasoline loan."

"Very good. How much gas were you going to buy?"

"A full tank. We want to attend our daughter's graduation."

The loan officer takes out a form.

"We don't usually advance money for a full tank of gasoline without some collateral. What were you planning to put up for the loan?"

"My house. It's in tiptop condition on an acre of land."

"And what else?"

"The house won't be enough?"

"Mr. Klingle, do you know what a full tank of gas costs these days? The bank demands more than just a house for collateral."

"I was afraid of that. What about my house and my 1980 Cadillac?"

"Are we talking about leaded or unleaded gasoline?"

Mr. Klingle says nervously, "Unleaded."

The loan officer looks at his chart, "That won't be sufficient. What else can you give us as a guarantee you'll pay back the loan?"

"I have a hundred shares of IBM, which is now selling at $340 a share."

"That just might do it. You'll have to leave the stock with us."

"I'll do that. I didn't know the bank demanded so much collateral for a gasoline loan."

"We consider these loans very high-risk ventures," the loan officer said. "When we first started giving them, people would take the money, buy the gas, use it up, and then default. Since there was nothing left in their tanks to recover, we've had to make sure that in the future we could get something else back in exchange. How long do you want to take to pay us back?"

"How much time do I have?"

The loan officer referred to his chart. "You can pay us over a period of 24 months, 36 months or string it out over four years. I am obligated under the 'truth in lending' law to advise you that we are permitted to charge 20 percent interest on gasoline loans. Of course, you can pay the loan back sooner, but there is a penalty."

"I think I'll be able to pay it back in 36 months providing my wife can get a job."

"All right. Here are the papers to fill out and these are for the gas station attendant to sign, attesting to the fact that he filled up your car with a full tank. When you bring in the deeds to your house, automobile, and the IBM stock, we will send the check directly to the gas station."

"Thank you very much, sir. You don't know what this gasoline means to me."

"Mr. Klingle, I wouldn't approve it if I didn't have faith in you. Besides, this bank believes people should have the good things in life today and not have to wait until they're old and gray before they can afford to buy a tankful of fuel."

Both men get up and shake hands. The loan officer says, "And don't forget—when you pay us back in 36 months we'll be happy to refinance another tank for you. Have a safe trip."

The Medicine Flackers

An Associated Press item says now that doctors have been given permission to advertise, they have gone one step further and are hiring press agents to get their names in newspapers and to arrange interviews on radio and television. One plastic surgeon mentioned in the news story said he knew at least 25 physicians who had retained publicity agents and he insisted there were hundreds more who had hired someone to flack for them.

I don't see anything wrong with it.

My friend Carl Bromberg, whom I consider one of the best press agents in the business, thinks that publicizing doctors will not only be financially rewarding for anyone in the public relations business but will also be challenging and exciting work. He told me:

"This is big stuff. We're going to have to think up items that the gossip columnists will take."

"Such as?"

"Something like, 'What well-known movie queen has stars in her eyes, thanks to Hollywood's new hot plastic surgeon, Dr. Cromley Barton, who, when last seen at Cedars of Lebanon Hospital, was lifting everything belonging to the wife of a top studio producer?' or 'Everyone at the UCLA Medical Center is still talking about the standing ovation Dr. George Catheter got last week on his smash kidney stone operation in the main UCLA Hospital Theater.

" 'Everyone who is anyone in the urology world was at the sellout opening. At a post-operation party at the Beverly Wilshire, Dr. Catheter said he thought it was the best thing he'd ever done, but hoped he wouldn't be typed as just another kidney stone surgeon.

" 'I'm getting a lot of offers, but I really have my heart set on removing a prostate.' "

"That's good," I said, "even Rona Barrett would use that one."

"Wait," Bromberg said, taking notes out of his pocket, "I've got more. Listen: 'Dr. Clem Dumbarton, the multimillionaire orthopedist, has just bought a 120-foot yacht which he says he hopes, for tax reasons, to turn into a hospital ship. "I plan to do all my slipped disc and tennis elbow operations at sea, outside the three-mile limit, so no one can sue me for malpractice," Dr. Dumbarton told friends.'

"And here's one you'll like," continued Bromberg, "it's in the form of a press release:

"'Dr. Rudolf Koenig, the jet set's favorite psychiatrist, announced at a press conference at Studio 54 that he would no longer take patients who want to tell him their dreams. "It takes too much time," said Dr. Koenig, "and if you've heard one dream, you've heard them all."

"'Dr. Koenig, who gets $150 for a half-hour session, also said that because of the heavy demands on his time he would no longer take neurotic or psychotic patients.

"'"It's a question of priorities, and as a doctor I want to devote more time to appearing on television talk shows."

"'Dr. Koenig won an Emmy for his outstanding performance on the *Today Show*, and he has been honored by the American Psychiatric Assn. for a recent profile done on him in *People* magazine.' "

"That's a beautiful press release," I told Bromberg.

"Medicine is a whole new ball game," he said. "I know many doctors, good people in their fields, who don't think they need a press agent. But they're finding out that when people have an appendectomy they want a name.

"No one is going to be impressed if you say you had surgery by somebody who hasn't at least been on the *Johnny Carson Show*.

"I had one doctor who came to me, and he was barely making $100,000 a year. I got him on the cover of *Parade* magazine, and now he owns his own hospital and shopping center in New Jersey."

Remedial Nuclear Energy

"Ladies and gentlemen, the class in remedial nuclear energy will come to order. Last week I gave you an assignment. You are the spokesperson for a major power company and there has been an accident in one of your nuclear energy plants. I will now see how well prepared you are. Mayberry, what is the first thing you would do?"

"Deny it."

"Yes, that would be the best response. But let us suppose the company has been obligated to inform the government that there was indeed an accident. The press has therefore been alerted and is on the scene. As spokesperson, Slayton, what would you say?"

"I would say, sir, that there has been a slight malfunction in one of the cooling systems of the reactor, but the problem is being dealt with and there is no danger to anyone because of the backup systems built into the plant, which are redundant but required by federal law."

"That's not bad, Slayton. Now let's go to phase two. Due to a series of human errors the valves have been shut accidentally, the secondary cooling system is not operating and the reactor is starting to overheat. This information has been leaked to the governor of the state and government officials, and you are asked about it. What would you say, Higginbottom?"

"I, I, ahhh, I would tell the truth."

"Wrong, Higginbottom! Wrong! Wrong! Wrong! Wrong! Why is Higginbottom wrong, Newcombe?"

"Because, sir, if the spokesman admits someone at the plant has made a mistake, he will open up the power company to millions of dollars' worth of lawsuits. The role of the spokesperson is to protect the company at all costs and minimize any accident, so hopefully the media will go away."

"Excellent. Then, Newcombe, what would you say in this situation?"

"I would say that our engineers are having a slight problem with an automatic pump and are therefore using a backup pump to cool down the reactor, which is still operating as well as possible under the circumstances."

"Prof. Stonewall, suppose the government inspectors are telling the press a different story? What should we do?"

"Well, Malcolm, now you've touched upon the core of the exercise. The credibility of the power company is being challenged by hostile outside forces. Let's see if there is anyone in the class who has any ideas. Altman?"

"I would say that the power company people are in a much better position to evaluate the situation than some outsiders who are just trying to frighten the public. I would add that if there were any danger the company would be the first to admit it, because we consider our major responsibility is to protect the health of our consumers."

"Well done, Altman. We're moving along. It turns out that a hydrogen bubble has formed in the reactor, blocking off the cooling water. This builds up pressure in the containment building. You are asked about this at the next press briefing. What do you say, O'Hare?"

"I wouldn't say anything, sir. I'd get the hell out of there."

"Very funny, O'Hare, but not as funny as the 'F' I plan to give you at the end of the semester. What you would say is that the situation remains stable, and although you had to release some gas out of the tank which was slightly radioactive, it is still much safer than if one had to have a dental X-ray.

"Now this is very important, so pay close attention. Some wise guy from the press is going to ask you who is going to pay for the plant breakdown and the cleanup. You will reply that the costs will be passed on to the consumers, because the company is not responsible for its own mistakes."

"Won't that cause a stink in the community, Professor?"

"Possibly, but it's the truth, and when you take on the role of a spokesperson for a large company it's essential that you always level with the customer."

Put on Your Life Jackets

Capt. Jimmy Carter, formerly of the U.S. nuclear submarine command, was standing on the bridge of the Ship of State staring through his binoculars. "Hard rudder right," he said.

The helmsman said, "It won't go to the right, sir."

The captain said, "All right then, hard rudder left."

The helmsman said, "It won't go hard rudder left, either, sir. What should I do?"

The captain said, "Let's drift until I talk to the crew." The captain grabbed the speaker, "Now hear this. This is your captain speaking. We are heading into rocky waters and I want all congressional chief petty officers topside immediately."

A surly band of CPO's came topside. "Gentlemen, I need your help. I can't steer this ship alone."

"Where are we heading, Captain?" one of them wanted to know.

"I'm not sure, but I'd like to stay on course."

"If you don't know where we're going, how can we help you stay on course?"

"Well, for a start I would like assurance that we have enough fuel to stay afloat."

"How much do we have now?"

"Lt. Schlesinger, how much fuel do we have?"

"I have no idea, sir. I keep getting different reports every hour. All I know is we're going to have to conserve as much as possible."

"Then I guess we better start rationing it," the captain said.

One of the congressional leaders replied, "How?"

"Lt. Schlesinger, do we have a plan?"

"Yes, sir. Here it is."

The chiefs looked it over, "We don't like this plan."

The captain said, "All right, we'll come up with another one. Lt. Schlesinger, do we have another plan?"

"Yes, sir. Here's a new plan."

The chiefs studied it. "This is worse than the other plan," one of them said.

"Then you people come up with a plan!"

"We don't know anything about conservation," one of them said.

"See here," Capt. Carter said grimly. "I'm in charge and you people must think about the good of the ship. We have to work together or we'll go on the rocks."

Ensign Hamilton Jordan came on the bridge, "Sir, we're taking on water."

The captain got on the phone, "Lt. Blumenthal, you're in charge of damage control. How much water are we taking on?"

"Well, I thought it would be seven percent, but apparently we screwed up. We'll be lucky if it doesn't go to 10."

"What happened to our plan to reduce the bilge in our tanks?"

"We thought we could keep the boilers from overheating but we were wrong."

"You're a big help, Blumenthal."

"Thank you, sir."

Capt. Carter hung up and said, "If we can only get through the Panama Canal we'll be all right."

Chief Tip O'Neill said, "I'm having trouble getting the crew to agree to go through the canal."

"Why?"

"The petty officers are being very petty."

"How can I command a Ship of State when no one wants to follow my orders?"

"Why don't you abandon ship?" Chief Kennedy suggested.

"You would like that, wouldn't you, Kennedy? It sounds like mutiny to me."

"No, sir, I'll support you as long as you're captain, but any time you want me to take over the wheel just let me know."

The helmsman said, "Captain, we seem to be drifting out to sea. Do you want to set a new course?"

"That's a good idea," the captain replied. "Which way is the wind blowing?"

"Port," someone shouted.

"Starboard," somebody else said.

"Fore," another voice offered.

"Aft," was the last reply.

"Good," said the captain. "Stand by your stations until I come up with another plan."

New Look at Mental Health

The nice thing about working on a newspaper is that you can always find a psychiatrist who will explain the state of mind of people during a crisis.

Last week a psychiatrist in California came to the conclusion that people get very depressed waiting in gas lines. The victims feel a great sense of loss, and it is very difficult for them to adjust to it. Some of them resort to anger while others withdraw into themselves.

These startling revelations could have great impact on the mental health of the country. But that's not all. This is only the tip of the iceberg.

A psychiatrist friend of mine has been doing a study of the attitudes of Americans toward the problems they face today. He talked to 100 people and these are some of the scientific conclusions he arrived at.

People are much happier with a full tank of gasoline than they are going to the hospital for an operation.

When you take a car away from a high school student, he will turn his frustration into anti-social behavior.

Status symbols in the country are changing. A person who gets 22 miles to the gallon in a Honda is much more emotionally secure than a man driving a large Lincoln Continental with a telephone attached to the dashboard.

When a person keeps saying over and over again, "Things will get worse before they get better," he is a candidate for a nervous breakdown.

The way to avoid stress is not to try to buy gas on Sunday.

People who dream that they are first in line at a service station usually have happy sex lives.

Those who dream that just when they get to the station the attendant puts up a sign CLOSED should seek help from Masters and Johnson.

Most people who hate oil companies have had happy childhoods. Those who have had unhappy childhoods never expected the oil companies to behave any differently.

When you allow someone to jump ahead of you in a service

station line, and you don't do anything about it, it usually indicates you had a weak father.

If you get out of your car and attack him with a monkey wrench it means you always had a supportive mother.

Those persons who are paranoid about the way the Department of Energy is handling the present energy crisis are not mentally unbalanced. Those who have delusions that the DOE is doing the best it can should be watched carefully and be referred for treatment at the earliest opportunity.

Crying is the healthiest solution to an energy problem.

Patting your gas tank when it is full of gas does not necessarily mean that you are a Dirty Old Man.

If you are a woman and find every service station attendant attractive, this does not mean you are a nymphomaniac.

Putting leaded gasoline in a car that requires unleaded fuel will eventually cause bed-wetting.

Those people who have a fear of running out of fuel and are constantly topping off their tanks are suffering from an incurable neurosis called Exxonphobia.

People who have no other way to get to work overcompensate for their inadequacy by taking the bus. But they are not dangerous to themselves or others and should be left alone.

A psychiatrist who is unable to get the fuel he needs can become just as emotionally disturbed as his sickest patient.

The Women Who Wait

It is only fitting as we celebrate Mother's Day that we honor those women who sit at home and wait. Some of them wait for the plumber, others for the electrician. There are women, as I write this, who are still waiting for rug cleaners, United Parcel, J. C. Penney, a tree surgeon or the appliance repairman.

These are brave women, unsung, afraid to leave their houses for even a half hour because the person they are waiting for might show up the moment they are gone.

Mrs. Katherine Davenport has been chosen this year to represent all the mothers of America who sit in a lonely vigil waiting for a repairman or a delivery driver who never comes.

I visited her home in Bethesda, Maryland, the other day to talk to her. She answered the door excitedly, but when I told her I was a journalist, her face dropped. "I was hoping that you were the linoleum man," she said. "I've been waiting for him for three weeks."

"That's not a long time."

"It seems like an eternity," she said. "He promised me he'd be here to lay the linoleum in the kitchen on April 23rd at nine o'clock."

"Have you heard from him since?"

"No, but I received a postcard from the Red Cross a week ago telling me he was well and that he was thinking of me." She showed me the card, which she apparently had read many times.

"Every morning I call the linoleum store and they say he's coming that day. I'm going out of my mind with worry. They get your spirits up and then by the end of the day they've sunk. Why do they say he's coming when they know he isn't?"

"I guess they don't want you to despair," I suggested. "We all need hope."

Mrs. Davenport twisted a handkerchief. "You don't know what it's like to just sit here waiting for the doorbell to ring. I don't sleep at nights because I have these nightmares that he took another job in Rockville. I keep wondering if he's getting enough to eat, or whether his truck has broken down, or even

115

worse that the linoleum I ordered never arrived. If he would just call and tell me he is all right, I could get through the days. But the uncertainty of it is driving me crazy."

"I'm sure he's all right or you would have heard from the Retail Linoleum Layers of America. Three weeks is not a long time to wait for a tradesman who promised to come on a certain day."

"But when he measured the kitchen floor he said he'd be back in a week. Why would he say that if he didn't mean it?"

"They all say that," I told her. "We once called a sewer man who said he would be there in two hours. He showed up alive and well six months later. When he finally came my wife asked what had happened, and all he said was, 'I got here as fast as I could.' Just when you give up all hope they do arrive."

"You're just saying that to make me feel better. Many of my friends have called repairmen who said they would come, and they've never been heard from again," she said as tears clouded her eyes.

"Have you thought about getting another linoleum man?" I asked.

"Every woman thinks about it," she said, "but what guarantee do I have that the second linoleum man won't do the same thing to me that the first one did?"

I didn't have an answer for her. I got up to leave.

She took me to the door. "Would you like to see the tape measure he left behind?" I said I would. She pulled open a drawer and with loving hands showed it to me.

"It's a beautiful tape measure," I said. "You were lucky to have even those few hours with him."

Ladies Always Tell

A day doesn't go by without a new book appearing on the market by some lady revealing every love affair she's had since she was 13 years old. The bigger the names in her memoirs, the hotter the property.

My friend Rock, a Hollywood star, says that it's taken all the fun out of seduction.

Rock took a beautiful young lady out to dinner a few weeks ago, and then she invited him to her apartment. When they arrived she said, "Pour yourself a drink while I slip into something more comfortable."

She returned in 12 minutes dressed in a black negligee, holding a yellow-lined legal pad and a ball-point pen, and sat down on the couch.

"You have beautiful eyes," Rock said.

The young lady started writing. "Don't go too fast," she said, "I can't take shorthand."

"I couldn't stop looking at your lips when we were in the restaurant—they were so succulent."

The girl gazed at Rock, bewildered, and then said, "How do you spell succulent?"

Rock spelled it for her and then said, "Do you mind if I turn off the lights?"

"No, but leave one on, otherwise I can't take notes."

"Why do you want to take notes?"

"Because," the girl said, "I want to remember this moment forever."

My friend continued, "I know you're not going to believe this, but I've never felt this way about a woman before. I want to crush you in my arms and feel your body pressed against mine."

"That's very good," the girl said, as she continued writing. "No one has ever said that to me."

"Will you stop taking those damn notes? You're making me nervous."

The girl stopped writing. "You look so hot, why don't you take your shirt off?"

Rock ripped off his shirt and the girl started examining him.

"What are you doing now?"

"I'm looking for scars on your body. It's so much more interesting if you have a scar."

"Oh my darling," Rock said, "do you believe that two people who meet for the first time can look into one another's eyes and know immediately that this is it?"

"Yes, I do. Isn't there a literary term for that?"

"It's called 'kismet.' "

"That's it," the girl said, writing it down. "I saw that once in a movie."

"We're wasting time, my beloved. Let me take you to paradise. I will bring you to new heights of ecstasy."

"Does ecstasy have one 'c' or two?"

"You're toying with my emotions," Rock cried. "Do you want me to beg?"

"Yes. That would be very good."

"I'm on my knees. Are you satisfied?"

"Oh, darn. This ball-point pen has run dry. Don't move from that position. I'll be right back with a new pen."

She quickly returned. "This is going to be one of the best scenes in my book."

Rock was incredulous. "You're writing a book?"

"Of course I'm writing a book. You don't think I play around without writing about it. What kind of girl do you think I am?"

My friend put on his shirt and said bitterly, "And I thought you were different from all the others. You don't want me—all you want is a chapter for your memoirs. How did a nice girl like you wind up in a profession like this?"

"It's a long story," the girl said tearfully. "But I met this editor from New York at a party and he said, 'How would you like to make some easy money, kid?', and the next thing I knew I had signed a contract for two hardcover books and a paperback."

Poor New Jersey

Almost everybody (well, maybe 53 percent of everybody) wants nuclear energy, but nobody wants nuclear waste dumped in his own backyard. Just the other day South Carolina refused to accept the waste from the Harrisburg Three Mile Island Plant. Gov. Hugh Carey of New York, who originally agreed that his state would take nuclear sludge, has now changed his mind. And so it goes.

Most states will take the energy, but not the radioactive garbage that goes with it.

When I queried people about where the stuff should be dumped, the consensus of opinion was New Jersey.

"Why New Jersey?" I asked a New Yorker.

"Because New Yorkers always dump everything in New Jersey. We've been doing it for years."

"Trash is one thing," I said, "but nuclear waste is another. I don't think it's nice for people who live in New Jersey to have all that nuclear matter piled on their shores."

"How would they know?" the New Yorker said. "They never go through their trash to see what's been dumped there. We built them the Lincoln Tunnel in exchange for letting us throw anything we wanted into their marshlands. New Jersey owes it to us."

"All you say may be true, but I know people who live in New Jersey, and they're adamant about not wanting other states to put nuclear refuse on their junk piles."

"So we don't tell them," he replied. "We'll throw it out the windows of the Metroliner at night when no one is looking."

"It seems so unfair to the Garden State," I said.

"What's unfair? They have legalized gambling in Atlantic City, haven't they? There has to be a trade-off for that."

"I don't follow your line of thinking."

"Las Vegas has legalized gambling, and the price they have to pay for that is to put up with atomic tests right outside the city limits. If you're allowed to build gambling casinos, you should be willing to put up with a little fallout."

"I hadn't thought of that. But let us suppose New Jersey says

119

no to accepting any nuclear waste, and even passes a law that anyone dumping it would be fined $100. What would you do then?"

"They wouldn't dare! New Jersey needs New York. Why do you think they've let us dump our garbage there for so many years? Don't get me wrong. I have nothing against the people who live there, but we have to be practical about this. If states like South Carolina are balking about accepting nuclear sludge, the only place left is across the Hudson River."

I found that Pennsylvanians felt the same way about it as New Yorkers. A man from Philadelphia said, "We've suffered enough in this state. You can't expect us to live with this contaminated material forever."

"Where do you want it to go?"

"What's wrong with Trenton?"

"But that's the capital of New Jersey!" I protested.

"All right, then Princeton. They were one of the first to come up with the idea of nuclear energy. Let them figure out what to do with the waste."

"That may be true," I said, "but don't you think each state should be responsible for its own sludge?"

"Not as long as there is New Jersey."

In Washington I called the Nuclear Regulatory Commission to ask if it would permit New Jersey to become a dumping ground for the other 49 states' nuclear garbage.

"Only temporarily until we can find a safer graveyard for it."

"But isn't it dangerous?"

"Not if you put the nuclear waste in Glad Bags. They last forever."

Autographs

I was sitting with Carol Burnett at the Kennedy Center the other evening at dinner when a lady came up, plunked a piece of paper in front of her and said, "My son will kill me if I don't get your autograph."

Carol signed it and the lady left with the paper clutched in her hand. Then Carol said to me, "Do you think she was serious?"

"About what?" I asked.

"Do you really believe her son would have killed her if she hadn't come home with my signature?"

"I don't know. I've heard people say it before. I guess you can't take a chance."

Carol said, "That's what I thought. Can't you just see the scene tonight if I hadn't signed her paper? The kid is waiting by the door and he says, 'Did you get Carol Burnett's autograph?' and the mother says, 'No, she wouldn't give it to me.' So the son picks up a shotgun and shoots her."

"It's obvious you prevented a matricide," I agreed.

We started talking about people and autographs. "I get threatened all the time," Carol said. "A man last week told me his wife would die if he didn't get a signature. He didn't say he'd kill her though he looked like he might. I felt like asking him how she would die, but I really didn't want to know."

"Have you noticed when people ask for autographs they rarely admit it's for themselves? It's always for someone in the family. A man asked me for one last month and said it was for his mother. I wanted to know his mother's name so I could autograph it to her, but he said he forgot."

Carol said some people are rather strange about autographs. "There is the type that always says, 'I've never asked for anyone's autograph before.' Then I say, 'Are you sure?' and they get very red in the face."

"I wonder why people want autographs?" I said.

"I think it's a question of credibility," she replied. "Some-one says, 'I saw Tim Conway in the restaurant,' and the person who is listening wants proof. No one believes anybody anymore."

"You're right," I said. "I was once dining in a Madrid restaurant with Cary Grant, and an American tourist came up to him while he was struggling with a plate of paella and said, "How about putting your John Hancock on this paper napkin?" Cary was furious and said, 'My name isn't Hancock.'

" 'I know that,' the tourist said.

" 'What do you want it for?' Cary asked.

"The tourist replied, 'My wife won't believe I saw you unless I have your autograph.'

"Grant stared at the man with steely eyes and said, 'What kind of relationship do you have with your wife, that she wouldn't believe you if you say you saw me in a restaurant?' The tourist went back to his table a broken man."

Many celebrities are so used to signing autographs that they do it automatically. The great football coach Vince Lombardi used to sit at the first table at Duke Zeibert's Restaurant in Washington. One time at lunch a little boy of 10 came shyly up to the table, and before he could say anything Lombardi took a menu and signed it for him. The boy said, "I don't want a menu. I want to borrow the catsup."

Another lady came up to Carol and said, "Can I have your autograph?"

"Who do you want it to?" Carol asked.

"Me," the lady replied.

Carol looked up and said, "Me, what?"

The lady said, "Just to me is enough."

SALT B.C.

The first SALT Treaty talks were held in about 750 B.C. As reported by the Prophet Isaiah, they took place between King Hezekiah of Judea and King Sennacherib of Assyria. The original draft of the agreement read, "All swords will be beaten into plowshares, and all spears into pruning hooks; nation will not lift up sword against nation and neither side will learn war any more."

When the wording of the treaty reached Hezekiah, there was an immediate outcry from his hawk advisers.

"We can't give up our swords. How do we know the Assyrians will not turn their plowshares back into weapons as soon as the treaty is signed?" said one general.

"The throw weight of the Assyrian spears is far superior to ours," another one cried. "This is a trick of the Assyrians so they can launch a first-strike capability against us."

A third adviser to the king said, "I cannot support a SALT B.C. Treaty of this kind. If we turn all our swords into plowshares, the Assyrians will have twice as many land-based plowshares as we have. Each plowshare could be mounted with 10 pruning hooks and be turned into offensive weapons which would bury every man, woman and child in Judea."

King Hezekiah was impressed with the arguments. He knew there wasn't a chance in Gomorrah of getting the treaty approved by his people unless there were guarantees that their sword and spear arsenals would remain intact.

He sent word to Sennacherib in Damascus that he wanted a limitation on the number of offensive swords each side could have, and he demanded the dismantling of defensive shields that the Assyrians had developed to deflect Judean steel.

Sennacherib, who had stockpiled thousands of swords and shields and had developed a new SS-18 spear which could be launched from a ditch, met with his advisers and worked out a strategy.

"We will tell Hezekiah," he said, "that as part of détente each side will be able to double the number of swords and spears in their arsenals, and both parties will be permitted to develop one more weapon of its own choosing. Even with this we will have superiority over them."

"What about the plowshares?"

"We will insist at this time that plowshares not be included in the arms limitation agreement. As you know, our new Backfire plowshares will be ready in six months. It will be an answer to their Minuteman pruning hook."

Hezekiah received the Assyrian proposals, which he knew would be rejected by the hardliners in his court. "What about verification?" one of them said. "How do we know the Assyrians will not put six blades on one sword?" another asked. "What would prevent them from turning their pruning hooks back into Mirved lances?"

Hezekiah knew he'd have to promise his army something in exchange for a SALT B.C. Treaty. "If you support me on this," he told them, "I will authorize the building of an MX system costing 30 billion sheep. This will enable us to hide our mobile spear throwers underground so the Assyrians will never know where they are. It will be the ultimate deterrent to prevent a surprise attack."

The Judean generals reluctantly agreed and King Hezekiah and King Sennacherib met to sign the SALT B.C. protocols.

It was the first SALT treaty negotiated by civilized people in history, and it has been the model for arms limitation agreements ever since.

Teddy in the Mirror

Teddy Kennedy looked into the mirror as he was shaving and said, "I have no intention of running for President of the United States."

He shook his head.

"I have no intention of opposing President Carter for the nomination in 1980."

It still didn't sound right.

"I have no intention of opposing President Carter if he is the nominee for President in 1980, and I believe he will be."

It needed a little bit more work.

"I stand by my previous statement that I am not a candidate for the presidency. I have full confidence in President Carter and will support him at the appropriate time."

He was still shaving the left side of his face.

"I have only one ambition in life and that is to serve the people of Massachusetts."

He almost cut himself on that one.

"I have not given my blessing to any 'Draft Kennedy' movement in the country. At the same time I cannot stop people from doing these things on their own."

He was now shaving under his chin. He paused, then looked in the mirror. "The Democrats already have a presidential candidate for 1980, and his name is Jimmy Carter."

He thought about that for a moment and rejected it. Then he said, "I don't know how many times I must answer the question, but I will try once more. There is no conceivable way I would enter the presidential race as long as Mr. Carter is in it."

He started shaving the right side of his face.

"The fact that I don't agree with President Carter on his national health program or his efforts to decontrol oil, or his cuts in the federal budget, which will affect every poor person in the country, as well as workers, farmers and the small businessmen, in no way changes my decision to campaign for him if he decides to run for another term in 1980."

Now he was getting somewhere. He looked into the mirror again.

"President Carter has made many mistakes in his first term in office, but overall I believe that, if given another term, he will be able to rectify those mistakes and with luck become a much better leader."

He discarded that one as he placed the razor on his upper lip.

"The party would be better served if its members stopped speculating about who its candidate will be in the next election. I will do everything in my power to stop the 'Dump Carter' efforts by misguided Democrats who feel we need a strong young leader who can restore confidence in our great American system."

Teddy looked in the mirror. The upper lip was clean. He took a washcloth and wiped all the excess shaving cream from his face.

He decided he had time for one more.

"The differences between the President and myself are being played up by the media. He knows I have every intention of ke~ping my word not to oppose him in word or deed. I shall speak my mind on the issues as I have done in the past. But this does not mean I want his job."

Teddy went into the bedroom, put on his shirt and tie and his jacket and then looked at his watch. He had another two minutes before one of his aides would pick him up.

He went back into the bathroom and took a final look into the mirror. He smiled and said, "On the other hand . . ."

A New Hospital Idea

Blackberry, who is a genius in the real estate business, came to me the other day with a brilliant idea. "Apartments all over the country are being turned into co-ops and condominiums. Why not do the same with hospitals?"

"Keep going," I said.

"Well, everyone knows that one stay in a hospital will cost you as much as a down payment on a house, and when you're discharged you have nothing to show for it, except possibly a scar. Why not allow patients to buy hospital rooms, as they do apartments, and then they could use them any time they wanted to?"

"But people don't use hospital rooms that often."

"So they can rent them out to relatives, friends or even strangers. It would be a tax-deductible investment, as long as the owners didn't use the room themselves for more than two weeks a year."

"You seem to have it all thought out."

"Look, the average hospital room comes to $300 a day; and you have to take whatever they give you. If you bought the room, you could choose your own view, decorate it the way you wanted to, and make it into a second home.

"You wouldn't have to sit through boring admission interviews, the nurses couldn't tell you what you could or could not do, and you would not have strange medical students waking you up day and night asking what's wrong with you. The initial investment might be high, but it would pay off in one short hospital stay."

"What about upkeep?" I asked.

"You would have to pay a monthly management fee, but most of that can also be deducted. Also, you could purchase a guaranteed parking place in the basement."

"It doesn't sound bad, but would the hospitals go for it?"

"Of course they would. Most hospital administrators are always trying to figure out how to fill their beds. If they went condominium they would have one less worry on their hands, and they could devote all their energies to medical problems.

Instead of treating patients they would be taking care of tenants, and it would make it so much more businesslike for everybody."

"What about semiprivate rooms?" I asked. "How would you turn them into condos?"

"Two families could purchase one and split it. Of course they would have to agree on the decor, and be willing to share the same bathroom, but I don't see this as a big problem. It's still cheaper to buy a semiprivate room in a hospital than to stay in one for three days."

"Blue Cross won't like your idea," I warned.

"Tough. Blue Cross should have thought of it first."

"What about people who can't afford to finance their own hospital rooms?"

"We could get them loans through the FHA. Our slogan is, 'Man's hospital room is his castle.' If people own their own rooms they'll take good care of them—keep the floors and walls clean, and wash the windows, and throw out flowers when they wilt. Now people don't give a damn the way their hospital room looks, because they know when they get better, they can walk away from it."

"It's a mind-blowing idea," I said. "Even Teddy Kennedy doesn't want to go that far in his national health plan."

"That's why it has to work. At first it will be a status symbol. People will say, 'You must come visit us at Mass General. We overlook the Charles River,' or 'If you're ever sick in New York and need a place to stay, please use our room at Columbia Presbyterian. We'll leave the key with the hall porter.' "

"It sounds like more fun than owning a yacht," I said.

"And a much better investment," Blackberry replied. "At the rate hospital rooms are going up around the country, you'll be able to double your investment in a year."

The Mustard Crisis

When it comes to the gas crisis, I regretfully have to admit that the media is part of the problem. A few weeks ago, Washington newspapers headlined on Friday that gas would be in short supply over the weekend. It was picked up by the radio and TV stations. Damned if everyone didn't pour out of their houses in panic and drive helter skelter to the nearest pump to fill up their tanks. Sure enough, the newspapers were right! There was a serious gas shortage on the weekend.

As I waited in line at my favorite station I couldn't help thinking of how people react to panic. Then I thought of my father and his friend Nat.

Nat had a grocery store around the corner from our apartment in Forest Hills on Queens Boulevard. My father stopped in every night during the dark days of World War II.

One evening as he was buying some milk and bagels, Nat whispered to him, "Mr. Buchwald, you heard about the mustard shortage?"

"There's going to be a mustard shortage?" my father said. "How do you know?"

"We've just been notified by Gulden's that our allotment has been cut by 20 percent. I won't be able to supply you with it as I have in the past."

The fact of the matter was that no one in the family ate mustard. I didn't like it, and neither did my three sisters. My father, as far as I could remember, never touched the stuff.

But struck with fear he said to Nat, "I've been a customer of yours for a long time, Nat. How many jars can you give me?"

Nat told him, "I can let you have 12 from my present shipment, but you can't tell anyone."

My father carried the heavy package home and unloaded the mustard in the closet. He happened to mention to a neighbor on the same floor what Nat had told him, and within a week it seemed everyone in Forest Hills had heard that there would be a mustard crisis in the United States, the likes of which the country had never seen.

Mustard started disappearing from shelves all over the area.

129

But my father was secure because he had his connection with Nat, who managed to save a dozen jars for him every time he went into the store.

The food closet in the apartment was jammed, and pretty soon the mustard took over space in the dish closet, and even the broom closet.

My sisters protested that there was no way they could eat all the mustard, even if the war lasted another ten years.

But Pop told them Nat knew more than they did.

Once the mustard crisis died down, Nat tipped off my father that Washington was going to cut back oatmeal production by 50 percent. Pop immediately bought every box of oatmeal in the store.

Another time it was tapioca, and then it was canned Argentinian corned beef. By some coincidence whatever wasn't moving in Nat's store suddenly was going to be in short supply.

I guess Nat's greatest triumph came the day he put a sign in his window saying: ONLY TWO CANS OF RHUBARB TO A CUSTOMER. There was a run on canned rhubarb in Forest Hills that old-timers remember to this day.

In fairness to Nat, he always took care of his old customers first, and my father managed to wangle two cases of rhubarb out of him, without anybody in the town finding out about it.

While the rest of the family thought Pop had been taken for a ride, he refused to hear one bad thing about his grocer. Years later when we were kidding him, he said indignantly, "Don't make fun of Nat, he gave us mustard during the war."

Brain Surgery

KUNMING, China—There are many ways to see China. If you are a tourist you get to go to museums, palaces and theaters. If you travel with the Secretary of HEW, Joe Califano, you get to see a lot of brain operations. The Chinese are very proud of performing brain operations with acupuncture. That and Peking Duck are their main specialties, and each hospital wanted to prove they could do it better than the one we had just visited.

In Kunming, the doctors permitted Califano to talk to a man while he was being worked on. It's hard to believe, but the patient was wide awake and in control of all his faculties as he conversed with the Secretary.

As I watched, I couldn't help thinking what the man would say when he got back to his commune that evening for dinner, with his head in bandages.

"Well, Wu Ling, what did you do in Kunming today?"

"I had a brain operation."

"What a great honor. How were you selected?"

"I was walking past the hospital on the way to the Chinese Herb Pharmacy, and two doctors came out and said, 'If you have nothing better to do would you like to stop in for a brain operation? It won't take long and it will help Chinese-American friendship.'

"I explained that I had several errands to make and suggested they find someone else, but they told me this wasn't an ordinary brain operation. It was to be performed for a visiting delegation of important Americans, headed by their Minister of Health. They told me it was also going to be covered by ABC and NBC television as well as correspondents from *The New York Times, The Washington Post* and *The Wall Street Journal*.

"Well, that changed the picture as far as I was concerned and I said, 'Count me in.' They took me inside, gave me a glass of hot tea and before I knew it I was lying on the operating table. Peering at me through glass windows in the ceiling were at least two dozen Americans, including their Minister of Health."

"You're making all this up, Wu Ling."

"May Chairman Mao strike me dead if I'm lying. The doctors started sticking needles into me, and before you knew it I could feel nothing. Then one of them started to cut off the top of my head."

"It didn't hurt?"

"Of course not. My head felt a little cool for a few moments, but I wasn't uncomfortable. But I haven't told you the best part. While they were sawing away, the doctors invited the Minister into the operating room to talk to me."

"I thought we weren't supposed to talk to foreigners after the March 1st edict."

"They told me it was perfectly all right. Patients having brain operations are not covered by the new law."

"What did the Minister ask you?"

"He asked me how I was feeling, and I told him 'fine.'"

"Then he asked me if I would like to visit the United States. I told him I'd like to very much because I knew the Americans were true friends of the People's Republic, and it was important for our Four Modernizations' Plan to have trade and technical assistance from the United States to further normalization between the two great nations. The doctors liked that."

"Did the Minister say anything else?"

"Yes. He told me a brain operation such as I was having would cost at least $3,000 in the United States, which is over 4,000 yuan, but he hoped to cut it down to $2,900 in his new health bill. Then he asked me if I had gotten a second opinion before I agreed to the operation?"

"And what did you say to that, Wu Ling?"

"I said, 'You've got to be kidding.'"

Help! Police, Help!

"Sergeant Riley, Fifth Precinct, Homicide Division, speaking."

"Sergeant, I would like to report a crime. Someone tried to poison my entire family."

"Are you sure?"

"I'm certain. I had my water and food analyzed by a laboratory and they were full of pesticides. Someone dumped the poison in our wells and rivers and not only my loved ones but all our neighbors may be croaking at this very moment."

"This is serious. Anybody have any grudges against you?"

"No one that I know of. Certainly we don't have enemies who would want to poison us."

"Maybe it's a crazy person who has some beef against the community. We better put out a dragnet."

"It's possible, but the person would have to have access to a lot of poison. Our pigs and cows are all sick and our horses are dying too."

"Let me get this straight. You think there is a mass murderer in your neighborhood?"

"Sergeant, I think there is a mass murderer in the county."

"You're not a kook, are you?"

"No, sir. If you check my record I am a very respectable person and have never been in trouble with the law."

"Okay, do you have suspects?"

"Well, the Frankenstein Chemical Co. is about two miles from my house and they've been dumping all sorts of sludge in the river.

"Sometimes it's green, sometimes a dark red and other times it's a deep brown. They do it mostly at night so no one will see them."

"Wait a minute. The Frankenstein Chemical Co. is a multimillion-dollar corporation with plants all over the United States. I know the men running the one in this county. They're lodge brothers of mine. Are you accusing them of poisoning people?"

"I know it sounds hard to believe, Sergeant, but I have this niece who works in the company's office and she has memos signed by two of the officers instructing the Frankenstein employees to dump all the waste in the river at night. The memos say that if anyone questions them about it to deny they did it, because if they get caught Frankenstein will have to close down the plant and they'll all be out of jobs."

"So what's the crime?"

"They're knowingly poisoning all of us. Isn't that a felony?"

"No, that's an environmental problem."

"Let me ask you something, Sergeant. If someone came into your house and started sprinkling arsenic on your food and fed your dog DDT and poured cyanide into your children's milk, would you arrest him?"

"Damn right I would, and I'd see he got sent up for life."

"What's the difference between that and a company doing the same thing to an entire community?"

"The police only deal with individual crimes. We have no authority to arrest company officials just because they have no way of getting rid of their pesticides."

"Then you mean the average citizen has no recourse when a large corporation knowingly tries to kill him?"

"If the government thinks they're doing anything wrong they have ways of punishing people who dump their waste in the wrong place."

"What's the punishment?"

"I think it's a $5,000 fine. It could be less. But you better be careful before you make wild charges such as you have."

"Why?"

"I can arrest you for harassing a respectable business establishment."

The War of the Chefs

SOOCHOW, China—It may have been Marco Polo who said it, but the best way of summing up traveling in China is: "If you don't eat it, or buy it—you have to climb it." In our travels with our beloved Secretary of HEW, Emperor Joseph Califano, we managed to do all three.

The Chinese, whose intelligence service is not to be underrated, had heard about Califano's renowned chef, and went to great efforts to top the meals that Joe serves in his dining room in his office on the top of the Forbidden City in Washington, D.C.

I had mentioned to our Chinese guides that I had dined at Califano's table, and therefore they were most curious to know if their meals were as good as the ones prepared by the famous Califano cook.

Apparently it was important to them in their bridge-building with the United States.

At a lunch in Soochow the table was decorated with cold hors d'oeuvres—the centerpiece was in the form of a crane consisting of razor-thin slices of whitefish and pine. This course was followed by a bowl of egg whites and shark fins.

One of the Chinese officials asked me how the dish compared with Mr. Califano's table.

"Just about the same," I said. "Secretary Califano's chef prefers Campbell's bean soup, but if he can't find white beans, he will use shark fins."

The next dish was "Beggar's Chicken," which had been cooked with herbs in clay for four hours.

They looked at me expectantly as I tasted it with my chopsticks. I finally said, "It's very nice chicken, though Mr. Califano's chef can do the same thing with hamburger. At least it tastes as if it had been cooked for four hours in clay."

The "Beggar's Chicken" was whisked away, and in its place appeared a "Sweet and Sour Mandarin Fish" surrounded by bacon and bean sprouts. Once again our Chinese hosts were waiting for an opinion.

"Truthfully," I told them, "I have never had 'Sweet and Sour

Mandarin Fish' at Mr. Califano's. He prefers his bacon decorated with lettuce and tomato on white bread. But I have had this delicacy in the HEW Government Cafeteria, and yours is definitely superior."

This pleased them very much, and we toasted each other with Mao Tai, the famous Chinese revolutionary firewater.

Following this course, we were served a piping hot bowl of prawn meat in winter melon soup. Six ducks made of egg whites, with tiny pieces of carrot for eyes, were floating on top.

"Surely," one of the Chinese said, "the Secretary's cook cannot make Mandarin winter melon soup with ducks."

"He can," I said, "but he only makes it when the Secretary is in a hurry and wants a fast bite, and his chef has orders to go easy on the ducks."

For dessert, we had three kinds of pastry, and then Soochow dumplings in a wicker basket. The dumplings had been sculpted in the form of tulips and contained almonds, sweetmeats and rice.

"I have to be honest with you," I told them, "even the Jell-O and Reddi-Wip Califano's chef serves does not compare with a Soochow dumpling."

My Chinese hosts were overjoyed and the message was translated all over the dining room.

It was time for the final toast. We toasted Chairman Hua and President Carter first. And then we toasted Secretary Califano's cook, whose cottage cheese salad with canned peaches, if not superior, was at least equal to that of any dish that could be concocted by the great chefs of the People's Republic of China.

Good as Gold

They used to be very quiet and you rarely saw one. But lately the gold bugs have come out of the closet. You can recognize them by the mad glint in their eyes.

My friend Bob Levin is one of them. He's hard to live with these days. This isn't just my opinion—it's his wife's.

She came to see me the other day. She looked as if she'd been crying.

"You've got to do something about Bob," she said. "He's gold crazy."

"Well, if he can afford it, it's not a bad investment."

"He can't afford it," she said. "He's putting everything we have into gold. He says it's the only safe thing left in the world."

"Maybe he's right."

"I told him I'd rather put some of it into food for myself and the children."

"What did he say to that?"

"He said, 'How can you think about food when South African Krugerrands are going up five percent a week?' I told him you can't eat Krugerrands, and he said, 'Maybe not today, but when gold hits $600 an ounce, we can have caviar for breakfast while everyone else will be starving to death.'"

"He sounds as if he's really got the bug," I said.

"Last week I told him I had to buy shoes for the children. I asked him for $50. He screamed at me, 'How can you ask for paper money when it's losing its value every day?' So I said, 'All right, give me a Mexican gold 50 peso coin instead.' He said, 'The gnomes in Geneva would really like that. They're counting on people like me getting out now, just when the market is going to soar.'

"I don't know what I'm going to do. The only thing we've bought for the house in the last six months is a scale. Bob spends his evenings weighing tiny bars of gold in cellophane wrappers. When I tell him to come to bed he says, 'Not until I find out what's happened in Tokyo.' The other night I asked him, 'What has Tokyo got to do with going to bed?' and he said, 'Everything. If you watch the Japanese bankers, you'll know where the dollar is going.' "

"What did you say to that?"

"I said I didn't care where the dollar was going as long as I could go with it—at least to a store. He said if I just held on for six more months we could buy the store."

"Where does he keep the gold?"

"In the house. He took the insides out of an old television set we have in the attic. Every day he calls up from the office and asks me to go up and check to see if it's still there. He doesn't even like me to go out anymore because he's afraid someone will break in while I'm gone."

"Why doesn't he put it in a safe deposit box in a bank?"

"Because he says the way gold is going the banks could close any day and he won't be able to get at his box."

"Has he seen a shrink?"

"He went once at my request."

"What happened?"

"He said he persuaded the doctor to put all his earnings into 10 gram bullion."

"I don't see how I can do anything," I told her as she pulled out some tissues to dry her eyes.

"I thought you could talk to him. He respects you and perhaps he'd invest in what you're investing in now."

"I don't think it would do any good," I told her. "My broker has me up to my ears in silver. I've got so much of it I can't even get it into my freezer anymore."

A New Weapons System

The Senate always feels it's doing its job when it votes more money for defense. But when it thinks of defense it imagines the funds will be used for some exotic weapon that the Russians don't have. What Congress doesn't like to do is appropriate money for simple things like boots, barracks and tents.

The Pentagon budget people are wise to what turns Capitol Hill on, so when they go up to ask for money for the mundane items that every armed service needs to survive, they disguise the requests as new weapons systems that will send the senators into orgasms of joy.

Col. Plotter was sent up last week to get an appropriation for new mess halls that the U.S. Army desperately needed. He knew he was in trouble if he asked for mess hall money because the Senate armed services subcommittee he was appearing in front of is interested only in new electronic hardware that can knock Moscow (or Havana) off the face of the map.

So instead of asking for funds for mess halls, Col. Plotter told the subcommittee the Army wanted to build 1,000 new MESS 112 All Weather Launch Pad Silos.

He unveiled a large drawing of the new weapon on his easel.

The senators studied it with interest.

Then one of them said, "It looks like a mess hall to me."

"Yes, sir," Col. Plotter said. "The configuration of the silo is quite similar to a mess hall, which makes detection of it from the air very difficult for the Soviets.

"The module was designed in a rectangular solid state complex to evade lethal enemy attacks."

"Do the Soviets have anything like it?" another senator asked.

"To our knowledge, sir, they are now working on a BORSHT 514-Silo which has twice the seating capacity of the MESS 112, but lacks the microwave oven throw-weight system."

"Don't evade the question, Colonel. Will we have parity or superiority if we go ahead with your weapon?"

"It is my opinion, sir, that if we don't go ahead on the MESS 112 immediately, our Army could starve to death."

"Tell us more about it, Colonel."

"All right. As you can see back here is what looks like a kitchen. This is the control center which feeds the passive integrated fuel supply into this section of the terminal which our people have dubbed the MESS line. The fuel is then transferred into aluminum software and moved by specially trained personnel through the line over to what appears to be tables, but are in effect armored air-to-ground missile shelters."

"When does the damn thing go off?" a senator said impatiently.

The colonel replied, "When the SPAM guidance system locks into the BORSHT 514 the roof opens and then it's goodbye Minsk, Pinsk and Kiev."

"Well done, Colonel," the chairman of the subcommittee said. "What do you estimate each MESS 112 will cost?"

"About $1 million per unit, sir, not counting the Cuisinart."

"Cuisinart?"

"That's our code name for the magnetic electronic back burner range."

"Colonel, you can tell your superiors as far as this committee is concerned you will get full authorization for 1,000 MESS 112s, and more if you need them. We won't approve the SALT II treaty unless we have them in our arsenal."

"Thank you, gentlemen. The U.S. Army has hungered for this weapon for a long time."

The New Status

Your status in Washington is no longer based on your title in government, nor how much entertaining you do, nor even if you come from Georgia.

You are now judged strictly on real estate.

I attended a party recently and my hostess was all aglow. "I want you to meet the most divine couple," she said. "These are the Schmertzes."

The name didn't ring a bell. "They bought a house in Georgetown in 1965 for $14,000 and it is now worth $350,000," she explained.

I got excited. "Forgive me," I apologized, "I didn't know you were *those* Schmertzes. I've been reading about you in the real estate pages. Didn't you get a mortgage for 4½ percent?"

"It was actually 4¾," Schmertz said modestly. "You know how real estate reporters tend to exaggerate."

Everyone gathered around the couple, while Sen. Teddy Kennedy stood in a corner all by himself. I looked around the room and couldn't believe my eyes. Coming in the door was Ziggy Wintermelon.

I went over to my hostess. "Marion, how did you ever get Ziggy Wintermelon, the condominium king, to come to your party?"

She just grinned mysteriously. "I told him Sam Freed might be here tonight. Wintermelon has been dying to meet him ever since Sam sold his mobile home in Potomac for $750,000."

"Is Freed coming?" I asked.

"He's already here, darling. He's talking to that man with the glasses and frizzy hair over there—I forget his name."

"That's Henry Kissinger," I told her.

"It's funny I don't remember inviting Kissinger. He really doesn't fit in with these people," she said.

"You certainly turned out the stars," I told her. "Isn't that Vic Orsini who just bought a million-dollar townhouse in the Kalorama section of Washington?"

"Yes, he closed on Friday. I believe he told me he's paying 12 percent for a 24-year mortgage which the bank insists it wants to renegotiate every five years. Vic's not too bright, but he's fun to have around."

"Why isn't anyone talking to Vice President Mondale and his wife?"

"They get free housing at the Naval Observatory. What could you talk to them about?"

"Marion," I said, "is it true the Stauntons sold their house in Alexandria for what they paid for it five years ago?"

"I'm afraid so. They seemed like such a nice couple, I don't know what got into them. Most people have dropped them, but I still say hello to her when I see her at Bloomingdale's."

Marion surveyed the room. Suddenly I saw her eyes stop. "I told Chief Justice Burger not to bug Charley Smith about buying a house in Mount Vernon," she said. "Warren knows perfectly well Charley can't discuss his projects while they're still being developed."

"Maybe Burger forgot," I said.

Marion took out her guest list. "Perhaps you can help me with the seating protocol. I have three Supreme Court justices, the Vice President of the United States, six senators and Carey Winston, the mortgage banker. Should I put Carey on my left or my right?"

The New Retailers

Where have all the radicals of the late Sixties and Seventies gone? Well, those who aren't working for IBM and for Chase Manhattan Bank are in retailing. You can walk down the main street of any large city now and see hundreds of outdoor stands set up where this generation of merchant princes is selling leather belts, carnations, jewelry, towels, art work and pressure cookers. They have not only joined the capitalistic system but have learned to beat it.

I was walking past Saks Fifth Avenue the other day and stopped in front of a stand with a sign tacked on the card table: MAX'S FIFTH AVENUE—ESTABLISHED SINCE JUNE 1978.

Max was selling T-shirts for $4 apiece. He was doing a good business and I had to wait a long time before I could have a word with him.

Finally, his girlfriend took over for him and we could chat.

"What does the fall look like?" I asked him.

"I'm optimistic in spite of the recession," Max said. "Our inventories are down and I believe the consumer is in a buying mood. Volume-wise we're ahead of spring, but profit-wise we're being squeezed by the high cost of card tables and pushcarts."

"Well, you certainly have a good location."

"Yes, we did a survey of the various sidewalks in Manhattan and decided that Fifth Avenue and 50th Street had a class clientele.

"We were first attracted by Saks Fifth Avenue's alluring window displays. They also have an excellent advertising department. We looked over Bloomingdale's but discovered that Alexander's, which is located next door, was underselling us.

"For a while we were set up on 34th Street, but we decided to upgrade our merchandise and appeal to the more affluent shopper. My girlfriend wanted us to put up our stand in front of Bergdorf Goodman, but I like to be in the shadow of St. Patrick's Cathedral."

"How does Saks Fifth Avenue feel about you selling T-shirts right outside their front door?"

"They haven't welcomed us with the enthusiasm you'd expect. Every hour Mr. Saks comes out and screams at me that he pays taxes and rent and provides air conditioning and heat and we're competing unfairly with him. I try to explain that we're good for his business. Our T-shirt stand attracts many upwardly mobile customers, and if they don't find what they want with us they'll go into his store. I don't know how many people we've sent into Saks, but it's certainly more than they've sent out to us."

"Nobody likes competition," I said.

"I don't understand him," Max said. "For years people complained because we were trying to overthrow the system. They said we were a bunch of bums that didn't know what it was to earn a living. So now we're part of the system and it's driving them up the wall. I've even offered to give Saks a discount on my T-shirts, but this only gets him madder. He wants me to move to Lord & Taylor's, but I told him I felt the location was too far down Fifth Avenue and they didn't have adequate parking facilities for my type of customer. I offered to merge with Saks on the condition they opened their books to me, but I was turned down. Frankly, I wasn't disappointed because I'd like to leave this piece of sidewalk to my son."

"Did you ever dream when you were trashing the Dow Chemical Co. in 1970 that some day you'd have a business of your own?"

"No, but that's what The American Dream is all about. Any person who is willing to work can start out on a slab of concrete in front of Woolworth's, and by perseverance and good luck wind up with his own card table in front of one of this country's finest department stores."

Just Tourists

It's hard to believe that the United States was unaware that there were "3,000 Soviet combat troops" in Cuba. The State Department's story is that our intelligence experts were caught by surprise. It was only after they "re-evaluated" their reports of the past five years that they concluded the Russians were there.

I managed to get one of the CIA's folders containing intelligence information from our man in Havana, a certain Miguel X, which explains why the United States was never sure that there were Soviet troops in Castro's Disneyland.

The first memo was dated August 12, 1974.

"Three thousand Soviet tourists disembarked from the passenger ship *Lenin* in Havana at 2 A.M. this morning. They were dressed in white wash 'n' wear seersucker suits, wore Panama hats and were carrying East German cameras and Ivanov submachine guns. I inquired of their tour leader, Lt. Gen. Vladimir Sokolov, what they planned to do in Cuba and he replied, 'We are from Kiev-Cuban Friendship Society to see beautiful country, sightsee and do cha cha cha with Cuban girls. We get five-year tour of country for package price of 995 rubles with breakfast included.'

"Do you want me to follow up? —M.X."

The reply to Miguel X was also in the folder and said, "It sounds like just another Intourist junket to us. If you can get anything you can pin down, let us know. Otherwise, due to budget restrictions, prefer you forget whole thing."

The next memo from Miguel X was dated December 3, 1976.

"Sorry to bother you, but was passing by Manzanillo and accidentally ran into Russian tourists. They have set up mobile homes with large saucer-shaped electronic equipment on top. Also saw 50 anti-aircraft guns, 200 tanks and heard artillery firing off in the distance. Ran into Gen. Sokolov in a bar in town and asked him how he was getting along. He bought me a vodka and said, 'Tour is going along fantastic. There is so much to see in Cuba we don't ever want to leave.'

"I asked what the saucer-like discs were doing on the mobile homes and he said, 'Is for television. Reception in this part of country is very lousy.' Then I asked him about the artillery firing. 'Is nothing but our people hunting wild boar. Look, we have license signed by Castro himself. Each tourist is entitled to one boar.'

"I can't put my finger on it but I think I was given a snow job. —M.X."

The answer from his superiors in Washington read: "Thank you, Miguel, for your report. We wish you wouldn't bother us with your suspicions that you were being lied to. It's obvious the Soviets have moved into mobile homes to save on hotel bills. The TV story makes sense to us. As for the anti-aircraft guns, they were probably left over from the Bay of Pigs. Because of new cut in budget, would prefer you mail your urgent reports via Mexico and not use straight cable."

The last message from Miguel X was dated May 1, 1979.

"The Soviet tourists held their Fourth Annual May Day Parade in the city of Batabano. Gen. Sokolov, who has been promoted to marshal, was in the reviewing stand with Fidel Castro. I managed to talk to him after the parade. He said he was having the best visit and the only thing he missed was black bread and borsch. He was thinking of opening a Russian-type restaurant which would cater to tourists like himself who were getting tired of Cuban food.

"The tourists put on quite a show for us. They divided themselves between the Red and Blue tour groups. The Blue group tried to capture the beach and the Red group repulsed them with mortars and machine guns. Of course they were using blanks. I don't know why I still think there is more to all this than meets the eye."

The final reply from Washington said: "Please stop wasting your time lolling around the beach with some bathers who just seem to be having a good time and concentrate on any military activity in the country."

Books Kill

What do the Russians fear from us the most? It's not our cruise missiles, our nuclear submarines, our B-52 bombers or our new MX system. They're afraid of our books.

This came to light once again when American publishers were invited to the Moscow International Book Fair. The Soviets confiscated 44 books (there could be more by the time this appears), including five editions of the *Best Pictorial Cartoons* from the years 1972, 1975, 1976, 1977, 1978, published by Pelican; all of Alexander Solzhenitsyn's books; *The Illustrated History of the Third Reich* by John Bradley (Grosset and Dunlap); *A Cartoon History of United States Foreign Policy* by the editors of the Foreign Policy Assn. (Morrow); *American Ballet Theater* by Charles Payne; *Hitler* by Joachim Fest, and George Orwell's *Animal Farm*.

When I read the news, I called up Boris, my KGB contact at the Soviet Embassy in Washington, and told him, "I've just microfilmed *The Complete Scarsdale Medical Diet* and I thought you might want to buy it from me."

He instructed me to meet him on a park bench near the Lincoln Memorial. He told me to bring along a bag of bread crumbs so we could pretend we were feeding the pigeons.

I made the rendezvous, sat down next to him and passed him the microfilm. He slipped me an envelope with ten $100 bills.

"This is very good work," he said. "What can I expect next?"

I replied, "I know a guy who works at the Discount Book Store in Chevy Chase. He has access to *The Complete Book of Running* by James Fixx. It will cost you, though. The guy thinks he's being watched by the manager."

"I'll ask my people in Moscow and get back to you," he said. "Do you have any word on whether Godunov, the ballet dancer, is writing a book?"

"No," I said, "but I'll try to find out."

"We're willing to pay a lot to discover this," he said.

"Why?" I asked.

"The sooner we know, the sooner we can ban it," he replied.

"Tell me, Boris, it must be impossible to keep books out of the Soviet Union that are printed in the West. Why does the Soviet Union go to so much trouble?"

He lit a new cigarette from the one he was smoking. "Books kill," he whispered. "We have the capacity to stop your planes and missiles and even knock down your satellites. But we have no defense yet against Fascist ideas. If certain books published in the West got wide circulation in the Eastern countries, they could become a threat to our national security."

"It must be terrible to be afraid of books. They look so innocent on a shelf. It's hard to believe they could do so much damage."

He lit another cigarette from the one he had already lighted and said, "It isn't the books, it's what is in them that we're concerned with. Our people are happy and love the Communist system. We don't want trash from the West to foment hatred and insecurity. The price of a true Marxist society is constant vigilance. Besides, you have no right to ask me all these questions."

"Don't get smart with me," I warned Boris. "I am your only source for an autographed copy of *Sophie's Choice*. I happen to know the author."

"I'm sorry I lost my temper," Boris said. "But we've been under tremendous pressure from Moscow. Several people who subscribe to the Book-of-the-Month Club managed to get visas to attend our book fair, and they're putting all the blame on us."

The Marines Have Landed

As a former U.S. Marine I swelled with pride last week when I saw the leathernecks hit the beach at Guantanamo Bay on television. It was a scene out of one of John Wayne's best movies. There they were, 1,800 men strong, covered by 80 newspaperpersons, television and radio crews brought to the island especially by the Defense Department to make sure that the world knew that President Carter was taking a tough stand on Cuba.

Of course, no Marine landing ever goes smoothly. For one thing weather held up the exercise and for another the time had to be set back when it was discovered that the television cameramen wouldn't have enough light to get the pictures they wanted.

But as the colonel of the operation said, "The landing went just like a ballet."

As with every military exercise there is a post-mortem in which the officers and sergeants thrash out their mistakes.

I'm sure it must be going on right now.

"Men, I'm proud of all of you. The Guantanamo exercise will go down in history with Montezuma and Tripoli. But we can't just congratulate ourselves on a job well done. We have to study our errors and learn from them.

"All right, let's start with the CH-46 helicopters.

"They were supposed to land by these NBC-TV cameras marked on the map here. Instead they landed over there where the print reporters were stationed. NBC lost a great photo opportunity, and we had to supply them with our own film to calm them down. Does anyone have an explanation for this?"

"Sir, we tried to get the ships as close to the NBC target as we could, but they set up their cameras on rocks. So we had to land 500 yards downwind from them. The producer wanted us to do it all over again, but we were short of fuel."

"I'll accept that excuse, but you were supposed to take this ledge by 1300 hours. You didn't get there until 1400. What went wrong?"

"We were pinned down by the *Washington Post, New York*

Times and *Wall Street Journal* reporters. Then the wire service people broke through our left flank and we had our backs to the sea. I told my men to dig in until we get some more PR reinforcements. Then we were ordered not to move out until the Mutual Broadcasting Company got an on-the-spot interview with every member of our mortar platoon."

"I'll accept that. Now we've had an official complaint from CBS that our Cobra gunships drowned out their sound, and they couldn't put an interview with one of our platoon leaders on the air. I gave specific orders—the Cobras were not to fly over CBS when they were filming."

"Fleet Headquarters gave us instructions, sir, to fly back and forth for the benefit of the ABC cameras as they wanted some action shots to go with the Frank Reynolds commentary. From the air it's very hard to tell the difference between CBS and ABC."

"I would now like to take up the still photography problem. When Alpha Platoon landed in their amphibious tanks on Zebra Beach the still photographers demanded the men point their guns toward Havana. Several tank commanders were confused and pointed them toward Miami. What the hell went wrong?"

"Our lead tank's gyro was out and by the time we got it fixed, the photographers had all snapped their pictures and disappeared into the bush."

"I never want it to happen again. One last thing. The *Women's Wear Daily* correspondent said she had been promised exclusive photos of the command post, but when she got there *People* magazine had beaten her to it. She was mad as a hornet and said *Women's Wear Daily* might never cover a Marine landing again. Gentlemen, this is the kind of goof that loses us a war."

Part IV

Trouble for Loan Sharks

One of the results of the high prime rate is that it is now cheaper to borrow money from the Mafia than it is from the Chase Manhattan Bank.

For years the Mafia prided itself on charging the highest interest in town. But thanks to the Federal Reserve actions of the past few months, the loan shark rates have become a bargain.

"Arnold the Adjuster," one of the major loan sharks in New York City, has mixed feelings about this turn of events.

"We naturally are delighted to be able to compete with Bank of America on their terms," he told me, "but the Cosa Nostra always prided itself on charging more vigorish (interest) than anybody else. People came to us when the legitimate banks turned them down. Now they're coming to us *before* they go to the banks. If we refuse to loan them the money then they have no choice but to throw themselves on the mercy of the Irving Trust Co."

"I should think you'd be delighted with this state of affairs," I told him.

"We would, except that in the past our loan department has dealt with individuals and if they couldn't pay we had sure-fire methods of collecting from them. Now the large corporations have heard our rates are cheaper and are coming to us for funds. How do you break the legs of the telephone company if they fail to pay you back?"

"I see the problem," I told him. "It must be difficult to go to IBM and say, 'If we don't get the money by Thursday, you'll never see your grandmother again.' "

"There are other difficulties," Arnold said. "Our main source of loan money came from Mafia families who didn't know what to do with their hidden cash flow. Now they can buy legitimate Treasury notes for higher interest than we are permitted to charge. So they've been withdrawing their deposits to buy bonds, thus drying up our money supply. At the same time they get very angry when the loan shark division doesn't show a profit."

"It must be killing you," I said.

"Loan sharking isn't what it used to be," he told me. "Our costs are going up every day. Our enforcers are demanding more money, the price of baseball bats has gone sky-high, and you have no idea what a bag of cement costs now. We've had to make big cutbacks. Before, if you borrowed more than $5,000 in a week, we gave you a free stolen toaster or TV set. But now you get the money without the gifts, and a lot of people are mad."

"At the same time," I said, "it must make you proud to know that you can undercut the Citibank on what they charge for a loan."

"It does and it doesn't. The Fed has screwed the money market all up. We don't know where we are from one day to the next. The legitimate banks never worried about loan sharks, because they always knew we charged three points more than they did. Now that our rates are lower, they're complaining to the FBI that we're hurting their business. The heat's on because Household Finance just can't stand the competition."

"Why don't you raise your vigorish above that of the banks? Then they won't have anything to gripe about."

"We don't want to drive the country into a recession. Our bookmaking and white slavery divisions depend on a healthy economy."

"So what are you going to do?"

"We're sending our people down to see the members of the Federal Reserve Board and explain what their tight money policies are doing to the 'under the counter' loan business."

"Do you think they'll listen to reason?" I asked.

"They have to. They have grandmothers too."

Three Coins in the Fountain

The Treasury Department is very mad at all of us. We haven't taken to the Susan B. Anthony dollar as their experts predicted we would.

Millions of dollars (paper ones) went into research to develop a coin that would replace the one dollar bill. The Treasury engineers worked in their cellars day and night to devise something that would grab the imagination of the American people. They finally came up with a foolproof design—a coin the size of a quarter with 11 sides and a picture of a suffragette on it. What more could the American people ask for?

Apparently a lot more. When the coin flopped, the only thing left for the Treasury officials to do was to call a meeting.

"Gentlemen, the Secretary is very upset. No matter how many Susan B. Anthony coins we put into circulation, people insist on using paper dollars. What can we do about it?"

"My staff has been doing some research to find out why the coin won't fly. Most men we've talked to say that if they have more than seven in their pants pocket they make a hole, and all the coins dribble out into the street. The young people say the dollars make a bulge in their jeans, and women complain if they take enough dollar coins to buy groceries they develop a bad back."

"That's nonsense. This coin was tested under the greatest stress conditions. We put $50 worth in a Deputy Secretary's pants pockets, threw him into the Tidal Basin and he didn't even sink. One of our women department heads carried 100 coins in her handbag for one week and except for black and blue marks on her shoulder where the strap hung, there were no signs of bodily damage. As for the young people complaining of bulges in their jeans from carrying the coins, my answer to that is, let them buy bigger jeans."

"I'm just reporting on what our research revealed, sir. If you ask me I think it's more psychological than anything else. The one dollar paper bill has George Washington's picture on it. The people can't tell Susan B. Anthony from the Queen of

England. They don't trust the coin because they are afraid it was minted in Canada."

"I agree with Merriweather. I tried to give one to a taxi driver the other day and he said, 'I only take American money.' I said, 'It is American money' and he said, 'Yeah, and Margaret Trudeau is the First Lady of the United States.'"

"I don't want to hear any more stories. We're stuck with billions of these coins and we're going to get them into circulation if it kills us. Now let's hear some constructive ideas."

"We could put them in cereal boxes as a promotion."

"Why don't we raise the price of a local pay telephone call to a dollar?"

"What about printing on paper dollar bills under 'In God We Trust' the words: 'This bill could be dangerous to your health'?"

"How about having Karl Malden do a TV commercial? He could be pushing a wheelbarrow and saying to the audience: 'Traveler's checks can be stolen—but nobody could carry off this wheelbarrow of coins. The Susan B. Anthony dollars. Don't leave home without them.'"

"Why don't we just use them to pay the OPEC people for their oil?"

"What good will that do?"

"They'll all get hernias and be so miserable they'll think twice about raising their prices."

Chomp, Chomp, Chomp

The Supreme Court agreed last week to decide whether you can patent a new life form created by man in a laboratory. It goes under the name of genetic engineering. One of the cases has to do with a scientist at General Electric who made a bacterium in the lab and called it Pseudomonas. The bacterium is capable of eating oil spills by breaking down the molecular structure of petroleum as it floats on the ocean.

I am not concerned whether you can patent Pseudomonas or not. What worries me is that the bacterium exists at all.

As with so many things scientists come up with, it sounds great in a test tube. Everyone hates oil spills, and if you can have hungry organisms feasting on the stuff it solves that problem.

But what happens after the bacterium eats up all the oil that is spilled? In a few days the Pseudomonas will start getting hungry again and going after oil that is being drilled up from the ocean floor. It will start chomping away at any fuel it gets its teeth in, and it's not inconceivable that as billions of them work their way through an oil field there will be nothing left to pump up but salt water.

Chomp, chomp, chomp—and there go all the reserves in the North Sea. Chomp, chomp, chomp—and it's goodbye to the oil in the Gulf of Mexico. Chomp, chomp, chomp—and you can kiss the petroleum off the coast of California goodbye.

The Pseudomonas can't tell the difference between oil spilled from a tanker and oil on the ocean floor. All it knows is that if it wants to survive, it has to eat. And one lousy tanker spill will not feed a family of bacteria very long.

If this isn't enough to make you nervous, what happens when the bacteria start clinging to the shoes of someone working on an oil rig? There is a big turnover in men who work on oceangoing rigs. After a while they long to drill on land. Suppose the rigger moves to Texas and wears the same shoes in the Panhandle. The bacteria will immediately start going down the well and chomp, chomp, chomp—it's arrivederci to Texas oil.

I know that someone will argue that the Pseudomonas won't eat oil unless it's mixed with salt water. But bacteria are very adaptable organisms, and if they can't swill their petroleum with salt water they'll take it straight.

Once the Pseudomonas gets into our domestic oil it's a short step for it to the refinery and then into your home heating tank. Chomp, chomp, chomp—and half the oil that cost you 90 cents a gallon will be digested by bacteria before it gets to your furnace.

I may be unfair to the Pseudomonas, or the man who created it. For all I know the bacterium may get its fill of oil spills and then die. But genetic engineering is a dangerous game, and when you start creating bacteria in a test tube you have no idea what they're going to feast on.

Today it may just chomp on tar balls off Cape Cod, but tomorrow it might decide that sweet oil tasted better. When it does it's shalom to Saudi Arabia.

The Human Body Shop

The big medical breakthrough of the Eighties will be the development of mechanical parts for the human body. We've seen the success of the pacemaker, plastic joints and hips, steel replacements for legs and arms, and artificial organs which do the work that was formerly left to human ones.

Perhaps I'm being too optimistic, but I predict that by 1989 half our bodies will either come from Dupont, U.S. Steel or Reynolds Aluminum.

It follows then that when our bodies are working well we shall all have to go to a garage, rather than a hospital, to have repairs done.

A man walks into George's Human Body Repair Shop:

"Can I help you, sir?"

"Yes, I'd like a tuneup and a grease job."

George takes out a repair slip and starts filling it in.

"Mind getting up on the rack so I can examine you?"

The man stands on a rack and George jacks him up a few feet. "How are the knees?"

"They seem a little sluggish when I jog."

"I'd better change the bearings and linkage," George says, as he writes on his clipboard. "When did you have these leg muscles checked?"

"About a year ago. Why?"

"They're starting to fray. We have a new steel-belted radial muscle which is guaranteed for five years."

"Do I really need them?"

"Depends if you ever want to walk again."

The man nods his assent and George scribbles on the sheet. Then he says, "How are the arms?"

"I have tennis elbow in the right one."

"We'll have to put in a new shock absorber. Are your finger joints okay?"

"They seem to be. I can still make a fist."

George examines the hands. "I'll have to put new points in your fingers. Your nails seem to be rusting."

"Look, I just came in for a tuneup. My body's 50 years old, and I don't want to put a lot of money into it."

"You notice anything else bothering you?"

"Well, my back hurts when I do situps. I hear this click, click, click every time I touch my toes."

George runs his hands along the man's back. "I was afraid of that," he says. "Your spine is all out of whack. We're going to have to replace it. We have a sale on back shafts that will last a lifetime or we replace it for you absolutely free. How's the head?"

"Fine. I have no trouble getting it together."

"You're losing a lot of hair. We better give you a transplant. We have a Lincoln Day special on new all-weather Orlon that is so strong you never have to wear a hat."

George keeps on writing on the pad. Then he says, "I don't think you're getting enough air into your lungs. I'll put in new valves. You're American, aren't you?"

"Of course I am. Why do you ask?"

"Because if you were a foreigner, we'd have to order the parts from overseas and it would take two months."

"Are you finished?" the man says.

"That should do it," George says.

"When can I have my work done?"

George looks at his schedule. "If you come in on Thursday morning at eight, I should have you out by 5 P.M. unless my mechanics find something I've overlooked."

"If you do everything you want to, can you guarantee that my body will be good for at least two more years?" the man asks.

"How can I do that?" George replies. "I'm not a doctor."

The Decline of S — X

"Sexual anorexia," the loss of sexual desire, according to people who keep up on such things, is becoming commonplace in American society. Apparently it is more prevalent in men than women. There are as many theories as to what causes it as there are sexual therapists.

One therapist blames it on *Monday Night Football*, which is now also shown on Thursdays and sometimes on Saturday nights.

"You can't expect someone who has listened to Howard Cosell for three hours to have a very strong sex drive," one therapist told me. "What worries all the people who deal with sexual dysfunctions is that more and more sports programs are being put on the air during prime time, and more men are complaining of headaches when they're ready to go to bed."

A woman sex therapist considers the new computer games a contributing factor toward sexual anorexia. She said, "You can play practically any game from backgammon to tennis on a toy computer now, and I find most of my male patients are happier trying to outwit a stupid machine then indulging in the pleasures of the flesh. Recently I tried an experiment in my lab. I had a beautiful girl in a black silk negligee sitting on the bed. Across the room on a card table there was a Simon Says computer game—the one that lights up in different colors and makes a lot of noise.

"Four of my five patients immediately went to the Simon Says computer and started to push the buttons."

"Well," I said, "at least the fifth person was healthy."

"I'm not sure. He confessed he was more attracted to the girl than to Simon Says, but that if I had offered him a radio-controlled robot he might have had second thoughts."

"Who would have ever dreamed that computers would replace sex?"

"I guess," she said sadly, "it's whatever turns you on."

Another member of the profession blames the loss of sexual desire on the proliferation of all the sex-oriented magazines.

"I can trace the decline and fall of the male sex drive directly

161

to the increase in the publication of *Playboy, Penthouse, Hustler* and all the other imitations. Men are reading more about sex and enjoying it less."

"Why is this?"

"They feel that since they've read about it, they've actually done it. Many men can now fulfill all their fantasies at the newstands for $2.50, which is much cheaper than paying for someone's taxi fare home."

One therapist (Washington has almost as many as California) told me that as men become more passive in their sexual drives, women become more aggressive.

"I have a lady friend who met a very attractive lawyer, and after a candlelight dinner and a visit to a disco, she said to him, 'Your place or mine?' The lawyer said excitedly, 'Mine,' and they played pinball until five in the morning."

"What's the answer to the problem?"

"Well, we know it isn't perfume," she said, "and it obviously isn't women's lib. We do know men's sexual appetites dwindle in direct proportion to the professional success of their mates. I would say the only answer is to return to a moralistic society where sex is considered forbidden fruit. Many of my colleagues will take issue with me, but if we indoctrinate young men with the fact that having a healthy sex life is a sin, they'll be inspired to give up their computer games and come to bed when they are called."

A Great Investment

Because of the uncertainty of the economy everyone seems to be buying things today "as a good investment."

My wife is no exception. The other day she came home with an Oriental rug the size of a postage stamp.

"How do you like it?" she wanted to know.

"It's beautiful," I said. "What's it for?"

"The hallway. I got a fantastic buy on it."

"Oh. Would I be out of line to inquire how much it was?"

"Six hundred dollars."

"You paid $600 for a rug that two people can't stand on at the same time?"

"It's a very good investment. Liz Stevens bought one just like it three years ago for $400 and it's now worth $3,000."

"You told me the dining room table you bought five years ago for $800 was a good investment."

"Well, it was. That table is now selling at Sloane's for $4,000."

"Okay, let's sell it then."

"Are you crazy?" she said. "Why would we want to sell our table?"

"Because we bought it as an investment and you never know when the market is going to drop through the floor on dining room tables."

"Then what do we do for a table?"

"We could buy another one for $800 and sell it in four years."

"You can't replace that dining room table for $800."

"Then why is it a good investment if you never intend to sell it? I might also ask the same question about this Oriental rug."

"The longer we hold on to these things the higher in value they'll go. We won't sell them until we need the money."

"Yes, but when that time comes, everyone else will also be broke, and there will be nobody to buy the rug," I said.

"The man in the rug store said he'd buy it back from us any time we wanted to sell it. That's how good an investment he thinks it is."

"Men in rug stores always say that. So do art dealers, and come to think of it so do jewelers. But have you ever tried to take something back to the person who says that?"

I could tell I wasn't getting to her.

"If you want to know the truth of the matter," she said, "I would rather have a small Oriental rug that will go up in value every year than a shag rug that will be worthless in a decade. Almost everything we own is worth five times what we paid for it."

"I say we liquidate, take our profits and run," I said. "That's what good investors do."

"Not on your life. The way inflation is going," she said, "the only protection we have is to invest in good things. Then we at least have security."

I called up Liz Stevens' husband George. "Would you be interested in buying a $600 Oriental rug for $1,000?"

"No," he said, "but I'll sell you a $3,000 rug for $400."

"That's what I thought," I said and hung up.

I sat on our $300 sofa which was now worth $1,200 and tried to figure out some other way to pay our gas bill.

The Most Valuable Doctor

The votes are all in, and the medical sports writers have just selected the Most Valuable Pro-Football Doctor of the year.

The winner is Dr. Bubba Klaus, who averaged 180 yards a game running on and off the field tending to injured players.

Klaus, a first-round draft choice from Johns Hopkins Medical School, was selected for the award not only for his scrambling and third-down stitching procedures but also for his emergency knee operations during time outs, which made it possible for a running back to return to the game for the next play.

His coach, Torga Strindberg, told reporters at the awards ceremonies: "Our medical scouts had been watching Bubba ever since he was an intern. He only weighed 150 pounds, which is pretty light for a football doctor, but he had the hands of a 270-pound plastic surgeon. He was overlooked by every other team in the league, and we picked him up for the price of two over-the-hill paramedics."

Asked what made Bubba such a great running doctor, Coach Strindberg replied, "He has no fear. As soon as he sees a player stretched out on the field, he'll leap off the bench and crash through the entire defensive line to get to him.

"And in an entire season, he's only fumbled his black bag three times. He also likes to block, which is rare for a doctor. I've seen him knock over three referees just to get to a wide receiver who had a cramp in his thigh. But it's not just his speed and strength which makes him a great football doctor —Bubba also has brains. When he sees that our defensive unit is pooped, he'll hold up a game for five minutes pretending one of our players has a cracked rib. Most doctors want to get their people off the field as fast as possible, but Bubba always sizes up the situation and he'll instruct our injured man to stay on his back until everyone gets his second wind."

A reporter said, "Howard Cosell on a Monday night game indicated Bubba is overrated as a football doctor and wouldn't be able to hold a candle to some of the great orthopedic men with the old Chicago Bears and Washington Redskins. What do you have to say to that?"

"Howard doesn't know the difference between an orthopedist and a pediatrician. He's had it in for Bubba ever since Howard came to him once complaining about hoarseness, and Bubba put his throat in a cast."

When receiving the trophy from NFL Commissioner Pete Rozelle, Dr. Klaus said, "I am honored to be named Pro-Football Doctor of the Year, but this award should be shared with many people, mostly the players of the teams who opposed us this season. Had it not been for their dirty tackling and vicious blocking, not to mention their roughing of our quarterbacks and kickers, I might never have gotten on the field at all.

"To those players on the opposition teams whose personal fouls against our boys made it possible for me to get into all the games—I say 'thank you' from the bottom of my heart."

A Tight Fit

As anyone who flies is aware, the airlines are putting more and more seats into their planes to make the flights more profitable. Some time ago, I wrote about a human engineer who was assigned to devise ways of packing as many people into a plane as humanly possible.

He was the first one to recommend putting seats in the luggage racks, and also tearing out lavatories to make more room for paying customers.

He also wanted to sell eight seats in the cockpit, but the Airline Pilots' Assn. protested and it was temporarily put on the back burner.

I met him on the shuttle flying from Washington to New York the other day. We were seated next to each other, our knees scrunched up to our chests and our shoulder blades sharply pressed into each other.

"You've done a marvelous job," I told him. "Who would ever have thought you could double the number of human bodies aboard an airplane in such a short time?"

He was observing everything going on and finally said, "I've been hired to figure out how to get 30 more seats in."

"It's impossible," I said, "unless you use the aisle."

"I can't use the aisle," he told me in disgust. "The CAB has some damn-fool regulation that you can't put seats in the aisle. The government is strangling the aviation business."

"Everyone seems as packed in as possible," I told him. "I guess you'll have to recommend that they fly bigger airplanes."

"I'm not being paid for that," he said. "My job is to get more seats on the planes the airlines already own."

"What about the freight compartment below?" I asked.

"I thought of that. But we can only get 12 seats in there and people might complain if their bags don't arrive on the same plane as they do."

"I guess there's nothing you can do then except make the people smaller."

He didn't realize I was making a joke. "We've been working

on that, but the few people we've tried our machine on squawked so much we gave it up."

"Well, you can't win them all," I said.

The human engineer was staring out the window. Suddenly his eyes widened. "Do you see what I see?"

"What's that?"

"The wing of the airplane."

"Of course I see the wing of the airplane."

"It looks pretty solid, doesn't it?"

"I hope so," I said. "Wait a minute—you're not thinking what I think you're thinking."

"Why not?" he said excitedly. "You could bolt in 15 seats on each wing and who would know the difference?"

"But wouldn't it be windy out there?"

"You'd put the seats facing the back so the people would be looking at the tail of the plane. On a clear day, the passengers would get a fantastic view of New Jersey."

"Are you sure people would agree to fly from Washington to New York on the wing of an airplane?"

He was writing furiously. "We'll give them 20 percent off their no-frills tickets, 30 percent if they fly as a family."

"I'm not certain you'll get many takers," I said skeptically. "The inside of the plane doesn't look like *Love Boat,* but at least we don't have to worry about the wind-chill factor."

"Look, years ago you would have screamed murder if you had had to fly with your knees on your chest. Now you accept it without a murmur. When you buy an airline ticket, all we promise to do is get you there. There is nothing in the contract which guarantees where you'll sit."

Something's Happening

One of the things I enjoy the most about the news shows on television is that you have to use your imagination watching them.

I don't seem to react much when the newspaper correspondent is actually talking to somebody. But I jump out of my seat when the reporter has failed to interview the subject he has been assigned to.

More and more of this is going on now. You've probably seen it yourself but haven't paid any attention to it.

Here's how it goes:

"For the latest report on medical fraud in the United States, let's go to Michael Mindlin in Thyroid, Long Island."

"Chester, I'm standing here in front of the $500,000 home of Dr. William Scalpel, who made $150 million from Medicaid this year by advising all his patients to go to a different physician for a second opinion. Dr. Scalpel is now in the house, presumably on the second floor, but he has refused to come out to talk to me. He arrived home at seven o'clock and drove his Mercedes into these closed garage doors behind me. Then I knocked on the front door over here but no one answered. I went around to the back and rang the kitchen doorbell and he refused to respond to my rings. Neighbors have told me that Dr. Scalpel will probably stay in his house all evening. This is Michael Mindlin reporting from Thyroid, Long Island."

"Good work, Michael, and now let's go to our White House correspondent, Janet Blonde."

"Chester, I'm standing here in front of the White House where Hamilton Jordan has yet to make an appearance. This is the fifth day that Jordan has not come out to talk to reporters. A White House spokesman said Jordan is very busy working on the crisis in Iran and the economy. Just before I went on the air a black limousine pulled up to the driveway behind me, and two people carrying briefcases stepped out and went into the side door."

"Did you notice who they were, Janet?"

"No, I didn't, Chester, and the chauffeur refused to say who he worked for. Both men are still in the White House and have been there for more than an hour."

"Thank you, Janet. We'll get back to you if they leave. Now let's go to an on-the-spot live report from Tom Stinch in front of New York Hospital."

"Chester, it's all quiet at New York Hospital at this hour. The Shah of Iran has been gone for a week, and hospital officials, who wouldn't let our cameras inside, say that it is now business as usual. An hour ago an ambulance brought in a lady who had broken her hip in the bathroom. I tried to speak to a nurse who treated the Shah, but she sent word down that she has been ordered not to talk to anybody about his stay here."

"Tom, where are Henry Kissinger and David Rockefeller at this moment?"

"That's the interesting thing, Chester. Kissinger is out lecturing and David Rockefeller's office said he had gone to the opera with his wife."

"Well, that puts a whole new light on the problem, doesn't it, Tom?"

"Yes, it does, Chester. If anything develops I'll let you know."

"Thank you. Now we will go to Nancy Dunsmore at the Supreme Court."

"Chester, I am standing in a pay phone booth two blocks from the Supreme Court and have been trying to call Chief Justice Burger to get him to comment on Bob Woodward's book revealing intimate details on how the justices operate. He hasn't returned my calls for three days."

"Why don't you try once more, Nancy?"

"All right. I'm putting 20 cents in and I am now dialing the number. It's ringing. 'Hello, this is Nancy Dunsmore from station WDFC. May I speak to the Chief Justice? He's in a meeting? Thank you very much.' Chester, he's in a meeting."

"Don't run out of dimes, Nancy. And now let's go to Al Kilduff at the Red Coach Inn in Detroit, where Jimmy Hoffa hasn't been seen for four years."

Leisure Will Kill You

This country is producing so much leisure equipment for the home that nobody has any leisure time anymore to enjoy it. A few months ago I bought a television tape recorder to make copies of programs when I was out of the house.

Last week I recorded the Nebraska-Oklahoma football game. When I came home in the evening, I decided to play it back. But my son wanted to play "Baseball" on the TV screen with his Atari Computer. We finished four innings when my wife came in the room and asked me if I would like to listen to the Vienna Opera on our hi-fi stereo set. I told her I was waiting to finish the baseball match so I could watch the football game I had recorded.

She said if I watched the football game for three hours, I would miss *Love Boat*. I told her I would record *Love Boat* and we could watch it later in the evening. She protested that *Casablanca* was showing on Channel 5 at 11:30 and she wanted to see it again.

"Don't worry," I assured her, "we can watch *Love Boat* late Saturday and *Casablanca* on Sunday morning when we get up."

"But if we watch *Casablanca* tomorrow morning when can we see the instant Polaroid movies you took of Ben yesterday afternoon?"

"We'll see them after we play backgammon on the new table."

"If we do that," my daughter said, "we won't be able to see the Washington Redskins-New York Giants football game."

"I'll record the Redskins-Giants football game and we'll watch it while *60 Minutes* is on the air. We can see *60 Minutes* at 11 o'clock."

"But," my son said, "you promised to play the pinball machine with me at 11."

"Okay, we'll play pinball at 11 and watch *60 Minutes* at midnight."

My wife said, "Why don't we listen to the Vienna Opera

171

while we're eating and then we can save an hour to play computer golf?"

"That's good thinking," I said. "The only problem is I've rented a TV tape for *Cleopatra* and that runs for three hours."

"You could show it on Monday night," she suggested.

"I can't do that. I have to return the tape Monday afternoon or be charged for it another week. I have an idea. I won't go to work Monday morning and we'll watch it then."

"I was hoping to use our Jacuzzi Monday morning," my wife said.

"Okay, then I'll tape *Cleopatra* and you can see it Monday afternoon."

"I'm using the set Monday afternoon," my son said, "to play digital hockey on the TV screen."

"You can't do that," I said. "I have to watch the *Today* show in the afternoon if I'm going to watch *Cleopatra* in the morning."

"Why can't you watch the *Today* show at dinnertime?" my wife asked.

"Because the Wolfingtons are coming over to hear me play 'Tea for Two' on the electric organ."

"I thought we might play computer bridge at dinner," my wife said.

"We'll play it after my encore," I assured her.

"Then when will we see *Monday Night Football*?" my son wanted to know.

"Tuesday," I said.

"Does that mean you're not going to work on Tuesday?" my wife asked.

"How can I go to work," I yelled, "when I've got so much leisure time on my hands?"

How to Buy a Car

WASHINGTON—Do you want to know why automobiles are not selling these days? I'll tell you why. I was looking for a car the other day to replace a gas guzzler I was unhappy with.

My first stop was at the Banzai dealership.

"I want a small car, comfortable, that won't use up too much petrol."

"Then the Banzai is for you. It has everything a big car has but you never have to fill the tank."

"I'm just looking, mind you," I told him. "I like the styling of the Banzai, but I might also check out a Brustein XLD."

"I understand," the salesman said, "but I think you ought to know the 1980 Brustein XLD has had eight recalls so far, and we're still in January."

"I didn't know that. Was it in the papers?"

"They keep things like that out of the papers. It seems if you have to stop for a red light, the seatbelt can give you a hernia. If you're looking for something hernia-proof, then you should get a Banzai with a sun roof."

I told him I'd be back. I went across the street to inspect a Hara-Kiri Sword. I told the man that a friend of mine had just bought a Sword and seemed happy with it. But I wasn't sure whether I wanted a Sword or a Banzai.

"The Banzai's a very good car," he said, "except the transmission keeps falling out of it. Apparently the people who made it give their workers sake instead of coffee when they take a break. Banzai workers are drunk all the time, except when they're out on strike."

I thanked him for the information on the Banzai and told him that although I planned to look at other cars I would probably wind up buying a Sword.

The next showroom I went to displayed the Achtung 489. The salesman told me each Achtung was guaranteed to give 35 miles to the gallon, and the doors could be removed and made into a bed. He asked me what other automobiles I had looked at.

I told him the last one I liked was a Hara-Kiri Sword.

"Do you have a family?" the man asked.

"Yes," I replied, "why do you ask?"

"Nothing," he said. "I just returned from a funeral of a family that had been driving a Hara-Kiri Sword. I still haven't gotten over it. The police said the steering wheel came off as they were parking in a shopping center. God, that family had so much to live for."

"That couldn't happen to an Achtung?" I inquired.

"I wouldn't be selling them if it could," he said, wiping the tears from his eyes.

I don't want you to think I just looked at foreign cars. My next stop was to check out a compact Stars and Stripes Zipper. The salesman took me for a drive in it. He drove past an auto dump filled with wrecked and crushed cars.

"It's full of 1978 Achtungs," the man said.

"Why?" I asked.

"No resale value," he said. "The only reason a dealer will buy them back is for scrap."

I liked the Zipper until the manager of the Rawhide dealership told me the ashtrays on it were wired into the electrical system and every time you put a cigarette out you got a shock. The people at the Hurricane showroom said the Rawhide's bumpers tended to fall off when it snowed, and the Grunt car dealer said the Hurricane had never been able to make it through a pothole without both axles breaking.

I decided the hell with it. I'll stick to my old Dowdy until I can find a new car that somebody has something nice to say about. Truth in advertising is one thing, but what's going on these days between competing automobile dealers is ridiculous.

The Pope as Statesman

My gripe today is with the Fashion Foundation of America, which has just voted Pope John Paul II the "Best Dressed Statesman of 1979."

I want to make it perfectly clear that I am a big admirer of Pope John Paul II and believe he should receive any honor bestowed on him.

But when it comes to clothes, I don't think he should be allowed to compete with people like President d'Estaing, Jimmy Carter, Deng Xiaoping, Margaret Thatcher or the Ayatollah Khomeini.

It just isn't fair to the other statesmen of the world to go up against His Holiness when it comes to clothing.

All John Paul's raiments are made by hand. I have it on the highest authority that he spends more money on one cape than Menachem Begin spends on his entire wardrobe. The cost of the Pope's slippers could shoe Madame Gandhi for the rest of her life.

When it comes to headgear, there isn't a statesman in the world who can hold a candle to one of the Pope's skullcaps.

No matter what you think of him personally, I believe it's unfair to make Fidel Castro run against John Paul II in the best-dressed statesman category.

There may be a few South American generals in full uniform who could make it a contest—Ferdinand Marcos is no slouch when it comes to dressing up for formal occasions, and the Royal Family of Saudi Arabia can get it all together when they have to. But except for Queen Elizabeth II, when she's opening Parliament, John Paul is in a class by himself.

The foundation tried to get off the hook when it announced the Pope as winner by saying it took "special note of the fact that the Pope added a light touch of fashion when he donned a Mexican hat during his trip to Mexico last year."

With all due respect to the Pontiff, even Henry Kissinger looks good when he's wearing a Mexican hat. The judges also said that John Paul II wears his robes far better than most recent Pontiffs have.

I don't believe this. Every Pope I've known looked great when he put on his vestments, because when it comes to papal attire, clothes make the man—man doesn't make the clothes.

Why am I getting so excited over this? The reason is quite simple.

I've always dreamed of making the best-dressed list of statesmen, ever since I bought my first J.C. Penney's polyester suit. This year I thought I'd be up against Giscard d'Estaing, Helmut Schmidt, Kurt Waldheim, Andrei Gromyko, Anwar Sadat and Zbigniew Brzezinski. I was sure I was a contender.

If I had known that Pope John Paul II was in the race, I would most certainly have asked the foundation to take my name off the ballot. It's like asking Princess Margaret to compete against Cher.

No Politics for Carter

"Is this Mr. Eldridge Winkler, chairman of the Flatbottom, Iowa, Democratic Party?"

"Yes, it is."

"Just a minute. The President of the United States of America would like to speak to you."

"Eldridge, this is Jimmy Carter. I am calling you from the White House, which I am unable to leave because of all the worldwide crises that are preventing me from campaigning during this election year."

"Yes, sir, Mr. President. It's very kind of you to take time out from your busy schedule, which must be consuming every minute of your day. Can I ask what you're calling about?"

"I just finished a meeting with the National Security Council concerning Iran, and I'm going into another meeting with the secretary of state over Afghanistan, and I was wondering how things were going in Iowa."

"You mean politically?"

"Of course not politically. I don't believe the President should get involved in politics at a moment like this. It's beneath him."

"If you say so, Mr. President. But why did you call then?"

"I was just thinking about you and all the loyal supporters in Iowa who did so much for me in 1976 when I first started running for the highest office in this land."

"You mean with all the things you've got to worry about, you've had time to think about Iowa?"

"I always think about Iowa. I can never forget your amber waves of grain and your corn which is as high as an elephant's eye, it reaches right up there into the sky."

"Now that you mention it, Mr. President, the people in Flatbottom would like to ask you about all that grain and corn. Why on earth did you put an embargo on food to the Soviet Union at this time?"

"Can you keep a state secret, Eldridge? If this leaked out, our whole foreign policy could be in jeopardy."

"Of course, Mr. President."

"The Russians can't be trusted."

"When on earth did you find that out?"

"About three weeks ago. They don't know what it is to keep their word. I'm glad I discovered it during my first term as President. It's given me a whole new insight into Soviet-American relations."

"But what do you do with all the grain and corn you told us to raise for the last three years?"

"Eldridge, I'm going to say one word to you now, but I don't want you to tell anyone where you heard it."

"I'm listening, Mr. President."

"Gasohol!"

"Gas-a-what?"

"Gasohol. I want all the farmers in Iowa to take all their grain and soybeans and corn and make alcohol out of it. Then I want you to take that alcohol and pour it into your fuel tanks. Then I want everyone to get in their cars and drive around with their headlights on and show the Soviets we mean business when they invade Afghanistan."

"Anything you say, Mr. President. Would you like to know how the Iowa caucuses are going?"

"No, Eldridge, I didn't call to talk about caucuses. I know the people of Iowa will do the right thing next week, in spite of the fact I have been too busy to further my own political fortunes in your great state. Goodbye, Eldridge. I'll pray for you."

"Is this Mr. Cameron Doolittle of the Mason City, Iowa, Democratic Party? Just a minute, I have the President of the United States of America on the line."

"Cameron, this is Jimmy Carter and as you know I am unable to leave the White House, but . . ."

Third World Friends

The Third World Flea Market was a beehive of activity.

Bamgambi from Gambia went over to Ahmad, the oil merchant, with his tin can. "May I have a quart of oil?"

"Of course, my friend," said Ahmad, "that will be $10 in gold."

Bamgambi searched his pockets. "Last week it was $7."

"Ah," said Ahmad, "that was last week. But this week we have had to raise prices because the First World is trying to take advantage of us."

"But I am of the Third World," Bamgambi said. "I can't afford to pay even $7 a quart."

"Well, you can blame it on the greedy Western merchants who are driving up the price every day. We Third World merchants have to stick together or the imperialists will have us by the throat."

"Excuse me, Ahmad, I don't mean to be rude, but it seems to me that YOU have us by the throat. If you and I belong to the same world, why can't you sell me your oil at a more reasonable price?"

"Have you gone mad, Bamgambi? Do you realize that the colonialist power brokers would love that? If we charged you a lower price than we charged the West, they would look at you as a second-class citizen from the Third World. The only way you can get any respect is to pay the same price for oil as the major industrial dealers."

"I see your point, Ahmad, and forgive me for questioning your logic, but we are running out of gold very fast, and pretty soon we will be unable to buy even one cup of oil. Without oil won't the industrial dealers think even less of us?"

"Bamgambi, all the oil merchants are aware of the hardships our prices are causing to our brothers in the Third World. We have agonized over it at length."

"And what conclusion did you come to?"

"We shouldn't put a cut-rate price on our friendship. If we charged you less than we did a Swede, you would think we were patronizing you. The fact that we make everyone pay the

179

same shows we respect you as much as we do a West German imperialist."

"You are very kind to think of us as equals. But that doesn't seem to solve the problem of how we can pay for your oil. Perhaps since we are of the same world you could give me credit until I can get on my feet."

"Now you have made me angry, Bamgambi. You think just because we're both brothers of the Third World that you can take advantage of our friendship? We have a strict cash-and-carry policy. Now do you want a quart of oil or don't you?"

Bamgambi handed Ahmad his last $10 in gold. "What choice do I have?"

"Here is your oil. If you come back tomorrow bring $12 in gold."

"You're raising the price tomorrow?"

"We have to eat, too."

Bamgambi picked up his quart of oil and started to walk away from the stall.

Ahmad said, "Are you coming to the meeting tonight?"

"What meeting?" Bamgambi asked.

"We're having a rally to protest the exploitation of the Third World people by the racist, money-grubbing industrial merchants who are holding all of us in economic bondage. Your support means a lot to us."

"Good Old World War III"

There is entirely too much talk about going to war these days. Strangers have been asking me lately, "Do you think there is going to be a war?" in the same tone they used not long ago to inquire if I thought there was going to be a recession.

I don't have any idea if there is going to be a war or not. But if there is one, it's not going to be like any other we've ever seen. The war we keep talking about these days has to do with another nuclear power and, therefore, it probably isn't going to live up to the nostalgia we all seem to have for World War II.

Before everybody gets too excited about us getting into another world war, I believe they should at least know what one could be like.

"Hello. Give me Bob Hope. Bob, how would you like to do a show for our troops in Yemen this Christmas?"
BBBBBRROOOOOOOOOOOOMMMMMMMMMMMM-MM!
"Never mind, Bob—there is no Yemen."

"Frank, I just wrote this great World War III song with Jimmy. Listen, 'Ivan, you s. o. b./Ivan don't mess with me. You may throw your weight around, but we will get up off the ground, Ivan . . .'"
BBBBBRROOOOOOOOOOOOMMMMMMMMMMMM-MM!

"Mrs. Miniver, I know this will be tough to take, but your son and husband were lost at sea. It's harder for those of us on the home front."
BBBBBRROOOOOOOOOOOOMMMMMMMMMMMM-MM!

"Elrod, I want you to know that all of us here at Four Corners are proud that you are going off to serve your country. Four Corners has always been the first to answer the bugle call when the enemy is at the door, and while we are safe and sound, there isn't a man here who wouldn't rather be in your shoes if he had the choice."

BBBBBRROOOOOOOOOOOMMMMMMMMMMMMM-MM!

"Hi, guys. Welcome to the Stage Door Canteen. Now who is the first sailor who's going to dance with me? Come on, don't be bashful—I may be the last girl you'll see for a couple of years. Anyone here from Oklahoma?"

BBBBBRROOOOOOOOOOOMMMMMMMMMMMMM-MM!

"And now, an important message for all Americans: Don't throw away your tin cans and scrap metal. Uncle Sam needs every bit he can get. Become a soldier on the home front, and give our boys everything they need."

BBBBBRROOOOOOOOOOOMMMMMMMMMMMMM-MM!

"My sakes and land-a-goshen! It's George, Paw. George is home. George, let me look at you. What are all those medals for?"

BBBBBRROOOOOOOOOOOMMMMMMMMMMMMM-MM!

"Men, here is where we are, and over here is where they are. Now we know they have tanks and machine guns. What we don't know is if they have tactical nuclear weapons. Fischetti, Goldberg, O'Brien, Nickapoulos and Hangdog. Your job will be to . . ."

BBBBBRROOOOOOOOOOOMMMMMMMMMMMMM-MM!

"I am here today to ask everyone as a patriotic duty to buy as many war bonds as he possibly can. I have been to the front and I have seen our boys. Their morale is high and every one of you would be proud of them. I asked our brave lads what they wanted most of all and they said just keep buying war bonds so they can get home as soon as possible. Now, let's have a show of hands of those who will buy $100 worth of bonds—I want to see a lot more hands than . . ."

BBBBBRROOOOOOOOOOOMMMMMMMMMMMMM-MM!

"Oh, Lawrence, before you go, I want to have your baby."
"Are you sure?"
"Yes, Lawrence, I'm sure."

"Gertrude, did you feel the earth move?"

"Yes, Lawrence, I did."

BBBBBRROOOOOOOOOOOOMMMMMMMMMM-MMMM!

A Chrysler or Else

All right, we've asked you as nicely as we could to buy a Chrysler car. First, Joe Garagiola offered you $500 off on any automobile from the Chrysler lot. Then Ricardo Montalban told you what a Chrysler product would do for your image.

Finally, Chrysler's own chairman of the board, Lee Iacocca, decided to go on the air and beg. Well, maybe he didn't exactly beg. He asked you to just compare the major American models, and if you didn't think a Plymouth or a Dodge or a Chrysler was superior, that was your business. But he knew when you tried the competition, you would be fair about it and go for his product.

Well, you didn't, so Lee made you an offer you couldn't refuse. You could buy the car, and if you didn't like it, you could return it within 30 days and get your money back.

You would have thought that the American people knew a good deal when they saw one. I mean, what more do you want Lee to do for you?

Since you didn't take advantage of his offer, I'll tell you what I'll do. I haven't cleared this with Lee yet, but I know he'll go along with it. After all, he dropped one billion big ones last year, and he has no choice.

If you buy a Chrysler automobile or truck within the next 90 days, we will give you a condominium in Florida, a four-year college education at Yale, Harvard, Princeton or MIT for any member of your family, a lifetime airline pass for any person over 21, a seat on the New York Stock Exchange and a quarter interest in the Alaska pipeline.

I know what you're going to say—you already have a car. That's not the point. Once you drive a Chrysler, Lee and I know you'll never drive anything else again. So, here's our last offer. We're not even going to ask you to buy a car. All we want you to do is to go to a Chrysler dealership and LOOK at one. Is that asking too much? Just stand outside the window and show some interest. If you do this, one of our salesmen will come out and present you with an original Rembrandt painting, signed by the artist himself.

If you decide to come into the showroom, and open one of the doors of our models, we'll give you a diamond necklace from Van Cleef & Arpels, valued at $100,000. And if you decide to take a spin in the car, we'll present you with the franchise to any football team in the National League.

We're being as nice about this as we possibly can. But if you still won't go out and buy an Omni, Volare or a Le Baron, then we will have no choice but to get tough.

We're going to put those automobiles on the road one way or another. If this means getting out there on the highway and smashing them into the car you are now driving and totaling it, so be it. I'm not saying we're going to do this, Lee happens to be dead set against it, but there are a lot of people in the company who want to take a hard line.

You can lose megabucks in this business for just so long and then your patience wears thin. So all I'm saying is you either buy a Chrysler car the easy way or the hard way. It doesn't make any difference to me. I'm not in this business for my health.

The Real Olympics

There is a lot more at stake in the Winter Olympics than winning gold medals for one's self and one's country. The real reason for holding the Olympics is to find new champions to do TV commercials.

While most of the world is watching the athletes for their skill and grace under pressure, there is a small group of men and women who are studying them to see if they have what it takes to do a 60-second commercial.

J. Walter Batten, who represents one of the largest advertising agencies in the United States, made me aware of this as we watched a downhill racing event on the super television screen in his den. "To me there is nothing as stirring in the world as a beautiful woman, dressed in a form-fitting stretch fabric, bent forward, plunging down a treacherous mountain, racing against the wind, risking her gorgeous neck to find the invisible red line and, finally, after getting to the bottom of the hill, ripping off her goggles, looking into the camera and saying, 'The thing we skiers worry about the most is chapped lips. Thanks to Crackproof, we don't have to worry anymore.' "

"It's sheer poetry," I told Batten. "What's your favorite Winter Olympic sport?"

"It's hard to say," he replied. "There are so many of them, and they each have something to offer. For sheer danger, I guess I'm partial to the bobsled. I can never get enough of the four-man teams who, without any regard for their own safety, take the dangerous curves and straightaways at 90 miles an hour, knowing that just one mistake could send them flying off the edge in a jumble of broken bones and concussions."

"That really turns you on?" I asked.

"No. Not that part of it. What excites me is the thought of putting a camera on their sled and filming the run. Then once they reach the bottom, they all go into the ski lodge and order four steins of beer. I want them laughing and pounding each other on the shoulders and having a good time, while the music comes up and a voice-over says, 'When the race with death is done, it's nice to know the thrill is still there in a Mogen's beer.' "

"I think I'm going to cry," I told Batten. "How do you feel about figure skating?"

"It has its place, if you've got the right client. I have to monitor the figure skating this year because I want to find a couple who have grace and dazzle. What we want to do is put a Quartex watch on the woman skater, and then have her partner swing her around by her legs in an arc, force her into a flying sit-spin, then have her do a double loop and, finally, fling her across the length of the ice-rink, and have her land on her wrist. Then we'll zoom in on the watch to prove it is still working and hasn't lost a second."

"No wonder everyone tries so hard to win a gold medal in figure skating," I said. "Do you have any interest in cross-country skiing?"

"Not really. Cross-country skiers don't sell anything for you. I don't know why the Winter Olympic Committee even bothers with them."

"That's Show Biz"

"FBI Casting. Agent Riley speaking."

"Riley, this is Charles Hawkins of the Atlanta office. I hear you're looking for someone to play an Arab sheik in the sequel to *Operation Abscam*."

"Where did you hear that?"

"I read it in *Variety*."

"Damn, we were trying to keep the sequel a secret. What experience do you have?"

"I played a French dope peddler in the *Marseilles Connection*, a Latin American arms merchant in *Buenos Dias, Señor Fidel*, a Swiss gnome in *Golddiggers of 1979* and the brother-in-law of Madame Marcos in *I'll Take Manila*."

"I didn't cast any of those stings," Riley said. "How were your reviews?"

"They were fantastic. Listen to this one by Rep. Greensleeves in the *Congressional Record*: 'FBI agent Hawkins certainly fooled me when I met him on the Eastern shuttle going to New York. He convinced me he was Mao Tse-tung's long-lost son, and gave me $50,000 to put in my briefcase until we got to La Guardia, because he said he didn't trust the stewardesses. I was never so entrapped in my life.' "

Hawkins continued, "Here is one from *Newsday* on Long Island: 'While the FBI's sting operation in Garden City left a lot to be desired, the casting of Charles Hawkins as a Mafia hit man was a stroke of genius. He brought life and excitement to what could have easily been a cliché role in the hands of a less-talented undercover man. It is a pity that the authors of this scam did not give Hawkins a bigger part. Had they recognized his talent, *Operation Sticky Fingers* might not have closed on Saturday night.' "

"I have some more," Hawkins said.

"No, that's okay," Riley replied. "How do you look on video-tape?"

"I'll send you a cassette of me bribing a food inspector in the *Little Caesar Salad Caper*. After my appearance as a crooked

188

female jockey, I received an Academy Award for 'best drag performance of the year in front of a hidden camera.' "

Riley said, "Your credentials seem to be in order. But the director is looking for a big name to play the sheik—someone a senator would pay money to see. We're putting $10 million into this production, and if we don't get any indictments out of it, we'll all be out of show business."

"Give me a break, Riley. I haven't had a good part since I played Robert Vesco's bagman in *Oh, Costa Rica*."

"I'll put your name in, but don't get your hopes up. Every agent in the bureau wants to play the Arab sheik. You get a rent-free house, a Cadillac limousine and a yacht for wild parties. It beats the hell out of playing an undercover numbers runner in the Bronx."

Truth in Jewelry

The newspapers and airwaves are filled with commercials urging people to bring in their gold and silver jewelry to stores and dealers. Jewelers are not selling but buying these days, and the public is showing up in droves with everything from diamond pendants to silver salt-and-pepper shakers.

While it is true that the buy-back value of these items has never been higher, there is a danger involved which I believe everyone should be warned about.

McCloskey's wife decided to cash in on some valuable pieces of jewelry that her husband had given her through the years. She was under the impression—and McCloskey had never denied it—that everything he bought her was worth a fortune. Accompanied by her friend Melba "for protection," she took it all down to a jeweler who was guaranteeing the highest prices in Washington.

The man behind the counter picked up one piece at a time, said "Junk," and threw it down.

Mrs. McCloskey was not only shattered by the man's contempt for her earthly possessions, but mortified that Melba was a witness to the embarrassing scene.

Melba promised she wouldn't say a word to anyone. What she really meant was that she wouldn't say a word to anyone until she could get to the nearest telephone.

When McCloskey got home that evening, his martini was warm and his wife was cold.

"Do you remember that beautiful gold necklace you bought me in Mexico City ten years ago?" his wife asked.

"The one we had insured for $5,000? I hope you didn't lose it."

"I wish I had," she replied. "I took it to the jeweler today and he said it was worth $20."

"That's ridiculous. The man who sold it to me in a dark alley off the Avenida de Montezuma said it was a priceless Inca treasure."

"You never told me you bought it from a man in a dark alley!"

"You never asked."

"Did you know that the pearl earrings you brought back from Beverly Hills were made by the Monsanto Chemical Co.?"

"I don't believe it. I paid $150 for them."

"And the silver family heirloom brooch you gave me for our wedding?"

"Plated?"

"Painted. I've never had such a miserable day in my whole life."

"Well, who told you to go to the jewelers? You were very happy wearing all that stuff before you found out what it was worth."

McCloskey's wife said, "But if my jewelry is a lie, maybe everything about this marriage is a lie."

"That's the stupidest thing I ever heard. We've been married for fifteen years, and just because some greedy jewel broker tells you your baubles aren't worth what you thought they were, there is no sense in thinking our marriage is on the rocks. The thing I have always loved you for is that you are not one of those hard, grasping women who counts her blessings in baubles."

"Well," McCloskey's wife said, "if something did happen with this marriage, I could always sell my diamond engagement ring."

McCloskey said nervously, "I wouldn't if I were you."

Sunny California

I came to Los Angeles last week for rest and recreation, only to discover that it had become a rain forest.

I didn't realize how bad it was until I went to dinner at a friend's house. I had the right address, but when I arrived there was nothing there. I went to a neighboring house where I found a man bailing out his swimming pool.

"I beg your pardon," I said. "Could you tell me where the Cables live?"

"They used to live above us on the hill. Then about two years ago, their house slid down in the mud, and they lived next door to us. I think it was last Monday, during the storm, that their house slid again, and now they live two streets below us, down there. We were sorry to see them go—they were really nice neighbors."

I thanked him and slid straight down the hill to the new location of the Cables' house. Cable was clearing out mud from his car. He apologized for not giving me the new address and explained, "Frankly, I didn't know until this morning whether the house would stay here or continue sliding down a few more blocks."

"Cable," I said, "you and your wife are intelligent people. Why do you build your house on the top of a canyon when you know that during a rainstorm it has a good chance of sliding away?"

"We did it for the view. It really was fantastic on a clear night up there. We could sit in our Jacuzzi and see all of Los Angeles, except of course when there were brush fires.

"Even when our house slid down two years ago, we still had a great sight of the airport. Now I'm not too sure what kind of view we'll have because of the house in front of us, which slid down with ours at the same time."

"But why don't you move to safe ground so that you don't have to worry about rainstorms?"

"We've thought about it. But once you live high in a canyon, it's hard to move to the plains. Besides, this house is built solid and has about three more good mud slides in it."

"Still, it must be kind of hairy to sit in your home during a deluge and wonder where you'll wind up next. Don't you ever have the desire to just settle down in one place?"

"It's hard for people who don't live in California to understand how we people think out here. Sure we have floods, and fire and drought, but that's the price you have to pay for living the good life. When Esther and I saw this house, we knew it was a dream come true. It was located right on the tippy top of the hill way up there. We would wake up in the morning and listen to the birds, and eat breakfast out on the patio and look down on all the smog.

"Then after the first mud slide, we found ourselves living next to people. It was an entirely different experience. But by that time we were ready for a change. Now we've slid again and we're in a whole new neighborhood. You can't do that if you live on solid ground. Once you move into a house below Sunset Boulevard, you're stuck there for the rest of your life.

"When you live on the side of a hill in Los Angeles, you at least know it's not going to last forever."

"Then in spite of what's happened, you don't plan to move out?"

"Are you crazy? You couldn't replace a house like this in L.A. for $500,000."

"What happens if it keeps raining and you slide down the hill again?"

"It's no problem. Esther and I figure if we slide down too far, we'll just pick up and go back to the top of the hill, and start all over again; that is, if the hill is still there after the earthquake."

The New Army

You would think that with the new emphasis on catching up with the Soviets, everyone at the Pentagon would be overjoyed. This is not so. The generals and admirals in charge of developing new sophisticated weapons are thrilled. But the officers who must train military personnel to use them are worried sick.

A recent Defense Department study revealed that 25 percent of all recruits in the three major services, after testing, had to be classified in the "low intelligence category." This means they could hardly read the instruction manuals that accompany the complicated weapons, much less understand how to fire them.

It has become painfully clear that even if we get all the new hardware that President Carter wants, the chances of a large number of our troops being able to understand how to use them will be minimal.

"Good news, Colonel. The XM-1 tank has just arrived."

"Very well, Sergeant. Instruct your crew on how to use it."

"Yessir————All right now, you chowderheads, hear this. This is the new XM-1 tank. It weighs 40 tons and can fire laser-guided missiles as well as artillery shells. Are there any questions?"

"Sarge. What's a tank?"

"A tank is an armored vehicle, capable of traversing any kind of terrain, and having the ability to destroy buildings, bunkers and people. It can go either forwards or backwards. It is the most feared weapon in ground warfare."

"Does it have an engine in it?"

"Yes, Klaus. That's what makes it go. I think the best thing to do is have you get into the tank and work it yourself. Here's the manual and the key to the ignition. I'll talk to you by radio. The range is over there where those large targets are. In order to aim the turret, you push the red button on the control panel, then sight the gun with the green button above the temp gauge, and finally, fire the gun by moving the safety lock to nine o'clock and the trigger mechanism to twelve o'clock, without taking your foot off the accelerator. Okay, you four over there, get into the tank and let's try it.

"Are you set? Start up———Okay, move out. No, Slocum, drive towards the range. . . . Slocum, you're heading for the PX. Turn it around, TURN IT AROUND. . . . Slocum, you just knocked down the PX building."

"Hey, Sarge, this is fun!"

"Slocum, aim your turret towards the targets. What button are you pressing?"

"This one, Sarge."

"SLOCUM, DON'T FIRE! YOU'RE AIMING AT THE OFFICERS' MESS. OH, NO. YOU JUST KNOCKED OUT THE SECOND FLOOR."

"Wow, Sarge—I wasn't even aiming at it. These laser guns are terrific!"

"Come back, Slocum. No, Slocum, don't back into the ammunition shack. Put the stick in drive, not reverse. Never mind—it's too late. Come back and we'll go over it once again."

"How's it going, Sergeant?"

"Just fine, Colonel. The men really like the new tank."

"Good. You better move your men out right away. Eye Company just got its new electronic-firing helicopter and wiped out F Company. We have no idea where they'll hit next. The whole base is on the alert."

"Yes, sir. Maybe this would be a good time to hold the remedial reading class."

"You better cancel it. The Navy just destroyed the base school with the new M-20 Cruise missile they got yesterday."

"What Do You Do?"

WASHINGTON—As you have probably read, Washington is a tough town for wives, especially when they go to dinners and cocktail parties. The first thing a woman is asked is, "What do you do?" If she admits to being just a housewife, the person who asks the question immediately loses interest in her.

A friend of mine named Lucy told me she got sick and tired of being asked the question, so she has come up with some replies that really throw the person who asked it.

Lucy said, "It came by accident one night when a man sitting next to me asked, 'What do you do?' I told him, 'I'm a paper clip inspector for the State Department.'"

"He said, 'You're kidding me.'"

"I said, 'I am not. They have to be twisted just right or the State Department papers won't stick together, and some of them could get lost. What do *you* do?' He just blushed and said, 'Nothing.'"

Lucy said, 'Ever since then, while I'm dressing to go out, I think of something to say for that moment when the inevitable question comes up."

"Give me some examples," I pleaded.

"Not long ago a woman who thought she was important asked me what I did and I told her, 'I'm a food taster for HEW Secretary Califano.' And at another party, a congressman put the question to me and I told him, 'I design white lines for shopping mall parking lots.'"

"I also told a general once that 'I run a halfway house for FBI informers.'"

"Those are very good," I said.

"My husband thinks I'm overdoing it," Lucy told me. "But he doesn't try to stop me. Once we were at a Georgetown party and all the people were full of themselves, dropping names and quoting VIPs they had spoken to that day. Then someone asked in a very patronizing way, 'What did you do today?' I said, 'I finished carving the last gargoyle on the Washington Cathedral. I thought the wind would blow me off the steeple.'"

"What did they all say?"

"What could they say? After that we were the quietest table in the room."

"Does anyone really get thrown when you tell them what you do?"

"All the time," Lucy replied. "A few weeks ago a commissioner from one of the federal agencies asked me the question and I said, 'I can't do anything for the moment until the grand jury decides whether or not to indict me. I promised to pay back the money, but my lawyer says the Feds still want to pursue it.' His eyes popped out of his head, and then I added, 'Maybe you can help me. You don't know any judges who can be bought in this town, do you?'

"What did he say to that?"

Lucy chuckled, "He said, 'May I get you another drink?' And I never saw him again."

She continued, "Newspapermen are the worst. If you're not 'somebody' they refuse to talk to you. Once a columnist who was working a room of an embassy stopped for a moment between ambassadors and asked, 'Who are you?'

"I told him, 'I'm from Lloyd's of London, assigned to watch Elizabeth Taylor's diamond necklace. If anyone makes a move toward it I have orders to shoot. Now get out of my way because you're in the line of fire!' "

"What did he do?"

"He couldn't keep his eyes off my pocketbook for the rest of the evening."

Oil Prices Unlimited

A lot of people are starting to get suspicious that the price of gasoline and oil in this country bears no relation to what is really going on in the OPEC countries.

This, of course, is not true. The oil companies have a very scientific method of computing fuel costs and are extremely careful in justifying every price increase in their fuel.

This is how one oil company does it, and I am sure the others follow similar guidelines:

Every morning at exactly 9 A.M., the Executive Committee for Price Raises meets in the private dining room for breakfast.

A typical session goes like this:

There are twelve men in the room laughing and joking.

Halberstam walks in and Middlecoff says, "You're late."

"Sorry about that," Halberstam says, "I just had a new grandchild."

"Congratulations. This calls for a celebration. What do you say, gentlemen, in honor of Halberstam's new grandchild we raise the price of regular gasoline by one cent?"

"Since it's his first grandchild, I say we should raise it two cents."

"No objections, so, done."

"That's damn decent of you. Wait until I tell Ella—she'll be thrilled. Where's Walker?"

"Walker's in the hospital with a kidney stone. We're praying he passes it."

"Maybe we should send him flowers."

"We thought we'd raise the price of heating oil three cents. That would do more for his morale than flowers."

"Great idea. Where's Burnside?"

"He's in New York getting the Advertising Man of the Year Award for his brilliant commercials proving the Windfall Oil Company makes less profits than the Public Television Network."

"Hey, let's surprise Burnside when he comes back by adding two cents a gallon to diesel fuel. We'll call it the Burnside Raise."

"It's done."

"I have a joke. If you guys laugh, you have to promise to up motor oil five cents a can."

"Okay, Kelly. But if anyone has heard it, you only get a two-cent raise."

"It's a deal. A guy goes into a doctor's office and the doctor says, 'You're very sick. I'm going to have to operate.' The guy says, 'I want a second opinion.' So the doctor says, 'Okay, you're ugly too.'"

Everyone slaps his thighs and Kelly gets the five-cent increase.

"Say, did we put up the price of airline fuel when the U.S. Olympic Hockey team beat the Soviets?"

"Yeh, I think we did—by 20 cents a gallon."

"Well, I don't know about you guys, but I think those kids played one helluva game, and I believe we should add another five cents to show those Russians what this country is really all about."

"You won't get any resistance from us."

"We're moving right along."

"I wish we could figure out one more reason to boost the price at the gas pumps this morning. Don't forget Monday is a holiday and we won't be meeting until Tuesday."

"Hey, look out the window, everybody. There's a red robin —the first one I've seen this year."

"That's good luck. What do you say we add three cents on unleaded Super Premium in honor of Jeremy seeing his first red robin?"

"All in favor, say aye. . . . Opposed? . . . The ayes have it. Well, it looks like we've had a good morning."

"Hey, we forgot the natural gas division."

"Didn't we give them a five-cent increase last Friday?"

"Yeh, but that was just to tide them over the weekend."

Behind Closed Doors

The Supreme Court is still wrestling with the question of obscenity. Last week it ruled that, while juries must vote what is obscene by the standards of the local community, they cannot include children as part of the community. The juror must decide not just for himself but for everyone in the area what should and what should not be permitted to go through the mails.

It's a helluva burden to put on somebody, as Melcher, a friend who is now sitting on a jury judging an obscenity trial, told me the other night.

Melcher said, "This is tougher than a murder trial. I'm not just sitting in judgment for myself. I'm representing the entire community, excluding children."

"That shouldn't be hard," I said. "Everyone in this neighborhood is against obscenity."

"That's what they say," Melcher said. "But they tell me one thing and then go out and tell Kinsey and Masters & Johnson researchers something entirely different. If we believe their statistics, there's more going on in this community than people will admit."

"How do you know this?" I asked.

"Well, I was trying to figure out some way of getting a fix on what the community thought was or was not obscene, so I took a copy of *The Joy of Sex* and went from door to door asking people what positions in the book appealed to their prurient interests."

"What was the result?"

Melcher replied, "Nobody would talk, but I sold 61 books."

"That's a lot," I admitted.

"Everyone tells me they're against X-rated movies, but *Deep Throat* is still playing at a downtown theater. It's had a longer run than *Star Wars*. Who keeps on going to the movies?"

"Probably people from Georgetown," I said. "Their morals are a lot looser than those of us who live in Wesley Heights.

I'd say they've been lowering the community standards in Washington by at least 10 percent."

"That's the problem," Melcher said. "The Supreme Court has ruled that a jury in an obscenity case must take into consideration the opinions of everybody in the community, from the 'most sensitive people' as well as 'deviant sexual groups,' before we come to a decision."

"What do they mean by 'deviant sexual groups'?" I asked him.

"Nobody has really spelled it out for us. Maybe it's people who go skinny dipping or who dress up in each other's clothes."

"We don't have anybody like that in our neighborhood," I said. 'I heard that's the sort of thing that goes on in Bethesda."

"But Bethesda is part of the community," Melcher said. "I have to think of them, too."

"Don't forget Chevy Chase," I told him. "They pretend to be straight, but I've heard the husbands go to massage parlors when their wives are away on summer vacation."

Melcher said, "That's my problem. Every time I think I've got the community standards down pat someone tells me something that throws them completely out of kilter. You've heard about the waterbeds at Watergate, haven't you?"

"Who hasn't heard about the Watergate waterbeds? You know something, Melcher? I think you're taking the Supreme Court guidelines on obscenity too seriously. If you try to figure out whether the guy is guilty or not by community standards you're going to go crazy. Send him up for life and forget about it."

"But the conviction could be thrown out by a higher court."

"Why?" I asked.

"Most of the pictures the defendant mailed were taken on Capitol Hill."

Washington Novels

The newspaper editors were in town last week, and one of the more interesting panels dealt with the "Washington Novel." The members of the panel were William Safire, who wrote *Full Disclosure,* Marilyn Sharp, who authored a mystery entitled *Sunflower,* Les Whitten of *Conflict of Interest* and Barbara Howar, who wrote *Making Ends Meet.*

Their conclusion was that the Washington novel is alive and well, mainly because all the ingredients for a novel are here —power, suspense and sex.

I've been trying to write a Washington novel for some time, but have not been successful, mainly because every time I think I've got a good fiction plot, someone else has already done it.

Here are some of the false starts I've had, which never got off the ground.

* * *

President Coeburn sat in the Oval Office. Stretched out on the couch was the beautiful, raven-haired, buxom Olga. She said to him bitterly, "Why do we have to keep sneaking around like this all the time? Are you ashamed to take me to the Gridiron Club?"

"Darling, you know I have to take my wife to the Gridiron Club."

"You always say that. But I know the real reason."

The President, in an exasperated voice, said, "What's the *real* reason?"

"I'm the Russian ambassador."

* * *

Congressman Blevens Bombast got into his new Toyota, which was parked in front of his modest Georgetown home. He looked forward to the drive up to Capitol Hill, as it gave him time to think about how he was going to balance the budget. Just as he was going to put his key into the ignition, Blevens noticed a large, unmarked manila envelope on the front seat. He opened it and found 600 fresh $100 bills. He looked around fearfully and then got out of his car and placed the envelope in the trunk.

Wiping the perspiration from his face, he got back into the car and started the most fateful journey of his life. He could go straight down Pennsylvania Avenue to FBI headquarters or turn left for the Beltway and keep driving until he hit Las Vegas. He thought of the trust the people in his District had in him. Then he thought of his wife and five children. There was no question about what he would do. He made the left turn and was surprised at that hour to find so few cars on the Beltway.

* * *

Secretary of State Clem Hapstead picked up the phone, and a man with a heavy foreign accent said, "This is Fotopick calling. We have the pictures you ordered."

"Oh, my God," said Hapstead, "How did you get them?"

"With a telephoto lens opening of f8 at 200th of a second."

"What will it cost me to get the negatives?"

"Jerusalem."

* * *

The man in the slouch hat and dirty raincoat was pretending to study a portrait of Mary Washington in the National Gallery when the uniformed guard took out his .45 pistol and fired three shots at him. The man fell to the floor with a thud. People rushed from all over as the guard hurried away to a phone booth. He dialed a number and then hung up. Ten seconds later, his phone rang. All the guard said was, "The deed is done." The voice on the other end of the line said, "Good. Now for your next clue, go to the Air and Space Museum and follow the instructions hidden in John Glenn's space capsule."

"You sure I'm going to win a prize?"

"Of course. Everyone wins a prize in the Reader's Digest sweepstakes."

Part V

I Want My Momma

The California State Court of Appeals may have made legal history. It overthrew the conviction of a man accused of a serious crime, because the police had refused to let him speak to his mother. The court said that in asking to see his mother, the suspect was indicating his desire to remain silent.

In the past, under the *Miranda* ruling, a person only had a right to ask to talk with his *lawyer*.

If the Supreme Court upholds the decision, many suspects may ask to talk to their *mothers*. But then again many may not.

Let's see why.

"Okay, Lefty. We caught you in the bank at three in the morning with your burglary tools. We'll make it easy on you if you confess."

"I want to see my mother."

"Ah, come on, Lefty. Don't give us that. Just tell us how you did it."

"I know my legal rights. Under *Miranda,* I'm entitled to talk to my mother before I say anything."

"He's right, boys. Get his mother."

Three hours later.

"Lefty, your mother's here."

"Hi, Mom."

"Archibald, what are you doing here? You were supposed to come to my house for dinner tonight."

"These guys busted me for allegedly breaking into a bank."

207

"Does that mean you're not coming to dinner?"

"It depends on how much bail money you have on you."

"Archibald, I'm very angry. I cooked a nice chicken dinner with mashed potatoes—just the way you like them—and baked your favorite mince pie with walnuts on top. You haven't been to dinner for a month."

"Mom, I've been busy."

"Is breaking into banks more important than seeing your mother?"

"Will you stop already? I spoke to you on the phone last week after they picked me up for allegedly stealing a car."

"Phone calls don't count. I want to see your face. You said you'd come last Friday."

"The guys and I had to open a jewelry store. It took much longer than we thought."

"It's always the guys. When I was sick in bed last year with the flu, did I get so much as one visit?"

"That's history, Mom. I was in San Quentin then. Was I supposed to fly over the walls?"

"A good son would have found the time. I knew once you left the house you'd forget me."

"Why do you keep bugging me? Do you realize that when they grabbed me, you were the only person I wanted to see? That says something, doesn't it?"

"Yes, but the only time you ask to see me is when you get arrested. It would be nice if you would ask to see your mother without taking advantage of the *Miranda* ruling. Maybe if you settled down with a nice girl, then I could see you in your home instead of the slammer. Of course, your wife would probably be ashamed to invite me to your house."

"If I was married, Mom, I assure you we'd invite you over to our place. Can't we just have a nice talk?"

"You don't look as if you're brushing your teeth. Maybe I should make an appointment with you with Dr. Berman, the dentist—just for your peace of mind."

"Okay, Mom, I guess our time is up. I enjoyed the visit."

"You call this a visit! The woman at the Information Desk in Macy's gives me more time."

"Goodbye, Mom— Detective, I'm ready to talk."

"I thought so."

"What made you so sure?"

"Ever since the new *Miranda* ruling, most guys, after one visit, would rather talk to us than their mothers."

The Complex Brain Drain

One of President Eisenhower's most famous speeches concerned a warning that the military-industrial complex should be watched at all times, or it would take the country for a ride. What Ike failed to foresee was a time when the military and industrial complexes would be competing with each other for the same personnel. As more and more contracts are handed out for the latest hardware, the industrial chaps are draining all the brains from the military establishment.

Here is how the military brain-drain works. Rudolph Heffenberg, an engineer with Armageddon Electronics, supplier of all digital dials on the new "Jaws" class nuclear submarine, goes out on a shakedown cruise with the crew of the USS *Snail Darter*. He is in charge of instructing Chief Petty Officer Rankowski on how to repair the dials at sea.

Rankowski, who has been trained at a cost to the taxpayers of $100,000, is a digital whiz, and can take one apart and put it back together with his eyes closed.

Heffenberg has been instructed by Armageddon to keep a look out for any good men who can be used to complete their multimillion-dollar, cost-plus naval contract.

Over a cup of coffee, Heffenberg asks Rankowski how much he makes as a chief petty officer.

Rankowski says, "Fifteen hundred a month, if you don't include food stamps. How much do you make?"

Heffenberg says, "Fifteen hundred a week and free membership in the country club of my choice. Rankowski, Armageddon Electronics needs men like you."

"So does the Navy," Rankowski says.

"But we need you more," Heffenberg says quietly. "The only way we can catch up with the Russians is if we build super submarines. And without digital instruments, they are worthless."

"Yeh, but who is going to repair the digitals once you people turn them over to the Navy?"

"That's not your problem, Rankowski. If you love the Navy as much as you seem to, then it's your duty to see our fighting

men get the best equipment that money can buy. You can't do
that when you're at sea."

"I don't know, I have 15 years in the service and I sort of
like what I'm doing."

"What about your family, Rankowski? How do they feel
about you being on a sub all the time? Wouldn't they prefer to
have you home every night eating steak and drinking good
scotch, and watching *Monday Night Football*?"

"My wife has mentioned it at times, but I still think I owe
something to the Navy."

"We all owe something to the Navy. It isn't as if you're
leaving it. All you're doing is making it possible for those who
are actively serving in it to have the equipment they need to
keep this country Number One. Forget the $50,000 a year
you'll probably be making in no time. If it was just money, I
would say, stay where you are. But I'm appealing to your
patriotism. We can't do the job the Navy wants us to do unless
we have the manpower to make their digitals. You don't look
like the type of person who would shirk his responsibility."

"I don't know. I believe I should talk it over with the CO."

"You do that, Rankowski. I'm sure he will tell you that I am
right."

"How can you be so sure?"

"Because as soon as he finishes his tour, he's coming with us
as a vice president."

"He is?"

"Yes. And so is the executive officer, the engineering officer
and the helmsman."

"Wow! You really made a clean sweep."

"You're the only holdout. If Armageddon can get a few
more good men like you, the U.S will have the best damn navy
in the world."

Garage Sale Fantasy

All over America people are holding garage sales. I don't know about you, but I can't pass one up. What drives people like myself to garage sales is that we all have fantasies that somewhere in the flotsam on display is a treasure the owner doesn't know he's got.

Here is my favorite garage sale fantasy:

I go to a garage sale at the Kreugers'. It's all junk, but as I'm about to leave, my wife whispers, "You have to buy something or they'll be very insulted."

"Why don't you buy that painting?"

"It's the ugliest picture I've ever seen."

"Yes, but we can always use the frame."

"But they're asking $15 for it," I protest.

"Offer them 10. It's five o'clock and you can see they're desperate."

I offer Kreuger 10 and he says stiffly, "Twelve-fifty, and all sales are final." I'm about to call him a crook when my wife nudges me in the ribs and I pay over the $12.50. "Do you have any newspaper to wrap it in?" I ask.

"We don't wrap," Kreuger says. "You bring your own wrapping to a garage sale."

I stick the painting under my arm and say to my wife, "Hurry up or we'll miss the N-2 bus."

We get on the bus, and seated across the aisle is a man in a pin-striped morning suit. I figure he's just been to a wedding.

He looks at me, and then casually at the painting I have leaning against my knee. Suddenly his eyes bug out.

"I beg your pardon. May I examine that painting?" he says.

I think he's going to make fun of me and I say, "What for?"

"Forgive me," he says, handing me his card. "I am from Sotheby Parke Bernet, the art auction house, and I could swear that picture is an original Applebaum."

"You are correct," I say. "It's been in my family for years. My Aunt Ada left it to us in her will."

The man from Sotheby's gets on his hands and knees and says, "It's the most magnificent Applebaum I've ever seen.

212

We've known of its existence, but we were unable to trace it after it was sold by the J. P. Morgan estate."

"The Morgans and my aunt were good friends," I say.

The Sotheby man takes a magnifying glass out of his pocket.

"It's simply fantastic. Do you know the history of Applebaum?"

"A little," I reply. "But our family has so many great paintings, we can't keep track of them all."

"Applebaum lived in Alaska, and spent forty years painting nothing but dog sleds. He never painted the dogs—just the sleds. For years he was ignored by the art world. But in 1950 he was rediscovered, and every museum in the world considers its collection incomplete unless it has one Applebaum hanging on its walls. What makes this picture so unique is that the dog sled was painted in the spring, when there was no snow on the ground."

"That's why my Aunt Ada bought it," I say. "She never did like snow."

"What are you planning to do with it?" the man from Sotheby's asks.

"Put it in our playroom with our Cézannes and Renoirs," I tell him.

"You wouldn't consider letting us auction it off, would you?"

"I don't know. We never like to part with a painting. How much do you think it would fetch?"

"We'd put a ceiling of two million dollars on it, but it wouldn't surprise me if it brought over five million. To my knowledge, it's the last Applebaum still in private hands."

"Well, then," I say, "it would be very selfish of me to keep it just for the family. I'll bring it to your offices tomorrow morning."

In my fantasy, the picture sells for $6,870,000—the highest price ever paid for a painting of a dog sled.

But the best part of my dream is when Kreuger reads the paper and finds out what I got for his painting, and starts banging on the front door, calling me a thief.

The last thing I say to him before I wake up is, "When you have a garage sale, all sales are final."

The Class of 1980

The class of 1980 is having a tough time finding jobs. Therefore, they have to lower their sights on what kind of positions they will accept. This is not only a burden on them, but also on their parents, who like to brag about what their children are doing.

I realized this when I attended a commencement exercise and overheard a group of parents discussing their children's plans now that they were graduating from college.

"What is your son going to do?" one of the mothers asked.

"He's getting a degree in economics, so he'll be driving a taxicab. We think he's very fortunate to get a position as a taxi driver right out of school."

"You must have pull."

"Well, his father did know a man who owned three taxis. At first my son said he wanted to get a taxi job on his own, but after pounding the pavements for a few months he realized it isn't what you know, but who you know in the taxi business that counts."

"What is your daughter Gertrude going to do?"

"She is getting a masters in library science and has already been offered a position as a waitress at Howard Johnson's. But she's holding out for a salesgirl's position at J. C. Penney. We warned her not to get her hopes up as we heard J. C. Penney was only hiring new sales personnel with Ph.Ds."

"My son Harry was most fortunate. In his senior year in law school he was recruited for an excellent position."

"With a private law firm?"

"No, with the Post Office as a mail sorter in their main branch office in Elkhart, Indiana."

"You must be very proud of him."

"It was worth the seven years of sacrifice. Isn't your daughter getting a degree in fine arts?"

"Yes. She made Phi Beta Kappa."

"What does she intend to do with it."

"She's had several marvelous opportunities, but the one that interests her the most is selling classified advertisements by

214

telephone for our local newspaper. The best part of the job, besides the security, is that she works on commission and in a good week can make $150."

"I'd like her to meet my son. He majored in biology and will be working for a landscape contractor mulching flower beds."

"She's been going steady with a boy in her graduating class who has a degree in business administration, and they hope to get married in the fall if he passes his test to be an airline steward."

"What is your son going to do, Sam, now that he has a civil engineering degree?"

"He lucked out. He was pumping gas at a Texaco station last summer, and they were so impressed with him, they offered to take him on full time when he finished his education. You should see him change a tire."

"We all seem to be pretty fortunate with our children," one of the mothers said. "We have a neighbor who graduated Summa Cum Laude from Harvard in public administration and she refuses to take any job that has been offered to her."

"What has she been offered?"

"The state of New Jersey offered her a toll booth on the Garden State Parkway, but she turned it down. She claims with her educational background she should at least be a meter maid in Trenton."

"Some kids have crazy ideas of what it takes to start out these days."

"Am I correct, Edward, that your boy is getting his doctorate in nuclear physics?"

"Apparently, the U.S. government still needs physicists."

"He wasn't hired by the U.S. He was hired by Pakistan."

The Hard Sell

It is no longer a secret that the American automobile companies are in a lot of trouble. They blame their woes on foreign imports, government emission standards, high interest rates and gasoline prices. Very few will admit the real problem, and that is that people aren't buying American cars.

The auto companies, for all their expertise, do not understand the consumer. They are making an appeal to his patriotism, offering rebates, and giving away autographed footballs.

It doesn't work. I don't wish to be presumptuous by telling the giant U.S. manufacturers how to move their cars, but this is a crisis and I believe they need all the help they can get.

What the American auto companies have to do is change their tactics and play hard to get.

This is how a dealer should treat a prospective buyer who comes into the showroom.

"Can I help you, sir?"

"No, I'm just looking."

"Go right ahead. None of these models are for sale anyway."

"What do you mean none of these models are for sale?"

"There is a six-month waiting list for anything you see in the showroom."

"I don't believe it."

"You haven't heard about the shortage, then?"

"What shortage?"

"There is going to be a big shortage of American automobiles in the next three years. We're only going to be able to take care of our regular customers, and they're going to have to take whatever we give them."

"But I need a new car."

"Everyone needs a new car, but there are just so many to go around. I'm terribly busy now. Perhaps you might try a foreign car dealer. I understand you can get a cheap import right away."

"But I don't want a cheap import. I want an American car."

"Everybody does. What makes you think you're so special that you should have one?"

"I'm an American and I have a right to own an American car."

"If you're going to become churlish you can leave the showroom right now. We don't have to put up with someone with a bad temper."

"I'm sorry I lost my head. If I gave you a $500 rebate would you sell me a car?"

"Sir, we don't accept bribes. There are people who have been waiting over a year for one of our cars. Even if Henry Ford himself called up and told us to give you one, we wouldn't do it."

"I don't want to beg. But I'm a salesman and I need an automobile for my work. Please give me a break. I'll take anything you've got in stock."

"Occasionally we do make exceptions for hardship cases. But we'll need a letter from your employer certifying that the automobile will be used for business and not for pleasure."

"I'll get it."

"And then we'll also have to have three references from people attesting that you are of good character and worthy of driving one of our models."

"I'll give them to you now."

"And, finally, you will have to sign a paper promising you will never reveal to a living soul that we sold you a car out of turn."

"My lips are sealed."

"Come into my office. I don't want anyone to see us concluding this sale."

"You're a good man, and I'll never forget this."

"If you don't mind. I can't stand a groveling customer."

The Exit Poll

There was a time in this country when a person's vote was his or her own business. But that was before someone invented the "Exit Poll." The Exit Poll is taken as the voter leaves the booth on election day, and makes it possible for the TV commentators to tell us what group voted for which candidate and why. It does nothing for the voting process, but it helps fill time on the air.

This is how the Exit Poll works. As Gradeson steps out of the voting booth at Public School 35, pollsters from the three major networks close in on him.

"Are you Jewish?" one of the pollsters asks.

"No, I'm not Jewish."

"You don't look Jewish," another pollster says. "Italian?"

"I'm not Italian. Hey, what's going on here?"

"Spanish American?" the third pollster asks.

"My grandfather was Irish and my great-grandmother came from Wales."

"Catholic or Church of England?"

"I happen to be a Christian Scientist."

"Great," says the first pollster. "We don't have anything on the Christian Science vote yet. Mind telling us how much you make a year?"

"I certainly do."

"Over $35,000 or under? You don't have to give us the exact figure."

"Listen, I'm illegally parked and if you don't . . ."

"Are you a college graduate?"

"I do happen to be a college graduate."

"Good, now just tell us your age and we'll get down to business."

"I'm 34. Who are you guys?"

"We'll ask the questions. Are you a registered Democrat or Republican?"

"I happen to be a Republican."

"That's better. The more you play ball with us the easier it will be on you."

Another pollster says, "Tell us who you voted for, Reagan or Bush?"

"I think that is my business."

"It happens to be ours, too. We have to get this information on the evening news, so just stop stalling."

"I happened to vote for George Bush."

"Why?"

"Do I have to tell you *why* I vote for Bush?"

"Of course. It doesn't mean anything if you just voted for Bush. The viewers have to know why the Christian Science vote is going for him."

"I voted for Bush because I didn't want to vote for Reagan."

"So your vote wasn't pro-Bush, it was anti-Reagan?"

"I also happen to like Bush."

"Why don't you like Reagan? Is it his age or is it that you don't trust him?"

"I don't dislike Reagan. I just think Bush would have a better chance of beating Carter."

"Then your Bush vote was actually an anti-Carter vote?"

"No, it was a Bush vote. It stands to reason if I'm a Republican I would like to see Carter beaten."

"Are you against Carter because of the way he's been handling foreign affairs or domestic ones?"

"Both. Now may I go?"

"How many bathrooms do you have in your home?"

That night Gradeson turned on his set to watch the evening news. The announcer said, "Early returns show that while Reagan and Bush are still running neck and neck, Bush is running surprisingly strong in the Christian Science neighborhoods by a margin of two to one, particularly with college graduates making over $35,000 a year who own their own homes and have an average of two and a half children. Bush's strategy of concentrating on Christian Science Reading Rooms apparently paid off, but Reagan campaigners were not willing to concede the state, mainly because Reagan was taking the Moonie vote particularly amongst those who hadn't finished high school and were making $14 an hour selling Bibles at the airport."

An Objective Panel

They recently assigned a panel of retired generals and admirals to find out what went wrong in the hostage rescue attempt in Iran. I can't think of a more objective board of investigators.

I have read as much as I could on the subject, and while I don't claim to be an expert, I have my own theory as to why the mission failed, and I hope the senior officers devote some time to it.

To me, it was all over the minute that tourist bus came down the road on its way to Tabas, just when the helicopters and C-130s were landing for refueling.

Let's replay the scenario that would have taken place if all the helicopters were operating. Remember that this was a 48-hour operation and depended on the element of complete surprise.

It is several hours after the bus has been stopped. The 31 Iranian tourists have all been herded onto a C-130 and flown off to some airfield in Egypt.

Mohammed Khafi, the owner of the Sheephound bus line, is waiting impatiently in Tabas for his bus to arrive. When it is five hours late, he goes to an official of the Revolutionary Council and says, "Something has happened, my bus is late."

Karim Jalaf says, "Your bus is always late. It probably broke down in the desert."

"That's what I'm afraid of," Mohammed says. "I have 44 tourists aboard, and if they have broken down in the desert they could all die, and I will have to pay for their hotel rooms in Tabas."

"So what do you want us to do?"

"Please go with me in a jeep down the road and see if we can find it."

"You must be crazy. We don't have time to bounce all over the place looking for one of your buses."

"But we need the bus to take our students to next Friday's anti-American demonstration in Tehran."

"I forgot about that. All right, Mohammed, I will find your bus."

Karim then orders three of his men and Mohammed into their jeep. They start driving down the road from Tabas to Tehran. Every time they are about to turn back, Mohammed urges them to go a little farther. Finally, they arrive at Posht-e Badam, the site of the airfield the Americans used for refueling. The bus is there, but there are no passengers.

Mohammed bursts into tears. "They have all left. They will never use Sheephound again."

One of Karim's men shouts, "Look, there are tracks leading to the airfield!" The five men follow the tracks. "It appears that they were picked up in a large airplane."

Karim looks sternly at Mohammed. "Are you sure your bus was not used to help the enemies of the Revolution escape?"

Mohammed cries, "May Allah be my witness, they were tourists!"

The men walk around the airfield. They find all sorts of equipment as well as fresh fuel on the ground.

Karim says, "Something is rotten in Denmark. We better let Tehran know about the bus and all the airplane activity. I can't believe anyone would go to so much trouble to kidnap 44 Iranian tourists."

From that moment on, everyone in the Iranian capital has been alerted, and while the commandos are putting their act together in the mountain hideout they were flown to, the element of surprise has been lost.

So, if the admirals and generals are going to be thorough in their investigation, the place to start is with the intelligence person who assured everyone there was no chance of any traffic being on the road where the rescue team would refuel. Anyone who reads thrillers knows that when you have 48 hours to pull off a sneak attack, the last thing you want to deal with is a busload of tourists, particularly if someone is waiting for it in Tabas.

A Strangelove Computer

As if we didn't have enough unthinkable things to think about—we now have to think about a computer going berserk at NORAD and starting World War III. The same computer has malfunctioned three times within the year, thereby alerting American forces to a Soviet attack that was not taking place.

I'm one of those people who believes war is too serious a business to be left to computers.

The day after the foul-up, a Blue Ribbon panel of generals and admirals was assigned to investigate what had gone wrong.

They were flown out to NORAD in Colorado Springs to question the computer about the mistake.

"Ask it," one of the generals said, "what went wrong."

The colonel started to hit the buttons on the computer, and the printout read, "AS FAR AS I WAS CONCERNED, WE WERE BEING ATTACKED BY SOVIET MISSILES AND I WAS ONLY DOING MY DUTY."

An admiral said, "Find out where it got its information."

The question was fed in and the printout said, "IT WAS JUST A FEELING I HAD. I NEVER DID TRUST THE RUSSIANS."

A general angrily went over to the keys and tapped in, "None of us trust the Russians, but at the same time, we don't want to start World War III."

The computer replied, "BETTER DEAD THAN RED."

"Your job is to give us information based on facts. You are not programmed to alert the entire nuclear defense network of this country just because you don't like Communists."

The computer answered, "IT'S TIME WE NUKE THEM BEFORE THEY NUKE US."

The general hit the keys again. "That is not a decision for a computer to make. You took an oath of office when you were installed, to alert us only if they fired their missiles first."

"HOW DO WE KNOW THEY WEREN'T GOING TO FIRE THEM?"

"That's not the point," the general tapped in. "You said they HAD fired them."

"I HAD THIS DREAM THAT THEY WERE GOING TO LAUNCH THEM. IT SEEMED JUST LIKE THE REAL THING. IF SOMETHING BAD HAPPENED, AND I HADN'T ALERTED ANYONE, I WOULD HAVE FELT TERRIBLE."

An admiral indicated to the general that he wanted to take a crack at the keyboard.

"Do you realize that this is the third time you have given us a false alarm?"

The computer appeared agitated. "ARE YOU TRYING TO SAY I DON'T KNOW WHAT I'M DOING?"

"No, but you have been working very hard lately, and the pressure can get to the best of us."

"I AM AWARE OF WHAT I WAS FED, AND AS FAR AS I WAS CONCERNED, THE DIRTY BOLSHIES HAD LAUNCHED THEIR MISSILES AT THIS COUNTRY IN A FIRST-STRIKE ATTACK."

"But you told us before that it was just a feeling, and you had no evidence to back it up."

"YOU'RE TRYING TO CONFUSE ME. YOU'RE ALL AGAINST ME BECAUSE I'M THE ONLY ONE WHO TAKES THE RED *&#@*! SERIOUSLY. I KNOW WHAT YOU'RE SAYING BEHIND MY BACK. 'CRAZY MARK VII. HE DOESN'T KNOW A REAL ATTACK FROM A FALSE ONE.' WELL, WHEN THE REAL THING HAP-PENS, DON'T SAY YOU DIDN'T HAVE PLENTY OF WARNING."

"Cool it," the admiral typed in. "You're only making things worse. You have a fine record in the service and we don't want to discharge you. But you're not giving us any choice."

"WHAT DO YOU WANT ME TO DO?"

"Could you at least show a little remorse for what you did?"

The final printout read, "BEING A COMPUTER MEANS NEVER HAVING TO SAY YOU'RE SORRY."

Letters for Losers

We always hear about the presidential candidates who made it. But there isn't much to say about the ones who didn't. What happens to them? They get letters like this.

DEAR GOVERNOR CONNALLY:

I happen to be the owner of a pizza joint in Green Forest, South Carolina. During your campaign you came into my pizza parlor and one of your staff said, "Governor, this is a great ethnic photo opportunity. Eat a pizza."

You said it was the best pizza you ever ate in your life and slapped me on the back. That's when we had our picture taken. I didn't give you a bill at the time because I figured if you ever made President, I could put the photo in the window. But since you didn't even get close, the food comes to $10.90 and the beer cost $15.75.

I would appreciate a check as soon as possible. Pizza doesn't grow on trees.

> Arrivederci,
> Giovanni Valenti

DEAR SENATOR BAKER:

While you were visiting the Sioux Indians, our chief presented you with a headdress and made you an honorary member of the tribe. He told the council that if you were elected, you would remember this gesture of goodwill and would look kindly on the Sioux when we came to Washington for redress. Since you dropped out of the race, we would like the headdress back so we can present it either to President Carter or Ronald Reagan. These Indian headdresses are hard to come by, and the chief made a mistake by giving it to you so early in the primaries. You can send it United Parcel as we don't trust the mails.

> Red Sunset, Chairman, Sioux
> Political Action Committee

DEAR MR. BUSH:

First of all I think you got a raw deal in New Hampshire when Ronald Reagan grabbed the microphone away from you and said he paid for it. I wonder if you have cashed my check for $500 yet? If you haven't, please let me know as I could use the money for something else. I sent it to you after you picked up all that momentum in Iowa. I'm not going to ask you what went wrong, because you're probably still trying to figure it out yourself. If you already cashed my check, perhaps you could have your treasurer send me one of his. I don't care where it comes from, as long as I get my $500 back.

> Best regards,
> Arnie Schmidlapp

DEAR CONGRESSMAN CRANE:

We are planning our American Express card commercials for next year—the ones that show a person saying, "You don't know me, but I carry an American Express Card everywhere I go, etc., etc." We were wondering if you would consider being one of our unknown politicians for next spring's campaign. If you are interested, we will send you a contract and tell you when you are on the schedule.

> Yours truly,
> Karl Malden

DEAR SENATOR DOLE:

I understand that you have withdrawn your name from nomination at the Republican Convention in Detroit. If this is true, does this mean I have no chance of becoming Secretary of Agriculture? The reason why I'm asking is that my wife has been house-hunting in Washington, and I better stop her from buying one if you're not going to get to be President. I know you told me not to get my hopes up, but frankly, Bob, you sounded in January as if you had the whole thing sewed up.

                                                                    Ezra

DEAR TEDDY:

   You can't keep track of everyone's campaign schedule in the family, but I've been in the coal mines of West Virginia for the past two months, making speeches for you. Someone just sent word down the shaft that you're not going to concede to Carter. Does this mean I'll be here until August?

                                                          Love, Jackie

Alice's Restaurant

Experiment time was over, and a bunch of white rats went to the lab commissary to relax.

An attractive rat waitress took their orders.

"I'll take a hamburger medium rare, lettuce and a slice of tomato."

"Sorry, we only have hamburgers, no lettuce and no tomatoes," the waitress said.

"Okay, honey," the white rat said, lighting up a cigarette, "anything you say."

Another white rat said, "When are you going to give up smoking? It makes me sick."

"When you get off the Pill, Flo," the rat smoking the cigarette said.

"I can't get off the Pill," Flo replied. "I'd lose my job." Then she turned to the waitress and said, "I'd like my hamburger rare and a glass of Perrier water with a twist of lemon."

"I'm sorry. All we have is water from New Jersey," the waitress replied.

"Skip the water," another white rat said to the waitress. "I'll have a cheeseburger and black coffee with no saccharin and what are you doing tonight after work?"

"Going to bed."

"Hey, that's no fun."

"It so happens I'm one of the rats who is *not* on the Pill. They have me on placebos," the waitress said.

"Forget I asked," the white rat said.

Another rat said, "You have any Valium malteds?"

"We only have Valium cherry soda."

"Okay, I'll have one of those and a hamburger just slightly singed on both sides."

"You want French fries with that?" the waitress asked.

"Are they cooked in saturated or unsaturated oil?"

"Saturated. What kind of place do you think we're running?"

"Don't get mad, I'm a heart patient," the white rat said.

"Oh, go ahead, Mike, have some saturated French fries," Flo said. "You only live once."

The waitress kept writing down the orders.

The last white rat was shedding hair all over the table, "Hey, Mathilda, what happened to your coat?"

"They've been spraying hair dye on me all day long. I think I'll have a tuna fish sandwich."

"We're out of tuna fish. All we have left is hamburgers."

"All right. I'll have a hamburger broiled."

"We only fry them here," the waitress said.

Mathilda sighed. "Give it to me fried but red on the inside."

In 20 minutes the waitress was back. She placed down the orders.

They all looked at their hamburgers.

"Hey, waitress," said Mike, "this hamburger's well done."

"So's mine," another one cried.

"Mine, too."

"Talk to the manager. I only work here."

The white rats were so hungry they decided to eat their hamburgers without complaining. Then they left.

The next night the commissary was completely empty. The manager said to the waitress, "Where is everybody?"

"Beats me," the waitress said. "All I know is a lab technician came in about an hour ago and asked me how many customers had eaten well-done hamburgers last night. I told him, and he ran out of here with a big grin on his face."

Cash and Carry

As controls on credit cards become more stringent, people are paying for their purchases in cash. Since most sales clerks in large department stores have no experience in handling money, they are now attending crash courses to learn how to deal with it.

One of the leading department stores in Washington permitted me to attend a class.

The instructor used slides to familiarize the clerks with the various denominations that they would be handling.

"Before the credit card," he said, "Americans used paper money when buying goods. Then plastic was invented and cash was abolished as a way of paying for goods in stores. Now, because of the credit restrictions placed on the customer, people are returning to the use of paper again, and you are permitted to accept it. Are there any questions?"

"How do we recognize the value of the currency?"

"That's a good question. Please watch the slides. First I will show you a one-dollar bill. Note that it has a picture of George Washington on it, and in the corner a larger figure one. This is the smallest denomination. It will not buy anything by itself but is used to supplement a purchase when the person uses the following bills: Here is a five-dollar bill with Abraham Lincoln's picture, and this is a 10-dollar bill with a likeness of Alexander Hamilton and a 20-dollar bill with Andrew Jackson on the face of it. We will deal with 50- and 100-dollar bills in the 'Advanced Cash Course.'

"Now, let's simulate an actual purchase so we get used to dealing with money. Frankie Kelly, you will be the sales lady, and Lizzie Diamond, you will take the role of the customer.

"Let us assume, Frankie, that Lizzie has just purchased a bathroom scale. Now go ahead."

Lizzie said, "I wish to buy this scale and I want to pay cash."

Frankie replied, "It is $25.60."

Lizzie handed over three 10-dollar bills.

Frankie inspected the money. "May I see your driver's license, please?"

"No, Frankie," the instructor yelled. "It is not necessary to ask to see a driver's license when someone pays cash."

"All right," Frankie said. Then she turned to Lizzie.

"Do you have any other identification?"

"Wait, hold it," the instructor said, jumping up. "When a customer pays cash you do not have to ask for identification."

"How do we know the money is any good? Lizzie could be using someone else's cash," Frankie said.

"We have to assume that the money is good and that it belongs to Lizzie."

I could tell Frankie was upset. She took a pen to write on the 10-dollar bill. "May I have your address and home telephone number?"

"Don't write on the money!" the instructor shouted. "It will only confuse the next person who uses it. Just take the cash."

"Shouldn't I call the Treasury Department and read off the numbers of the bills to make sure Lizzie isn't a deadbeat?"

"It isn't necessary," the instructor said. "You see, on each bill it says, 'In God We Trust,' so when a customer pays with cash, you have to trust her."

"You mean I don't even have to call my supervisor to initial the bills?"

"No, you don't. Just write out a sales slip and then deposit the bills in the register."

"I don't think I'll ever get the hang of it," Frankie said in tears.

"Of course you will. Now for the next two hours, we will discuss the key to the cash system, which is called 'making change.' Has anyone in the room ever made change before?"

No one raised a hand.

Muskie and the French

Secretary of State Edmund Muskie has a lot to learn about diplomacy, and there is no better place to start than with the French.

Recently he made a boo-boo by attacking President Giscard d'Estaing for meeting with Leonid Brezhnev in Warsaw without first telling the U.S. What irked Muskie most is that he had just received a dressing down from the French foreign minister because the U.S. was failing to consult with France.

The other item that got the Secretary's dander up was France's decision to go to the Olympics in Moscow.

What Muskie must learn is what any tourist who has been to Paris knows, and that is, if you want to get the French to do something, you have to indicate that you desire them to do the exact opposite.

For example, when the Secretary was in Brussels, he should have taken Foreign Minister Jean François-Poncet aside (the French love to be taken aside and whispered to) and said, "Mr. Minister, I must tell you this in the strictest confidence. We want the French to go to the Olympics in Moscow because we believe that your athletes are the only ones who can beat the Russians. President Carter has asked me to instruct you that no matter what he says publicly, he believes privately it is in the best interests of the West if you compete."

François-Poncet would have said, "Of course, we want to do what's best for the West. We will send a team." Then he would have excused himself and got on the scrambler line to President Giscard.

"Monsieur le Président, I have just spoken to Secretary of State Muskie, and he informs me that the U.S. wants France to go to the Moscow Olympics."

"Alors. This means, of course, we *cannot* go. Are you sure they want us to attend?"

"Yes. Monsieur Muskie took me aside and told me it is in the best interests of the Allies if the French appear at the Games."

"We shall see what is in the best interests of the West. If

231

Carter thinks we will go to Moscow just because he wants us to, then he will be very disappointed. Frankly, Jean, I intended to send our team, but now if I wanted to, I couldn't, as we would only be playing into American hands."

"Exactly my thoughts, Monsieur le Président. Muskie must take us for fools."

"What did you tell him?"

"I told him we would gladly send a team to the Olympics if the U.S. thought it was the right thing to do."

"Good. Tomorrow I will announce that we have no intention of sending one and never did. I shall say France intended to boycott Moscow long before the United States thought of the idea."

"I can't wait to see Muskie's face when you do it. Do you intend to meet with Leonid Brezhnev in Warsaw, Monsieur le Président?"

"I haven't made up my mind yet. What do the Americans want me to do?"

"I will find out and report back."

François-Poncet would then go back to the foreign ministers' meeting and take Muskie off into a corner (the French always like to take people off into corners) and say, "I have just spoken to Giscard and he wants to know how the Americans would feel if he met privately with Brezhnev in Warsaw."

Muskie should have said, "An excellent idea. It's best to keep communications open, and who would be better at it than Giscard. Tell your President to arrange a meeting as quickly as possible."

Once again, François-Poncet would excuse himself and get on the line to Giscard.

The French foreign minister would say, "They want you to meet Leonid as soon as possible."

Giscard would say, "What gall! How dare the Americans tell the head of the French republic who and who not to meet with! I will go to Warsaw, but I will turn my back on Brezhnev and refuse to so much as shake his hand."

"Well said, Monsieur le Président. It may be a slap in the face to the Russians, but it will be a bigger slap in the face for the Americans. Vive la France!"

"Vive la France to you, Jean."

So there you have it, Secretary Muskie. This is your first lesson in dealing with the French. If you tell them what you don't wish them to do, they'll do it every time. That's why they're called French.

Mr. Chairman

"Mr. Chairman, Mr. Chairman."

"Will the gentleman in the living room in his undershirt please sit down. You are out of order."

"Don't tell me I'm out of order. You know the only reason you're going through this charade is because of the television audience."

"What seems to be the problem, sir?"

"I want to see the reruns of *Charlie's Angels*. Why can't you people hold your convention in the daytime when everyone is at work?"

"That's impossible. It would mean preempting the soap operas, and our female viewers would never stand for that. Besides, this is a very historical moment on television. We're nominating the person who may be the next President of the United States."

"Who's that?"

"Ronald Reagan."

"No, you got it all wrong. It's Jimmy Stewart for President —Ronald Reagan plays his best friend."

"We know what we're doing. Ronald Reagan for President —the part's all sewed up. Now will you please sit down so we can get on with the speeches?"

"I'd rather see *The Gong Show*—and I hate *The Gong Show*."

"If you don't keep quiet, sir, we'll make you listen to Sen. Charles Percy."

"I'll be quiet."

"All right. Now, ladies and gentlemen, we have a real treat in store for you. How would all you Americans like to have the Panama Canal back? You would? Well, it's now possible. If you vote for Ronald Reagan in November, we will send you absolutely free, without any obligation on your part, the Panama Canal, as well as all the locks that go with it. Just think of it, the canal that you've always dreamed of is yours, once you put Ronald Reagan into the White House."

"Mr. Chairman. Mr. Chairman."

"Sir, we only have four hours of prime time and we would appreciate it if you'd . . ."

"What happened to the tax cut?"

"We're coming to the tax cut, sir, right after we return from Clare Boothe Luce. Why don't you go and take a nap and as soon as we get to the tax cut, we'll wake you up."

"I don't wanna miss anything. You go right ahead with whatever you were planning."

"We have a film on Ronald Reagan as a young man."

"Beautiful! I'm glad I didn't go bowling tonight. Are we going to get a tax cut and a balanced budget at the same time?"

"That's our big secret. If we told you that you might turn off the set and go to bed."

"Give me a hint."

"Well, we've shot it three different ways like they did *Dallas* so it will be kept a mystery. In one version you get the cut and the balanced budget. In another you get the cut and a larger deficit, and in the third, you get the cut AND the Panama Canal as well."

"Is it true Ronnie wants to give the People's Republic of China to Taiwan?"

"Ronnie's always had a warm spot in his heart for Taiwan. He has all his American cowboy boots made there."

"Doesn't everybody? Hey, do you mind speeding it up? Maybe if you wind up early I can get to see Johnny Carson."

"We still gotta lot of business to attend to."

"Such as?"

"Ronnie is going to do his welfare cheaters number."

"Again?"

"It still plays in Peoria."

Coffee, Tea, or Talk

When it comes to "Truth in Advertising," "Truth in Lending," and "Truth in Consumerism," I am ready to man the barricades to fight for the public's right to know. The only area in which I do not believe people should be informed about *anything* is when it comes to "Truth in Flying."

In the past, I have criticized airline pilots who insist on getting on the loudspeaker of their planes and giving the passengers a sightseeing tour of the United States.

"Well, folks, we're now flying over Kansas, which you can't see because of the cloud cover, and pretty soon we'll be crossing the Mississippi, which just keeps rolling along, etc., etc."

I thought that was pretty bad, but it's nothing compared to the pilot who feels his passengers are fascinated about the technical aspects of flying.

I was bouncing around the country last week on three different airlines, and I learned more about planes than I ever wanted to know.

We were sitting at the gate at La Guardia when the pilot said, "I guess you folks are wondering what the holdup is. We have a lil' old leak in the hydraulic system, and the mechanics are trying to find it, because once you put these big birds into the air, they need all the power they can get. And while we have a backup system, I think I'll let them fix the leak, just so this lil' old red light up here on the panel will go off."

Ten minutes later: "This is the pilot. Well, it wasn't a hydraulic leak after all. It seems to be a lil' old electric short in the black box. They should be able to repair it in a jiffy by going in under the nose wheel and splicing the wires that control the afterburner gauges. The reason for the delay is that the pilot who flew this plane into La Guardia failed to report the malfunction. All he complained about was that one of the rear wheel tires had blown out, and that's been changed, so once we get the electrical wiring situation straightened out, it will be all systems go."

Fifteen minutes later: "Everything appears to be A-O.K.

now. The red light is out and the hydraulics seems to be working fine, though the real test is when we get into the air. But we don't expect any trouble, so relax and enjoy the flight. I'll be back to you as soon as we're airborne, and if I see any red lights on the panel, you'll be the first to know."

A few days later, I flew from San Francisco to Chicago. It was a different airline and a different pilot. We were somewhere over Colorado. "Hi, folks. Well, so far we've had a very pleasant trip, but planes in the area are reporting heavy turbulence ahead. Ordinarily, we'd try to fly around the storms, but in this case they seem to be spread over such a wide area that we're just going to have to go lickety-split right through them. It's going to be a little bumpy, but these planes were built to take it, and could even fly through a tornado if they had to. If you look out the window you can see the lightning and black clouds all around us. You have to expect this kind of weather in the summer in this area, as well as lots of hailstorms. So fasten your seatbelts and maybe you'll all have something to tell your grandchildren about."

The next day I had the fun of flying from Chicago to Upper Michigan. The pilot hadn't given us much information on how he was doing, and I was starting to get a little worried. But as we were making an approach for a landing at Travis City, he suddenly veered off to the left, gunned his engines and started to climb.

"That was a close one," he said over the loudspeakers. "Those of you on the right side of the aircraft probably saw the little single-engine plane which decided to land at the same time we did. Apparently the people in the tower were asleep, or maybe they thought we would both enjoy landing on the runway at the same time. In any case, I think we'll make another pass and hope this time we can set this thing down without a Piper Cub trying to knock our tail off. I don't want anyone back there to worry, because I'm going to report the plane as soon as I get on the ground. I'm going to have a few choice words to say to the tower as well."

I'm certain that there must be passengers aboard our airlines who are grateful for all the news they can get on how the pilot of the plane is faring. But I've yet to meet one. Most of us still believe that Truth in Flying is for the birds.

A New Awards Show

No one wants to say it out loud but all the award shows on television are getting to be a bore. Whether it's the Oscars or the Tonys, the format never seems to change. "May I have the envelope, please— The winner is—"

"Oh my goodness, oh my gracious, this is the greatest moment of my life—I want to thank my producer Ron Christmas, my agent Eddie New Year, the cast, the cameramen, the sound mixer, my chauffeur, the woman who comes to clean my apartment twice a week, the Beverly Hills Fire Department, the boy who delivers my newspaper, my mother, my father, my third husband and his two children by a former marriage, Thomas Alva Edison, the Mormon Tabernacle Choir, Burger King, who always let me have it my way . . ."

The producers of these shows know they're up against the wall and they are searching desperately for a new format to hold the audience's interest. I believe I may have one for them.

Instead of announcing the winners at shows such as the Academy and Tony awards, they could announce the losers.

This is how it would go:

"The nominees for the best actress are Lila Crane in *Valium*, Sylvia Riff in *Light My Beer*, and Dora Tremble in *Roller Skate Hustler*. And the big loser is Lila Crane who starred in *Valium*."

"I am delighted to accept this award because it gives me an opportunity to mention all the no-talent people who participated in the making of *Valium*. I don't know where to begin when it comes to blaming people involved with this picture. There were so many of them I'm sure I'll forget someone's name.

"To my lecherous producer Sam Tolstoy, who pursued this project for 13 years before he found a studio dumb enough to put up the money, I would just like to say it was a lousy script to start with, but you managed to mess it up even worse. To my director Gary Ack, who doesn't know one end of the camera from the other, I advise you to go back into your father's slipcover business. To the cast, who sabotaged every scene I had, I will see all of you at a Screen Actors Guild hearing where I've preferred charges. And to my astute husband-manager, who persuaded me to play in this turkey, I want the house in Bel Air, custody of the dogs, and a complete accounting of all the money I've made in the past 10 years. If you have anything to say to me after tonight, you can tell it to Marvin Mitchelson, my lawyer."

"Thank you, Lila, and now for the best actor of the year, the nominees are Rock Hammer for *Drowning*, Jeff Holster for *Far Too Many Indians*, and Dan Lava for *The One-Legged Place Kicker*. And the loser is, Dan Lava."

"I'm proud to stand up here and accept this award, not because I believe that I am the only loser in this business. Everyone who was nominated is a loser. I saw Rock Hammer's performance in *Drowning* and had to walk out of it. Jeff Holster's portrayal of a half-breed sheriff set the motion picture business back 20 years. They both deserve to be up here with me tonight. As for *The One-Legged Place Kicker*, I have nothing to apologize for. I did it for the money, which in this business is the name of the game."

"Let's hear it for a great actor, Dan Lava. And now our final award for the best picture of the year, the nominees are *Two Tickets to Picasso* produced by Sy Custer, *The Incredible Tax Shelter*, producer Merrill Linch, and *Ashes Over Portland*, producer Chauncey Campbell. May I have the envelope, please? The big loser is Merrill Linch.

"Accepting the award for Merrill Linch, who could not be with us tonight, is E. F. Houghton."

"Ladies and gentlemen, Merrill wanted to be here this evening in the worst way. But as you know he's doing one to 10 in the Allenwood Penitentiary for padding the books and writing bum checks to pay the cast. *The Incredible Tax Shelter* was a labor of love as far as he was concerned, and although it brought in $60 million at the box office, it never made back its negative cost. Why a jury refused to believe this is something Merrill will never understand.

"To the talented people associated with *The Incredible Tax Shelter*, who were cheated out of their profits, Merrill has asked me to say you've been great sports, and as soon as his parole comes through he'd be proud to make another film with each and every one of you."

Nostalgia in Detroit

The theme for this year's Republican convention, according to California's Lt. Gov. Mike Curb, who is in charge of the show, will be "nostalgia." Since there is no contest, and not even an expectation of a fight, the networks will have to cover 15 hours of entertainment.

The biggest burden will be on the TV anchormen and the floor reporters in Detroit, who will have to create the excitement in order to keep their listeners.

I now take you to the producer's booth of CBS in Detroit where all the action will be directed. It is opening night of the convention.

The producer, sitting in his chair, is staring at all the TV monitors, not only those of his cameramen, but also NBC's and ABC's.

He says, "I want a tight shot of Kate Smith singing the 'Star-Spangled Banner.' Then we go to the floor and talk to the delegates."

The director says, "John Chancellor and David Brinkley are coming up with an exclusive interview with Dorothy Lamour."

"Dammit, who do we have?"

"Lesley Stahl is standing by with Liberace."

"Okay, we'll take it, then go over to Ed Bradley. He says Roy Rogers has agreed to talk with him."

"Walter wants to know when he can talk to Alf Landon."

"Tell him after we show the excerpts from *Bedtime for Bonzo* with Reagan."

"Oh my God, ABC has talked Esther Williams into taking a swim at the YWCA with Barbara Walters."

"Get a camera crew over there right away."

"What happened to Harry James? Weren't we going to have a medley of songs from the Forties?"

"He follows Ethel Merman."

"Okay, let's go to Walter in the booth and let him do the two-minute piece he wrote about *Lassie* and the different Presidents she served under."

"ABC is coming up with Sander Vanocur and The Andrews Sisters in the Illinois delegation."

"Where's Harry Reasoner?"

"He's trying to get over to Shirley Temple."

"It's too late. Tom Brokaw has her on NBC."

"What's going on at the platform?"

"They're honoring Herbert Hoover's granddaughter. Do you want it?"

"Sure we want it. Tell Bob Schieffer to hold off on Rudy Vallee. We can get him any time."

"Bill, there's something going on in the Mississippi delegation. Everyone is standing up. Lesley wants to talk to you."

"Come in, Lesley."

"Bill, Mississippi has a barbershop quartet, and they're singing 'Sweet Adeline.' The chairman is trying to gavel them down. Florida is protesting because they were told no barbershop quartets would be permitted on the floor."

"Great work, Lesley. I'll send over Reasoner to cover Mississippi. You stay with the Florida delegation in case they decide to walk out."

"Hey, Bill. Greer Garson has just grabbed the mike on the platform and she's doing a scene from *Mrs. Miniver* three times."

"Barbara Walters has Joe DiMaggio in the booth."

"Chancellor is now talking to Ginger Rogers and Fred Astaire."

"Does anyone know where Mary Pickford is sitting?"

"She's dead, Bill."

"Oh, yeah. I guess we better go to the commercial."

Justice Is Served

The justice system in this country seems as loused up as everything else. One of the reasons for this is that the law provides that anyone who has a legal dispute involving more than $50 is entitled to a jury. Most jurors can deal with personal injury and liability cases. But you have to have an MBA from Harvard, a law degree from Stanford, and an accounting diploma from the Wharton School to be able to follow the complicated suits that ordinary citizens are required to adjudicate these days.

How can the average jury understand the issues in a multibillion-dollar corporation lawsuit?

A well-known trial lawyer told me they can't. Most juries involved with any business litigation make their decisions based on things other than the thousands of pieces of evidence and months of testimony that neither they nor the judge understand.

This is how it goes in the jury room, he told me.

"I think we should find for the plaintiffs."

"Why?"

"Their chief lawyer always looks so fresh and neat, no matter how hot it is in the courtroom."

"I'm for throwing out all the charges. The defense has a woman lawyer on the staff, and I think if we voted for the defendants it would encourage large corporations to hire more women lawyers."

"That's the most stupid reason I ever heard for judging a case. If we're going to play by those rules, we have to take into consideration that one of the plaintiff's executives has a bad limp. Why not give the billion dollars to them for hiring the handicapped?"

"Wait, we're getting away from the evidence. Let's go over it again."

"Are you crazy? No one in this room knows what anyone out there was talking about."

"Okay. Let's *not* go over the evidence. How do we arrive at a decision?"

"I'm for giving the nod to the plaintiffs. Their backup lawyer always came over to us when he wanted to make a point. The defendants' lawyer preferred to address his remarks to the judge. If he wants to win, the defense counsel should have paid more attention to us."

"You're too sensitive. Only the fat defendants' lawyer ignored us. The cute one with the horn-rimmed glasses spent a lot of time leaning against the jury box. He had beautiful eyes."

"But he had a beard. I'd never trust a person who sports a beard."

"My son has a beard."

"I thought as much, and while we're on the subject—I don't trust you either."

"Hold it. We've been together five months. Let's get a decision so we can all go home. How do you vote?"

"How is she voting?"

"I'm voting for the plaintiffs."

"Then I'm voting for the defendants."

"I told you she couldn't be trusted."

"We're never going to see our loved ones again. There has to be a compromise. I suggest we give the plaintiffs half of what they are asking."

"Why?"

"Do you remember when the president of the injured company testified? His entire family sat in the first row for five days. I thought that was very loyal of them. You don't see families that close anymore."

"Are you planning to give the plaintiffs a half a billion dollars because their chief executive officer has a nice family? How do you know what goes on behind closed doors?"

"I agree. Besides, the defendant company's chairman of the board wore his Shriners pin when he took the stand. I happen to be a Shriner, and I'll take a lodge brother's word against anyone who drags his kids out of school to sit at a trial."

"We appear to be split on a verdict. Shall I report to the judge that we can't come to a decision?"

"Don't do that. He'll make us read the court transcript again. I say we flip a coin. Heads we find for the plaintiffs—tails for the defendants."

"Okay, as long as she takes back what she said about men with beards."

"I take it back, but only because I believe justice should be served."

Take My House

Everyone knows that Californians are different from the rest of us. They were the pioneers of pyramid games, they invented the candlelight dinner and hot tubs, and they were the first to put Gucci shoes on their roller skates.

Californians are into something new now. It's called "real estate." It isn't what you are or whom you know that counts anymore. It's how much you're asking for your house.

I didn't realize how much real estate values mattered in people's lives out here until a very nice lady took me to lunch in the Malibu colony at a $2 million shack which resembled the stockade in *The Bridge on the River Kwai*.

The guests were all gathered around the small swimming pool and my hostess introduced me to the people. "This is Ted and Jane, who are asking $95,000 for their villa in Ventura; Bob and Alice, whose English Tudor is now on the market for $1 million five; Don and Phyllis, who turned down $2 million one for their Spanish hacienda in Brentwood; and Mildred, who just split with Sam and is showing her $850,000 redwood contemporary by appointment only."

They seemed like really nice people.

The hostess apologized because lunch was late. "We're still waiting on Henry and Roz, who have just listed their Tarzana colonial for $2 million six, and Allen and Marjorie, who won't take less than $1 million seven for their place in Laurel Canyon."

"They're worth waiting for," I said.

Most of the people were in the movie and television business so I expected some hot gossip about the stars which I could take back East with me. But it was not to be.

The table conversation went like this. "Rhonda left Johnny's fabulous $2 million panoramic hillside retreat with four bathrooms and an indoor Jacuzzi and moved in with Herb in his $500,000 condominium with a wet bar on Wilshire Blvd."

"What a fool. Rhonda is always trading down."

"When Rhonda falls in love you can't talk any real estate sense into her at all."

"Someone told me the Saudi Arabians are moving into Culver City."

"I can't believe it. They haven't gobbled up Bel Air yet."

"Do you know the mobile home on the highway near Trancas?"

"You mean the one that was set up after the waves washed away the seven-figure Cape Cod on the dunes?"

"The mobile went for $1 million six."

"I thought it had been condemned by the zoning people."

"It had. That's why it was sold so cheap."

I tried to get into the conversation.

"What's Johnny Carson really like?"

"Six million for his home in Beverly Hills, and $1 million eight for his house on the beach."

"How about Candice Bergen?" I asked.

There was dead silence at the table. Finally, someone said quietly, "Off the record?"

"It won't leave this patio."

"Candice sublets."

You Can Now Sue Your Spouse

With all the bad news on the front pages lately, there was good news for husbands, wives and lawyers a few weeks ago. The Massachusetts Supreme Court ruled that a wife could sue her husband for negligence if he did a lousy job shoveling snow and ice off the sidewalk in front of their house.

The case, and I did not make it up, concerned a Shirley Brown of Wakefield, Massachusetts, whose husband William got up at 7 A.M. on December 21, 1978, and shoveled the sidewalk before he went off to work. At about 8 A.M., Mrs. Brown left the house and slipped on the shoveled walk, breaking two pelvic bones.

Mrs. Brown charged that William was "careless and negligent in the maintenance of the walks" and failed to leave them in a safe condition for his wife. She also maintained in the suit that it was part of her husband's duties and responsibilities to keep walks clear and to spread sand and prevent them from getting slippery.

For years courts have been reluctant to allow spouses to sue each other for negligence, so *Brown v. Brown* opens up a whole can of beans for married couples, the legal profession and insurance companies. If there is a plethora of *Brown v. Brown* cases, all homeowner policies will have to be rewritten and the rates could go sky-high.

If a wife can sue a husband for neglecting his household chores, there is no reason why a husband can't go to court when a wife neglects hers.

Let me give you some examples based on personal experience:

Under English common law, one of a wife's duties is to put out the trash. Recently I was playing with the dog and tripped over a Hefty bag my wife had carelessly thrown in the driveway. I scraped my elbow badly. Had the *Brown v. Brown* case come down earlier, I would have immediately called my lawyer, Edward Bennett Williams, and started the legal ball rolling. But being ignorant of my rights all I did was warn her that if she couldn't do a better job with the trash, I would no longer permit her to watch television after she did the dishes.

I have always maintained that it is a wife's duty to repair anything in the house that goes wrong. I hate to spend money on electricians and plumbers when it isn't necessary. A month ago I asked her to change the motor on our garbage disposal unit, a simple job that any housewife should be able to do. When I came back from playing tennis all the parts of the motor were on the floor and she was crying.

I had to pay $250 to get a man in to do it right. This was an open-and-shut case of negligence in maintaining household equipment, and I can't believe that any all-male jury in the land would not have ruled in my favor had I known I could have taken the case to court.

I believe one more example is sufficient to make my point. Three weeks ago my wife was on a ladder painting the ceiling when I walked by on my way to the kitchen to get a Lite beer. I happened to accidentally brush the ladder and the can of paint came tumbling down and fell on my toes, causing me anguish and pain. Having failed to put up a sign warning passersby that she was painting the ceiling made her guilty of violating every safety regulation in the book, and if I had known about the Massachusetts Supreme Court ruling I would have slapped her with a subpoena on the spot.

There are people who say *Brown v. Brown* could endanger the sanctity of marriage. But I believe it could bring people closer together. Many divorces come about when one party thinks that he or she has been injured by the other. Now that one spouse can go to court and sue the other, there is no reason to break up. If, as the song says, "You Always Hurt the One You Love," it's Mutual of Omaha's problem, not ours.

Won Ton Ronnie

"OK, Ronnie, can we go over it once again? This is the People's Republic of China. It has one billion people and because it is scared silly of the Soviet Union it is tilting toward the United States."

"And what about the real China?"

"It's not called China. It's called Taiwan. It's this little island on the map over here. There can't be two Chinas."

"There were two when I was on *Death Valley Days*."

"Well, all that has changed."

"Who changed it?"

"Nixon and Kissinger. They decided that recognizing a China with a billion people would upset the Russians a lot more than pretending this island over here was the real China."

"What about Chiang Kai-shek's plans to invade the mainland and take Peking back?"

"Ronnie, Chiang Kai-shek is dead."

"What a pity. I better send George Bush to his funeral."

"He died some time ago. Besides, George is now in the People's Republic of China—that's this big area here—talking to the Chinese leaders who run the country."

"What's he doing there?"

"He's trying to explain to them that you didn't mean what you said about two Chinas."

"He has some nerve. Has anyone done the security check on him?"

"Ronnie, I know you like to live in the past. But if you become President you have to think of the future. Nixon would have never recognized the People's Republic of China if it hadn't been in the United States' national interest."

"But what will I tell all my friends? They were all hoping that when I became President I would free mainland China from Communism."

"Your friends will understand if you just show them this map. Explain to them that even Taiwan has faced up to the fact that there can't be two Chinas, and is willing to go along with the status quo, providing the People's Republic doesn't move in on them."

"I don't trust Mao Tse-tung and never have."

"Mao Tse-tung is dead, Ronnie."

"We'll send word to George Bush not to go to the funeral."

"Mao died a long while back. We don't have to deal with that problem."

"Why didn't someone inform me? This could be a golden opportunity to attack the mainland. We could send our Marines up there through Vietnam and surprise them."

"We're not in Vietnam anymore, Ronnie. We've been out of there since 1975."

"How can I be President of the United States if nobody tells me these things?"

"That's why we're having this briefing. We want you to be up on events. We want you to be up on everything. A lot has happened around the globe since World War II."

"I don't like it one bit. The next thing you know mainland China will want to send over a Ping-Pong team. What do I tell the other China then?"

"You'll think of something, Ronnie. We're not making you America's greatest statesman for nothing."

The Invisible War Machine

I am one of those reporters who will buy any conspiracy theory, providing it's leaked to me. The latest one was planted by a friend, Art Kranish, concerning the "Stealth" bomber, known as the invisible plane because the Soviets cannot spot it with their radar.

There has been a tremendous political flap over the fact that the Pentagon had confirmed we were building it. Many irate retired generals and admirals have said that the leak will give the Soviets a 10-year start to come up with a system for making the invisible bomber visible. It has been called by the Republicans "one of the greatest security blunders in American history."

Maybe. But Kranish has another theory.

Here is how he presented it to me. "The only way we can win the arms race with the Soviets is if they go broke first. Since it is too expensive to build everything to fight an all-out war, the Pentagon chiefs have come up with a new plan. They are going to purposely leak stories about weapons they have no intention of building, so that the Soviets will spend zillions of rubles and thousands of man-hours devising ways of combating them. The Russians will be so busy trying to come up with an answer to the Stealth bomber that they won't have time to develop one of their own."

"But that's dirty pool," I said.

"We have no choice. We have to play hardball in order to catch up with them. You saw the shock in the U.S. when we announced we were working on the Stealth bomber. You can imagine how it must have hit the Kremlin. They've probably rounded up every scientist in Minsk, Pinsk and Smolensk to come up with an answer to it."

"What happens when the Soviets discover we have no intention of building an invisible bomber?"

"Then the Pentagon will leak a story that they are going to build an invisible submarine instead. The Soviets will have to scrap all their electronic defenses for the bomber and start right from the beginning trying to figure out how to spot an invisible submarine."

"It makes a lot of sense, particularly since it won't cost any money. But won't the Soviets wise up eventually and be suspicious of the Pentagon leaks?" I asked.

"Exactly. At some point, the Russian military intelligence, which was burned by so many U.S. defense leaks, will start to ignore them. That's when our military boys make their move. They will leak that they have decided to build an invisible aircraft carrier. The Soviets will think this is more 'disinformation' being put out by our side, and will do nothing about it. But this time we'll go ahead with the plans, and the commies will wake up one morning and see hundreds of invisible aircraft carriers off their shores."

"If they're invisible how will they see them?"

"Because we'll deny they are there. The fact that they can't see them will put the fear of God into the Russkies and will bring them to their senses."

"Why can't the Soviets do the same thing to us?"

"Do what?"

"Leak a story that they're going to build an invisible bomber and have us spend billions of dollars to build a system to stop it."

"They have done it. That's where the Pentagon got the idea in the first place."

"One last question," I said. "How do I know that you're not leaking this story to me because we really intend to go ahead with the Stealth bomber and we want the Soviets to believe we're not?"

He replied, smiling, "That's for me to know and for you and the Soviets to find out."

The Hijacker Special

There seems to be a rash of airplane hijackings to Cuba lately. One can only gather that the hijackers are disappointed refugees who are homesick for the old country and want to get back there as fast as possible.

This is understandable but very inconvenient for people who are on the same plane and have no interest in seeing Havana.

The U.S. government is doing everything to beef up security and weed out the would-be hijackers, but with little success. It seems to me that they are overlooking the easiest and cheapest solution to the problem.

Instead of trying to stop hijacking, we should provide free air transportation back to any Cuban refugee who doesn't want to stay.

Major fields in Florida would have planes on a 24-hour standby basis, and all the disaffected Cuban would have to do is call a toll-free number and make a reservation.

The planes would be provided by the airlines, who would save thousands of dollars by giving this kind of service rather than deal with the rerouting of a hijacked plane and the irate passengers that are on board.

This is how the "Hijacker Money-Saving Plan" would work:

As each refugee disembarks in Key West or some other port of entry, he would be handed an airline schedule which would say: "Fly to Cuba. Delta Is Ready When You Are."

Let us assume that Raoul Domingos has just set foot on American soil and doesn't like what he sees. A red-jacketed agent will greet him on the dock and ask if he can be of help.

Raoul will say, "I don't like it here and I want to go home."

"No problem," the agent will reply. "We have a DC-10 leaving for Havana in an hour. Do you want to go first class or tourist?"

"I have no money."

"The flight is free. We serve a champagne luncheon and we're showing *Smokey and the Bandit*."

If Raoul replies, "I want to see my cousin in Chicago first," the agent will say. "You can still fly back to Havana after that.

Just go to any airline office and tell them you're a potential
hijacker and they will give you an airline ticket to connect you
with one of our shuttle flights leaving on the hour from
Miami."

"Do I have to change in Atlanta?"

"Everyone has to change in Atlanta. But one of our federal
marshals will meet your plane and escort you to the right gate
and help you with your baggage."

"I may want to see Disney World first."

"Be our guest. Air Florida has a red-eye special leaving
Orlando at eleven o'clock in the evening. It will get you into
Havana by one o'clock in the morning."

"Do I have to make a reservation in advance?"

"Of course not. Just show up at the airport and they'll leave
whenever you're ready."

Having been informed that there is no need to hijack a plane
to get home, Raoul and the people like him will have no desire
to do anything illegal to return to their motherland.

It is only fair to mention that most Cuban refugees who have
arrived on these shores do not have any desire to return to Mr.
Castro's socialist paradise, and no one should be given a free
ride back against his will.

But there are a few such as Raoul who find the U.S. does not
live up to their expectations, and we owe it to them to see that
they get back to Cuba safe and sound.

To publicize the new U.S. to Cuba service, the airlines
could buy billboard space all over the country which would
say: AMERICA: LOVE IT—OR CONTACT YOUR NEAREST TRAVEL
AGENT FOR FURTHER INFORMATION.

They Did a Great Job

As a member of the print media, no one stands in as much awe as I do of the electronic media. It is not when they have a good story that they're at their best—it's when they have no story at all and have to stick with it that they really shine.

All three networks excelled last week at the Democratic convention.

I guess the highlight was Wednesday evening. I was watching one of the major channels and there was absolutely nothing going on. The network team rose to the occasion.

"Let's go now to Tammy Dumberton. Tammy, you had an earlier report that nothing was going to happen in the next hour. Can you confirm that for us?"

"Yes, Lester. I've been talking to the Rhode Island delegation and they have told me they don't plan to do anything."

"That's very interesting, Tammy, stay with it. Let's go to Carlton Finks, who is talking to a lady delegate from Delaware."

"Lester, as you know, nothing has taken place here for the last two hours and with me now is Mrs. Cynthia Grogan, a Carter delegate from Delaware who says she has nothing to say. Mrs. Grogan, is this true?"

"That's correct. On behalf of the entire delegation from Delaware, I have no news to report."

"I'm sorry, Carlton, I have to switch to the Waldorf where Temple Star has the latest news on what is going on at Kennedy headquarters."

"Lester, it's too early to say, but I've talked to one of the senator's campaign aides who was closeted in the suite and he said none of it means anything. I'm trying to get confirmation on this now."

"You do that, Temp, and we'll get back to you. Now let's go to Eldon Lloyd, who has been standing out on Eighth Avenue and can give us an up-to-date report on the situation there."

"Lester, the traffic on Eighth Avenue is moving very well. Three buses have passed by in the last half-hour going north, and about six minutes ago I saw a 1961 Buick. You don't see many of those around anymore. There is something going on in Pennsylvania Station. I believe an Amtrak train is running late, but none of the Amtrak people will talk about it."

"Eldon, will you hold off on that Amtrak report? We've had a bulletin that they've run out of coffee in the Garden concession stand just below us. Ron Peterson is trying to get over there now. Ron, can you get to the stand and check it out?"

"I'm working my way over now, Lester. As you can see, the floor is jammed with people. Okay, here I am. Sir, is it true your concession has run out of coffee?"

"Yes, we have. Hi, Mom and Dad and Danny and Eddie and Sue and the guys at Feagan's Bar."

"What do you plan to do about it?"

"Nothing."

"I guess that clinches it, Lester. It could be the biggest nothing story we've had so far."

"It certainly could be. Well, as you have seen and heard, there is nothing going on here, and we'll stay with the story until its conclusion. In a moment we'll be back with the latest coverage of the Democratic convention on our 72nd hour in captivity."

The Greatest Chinese Mistake

It was inevitable that once the People's Republic of China opened its doors to the Western nations, it would be corrupted by our evil ways. This thought occurred to me when I read in the newspaper that the National People's Congress had just passed its first income tax law, "to safeguard China's economic interests." The leaders of the People's Republic have assured the populace that the law, in its present form, only affects 21 out of China's one billion population. The reason is that the bill provides for the equivalent of a $6,575 annual exemption, and except for the 21 Chinese performers, artists and writers, no one makes that kind of money in the nation.

Let the people of the People's Republic beware! You may be safe this year, and possibly next, from the Chinese IRS, but there has not been an income tax bill ever passed that hasn't eventually included the majority of the country.

I can see a meeting of the 1982 National People's Congress. The Communist Finance Committee is scratching for revenue.

"Comrades, it is urgent that we raise another billion yuan to pay for our cradle-to-the-grave birth control program."

"The only way to do this is to lower everyone's exemptions and raise the rate of the income tax. We will assure the people that instead of 21 people being affected, only 100 million out of one billion will have anything to worry about."

"Of course, why didn't I think of that?"

Six months later, the deputy finance minister returns from a trip to the United States and reports to the party, "Comrades, I have seen a wondrous thing in America—a thing that no Chinese person would believe."

"So tell us, Weng Pu, what is this wondrous thing?"

"I have seen a machine that takes the income tax out of a person's salary before he receives a check."

"You are a capitalist toad liar, Weng Pu. No such machine could do that."

"I swear on—who's in power this week?"

"Jiang Xang?"

"I swear on Jiang Xang's head that I am telling the truth. I went to a U.S. zipper factory and asked a foreman how much salary he made. He said $450 a week. Then someone handed him his check and it was for $200. The head of the factory said a machine took out the $250 and mailed it to the government."

"If we can get one of these machines," a worker in the Finance Department said, "We could lower the tax exemption and only 300 million people would have to pay any income tax."

"The Treasury Department gave me one as a gift," the deputy finance premier said. "We can start right away."

Of course there would be a certain uproar about the tax, so the Chinese IRS could throw in a few tax-deductible items. For example, if you had lunch with someone and talked about "the gang of four," it would be considered a business meal and could be deducted. If you took the head of your commune to the Peking Opera in hopes he wouldn't make you clean out the horse barns, that would be a legitimate entertainment expense.

And if you used your air-raid shelter to store rice, it would be considered a tax shelter until there was an air raid.

Bureaucrats being bureaucrats and politicians being politicians, I predict that by 1990, one billion Chinese will be paying income taxes, except for 21 people, who will be in the oil business.

It is not my place to criticize the National People's Congress in Peking, but by starting an income tax in their country, they have opened a Pandora's box that can never be shut. The moment you slap a personal income tax on your people, you invite H. & R. Block to invade every commune in the land.

Election Year Whoppers

The biggest lie in the world is, "The check is in the mail"—except during an election year, and then you get some whoppers to top even that.

"I promise, if I am elected, that you will get a tax cut, and I will also balance the budget."

"When I become President, the Russians will know we mean business."

"I guarantee that everyone who wants to work will have a job."

"I will give you less government—not more government."

"My goal is to see that all the people get medical care at a price they can afford."

"Let's make no mistake about this. I am for the farmer."

"My first priority will be to see that everyone gets decent housing at reasonable interest rates."

"I intend to take strong measures to insure that every worker in this country shares in the fruits of his labor."

"My first concern is to cut red tape and to encourage business to make profits so we will have a strong economy and compete with overseas imports."

"I will not appoint anyone to public office for political reasons."

"My Vice President will be in on all my decisions."

"I will work closely with Congress and keep them advised about every foreign policy decision I make."

"My staff will be kept to a minimum and my door will be open to the cabinet members at all times."

"The sick and the elderly will have someone in the White House who cares about them."

"I intend to take the high road in this campaign and not deal in personalities."

"I will never lie to you."

"The only reason I have sought this office is that I believe the country needs leadership."

"This is the best kosher frankfurter I've ever tasted."

"I would say, with a few exceptions, that the media has treated me fairly."

"I intend to rebuild every American city in this country."

"Anyone in my administration who commits an impropriety will be immediately dismissed."

"My first act in office will be to make us self-sufficient in energy."

"No one will go hungry as long as I am President."

"Make no mistake about this. I'm for the small business-man."

"I will see to it that women are treated as equals with men in job opportunities, pay and respect."

"I have spoken to the people and I have listened to what they have to say."

"This is the best chicken gumbo I've ever tasted."

"I can't do the job without your prayers."

"I can't do the job unless you elect Hap Gable as congress-man from this district."

"Make no mistake about this. I'm for the American Indian."

"I read a book about Abraham Lincoln last night and I came across this passage."

"It doesn't matter to me personally if I win or lose, but it does matter to this great country of ours."

"I know what it's like to be poor."

"My remarks were misconstrued by the press, and I had no intention of offending anyone."

"Make no mistake about this. I'm for the coal miner."

"If I am elected, I will listen to the best minds in this country."

"This is the best enchilada I've ever tasted."

Part VI

The Guru Speaks

Whenever I get worried about the economy, I go up to the top of the mountain to see the Great Exalted Economist.

Last week I found him seated cross-legged in front of his cave in his Pierre Cardin robe reading *The Wall Street Journal*.

I placed a fresh sirloin steak at his feet and bowed.

"Oh, Master," I said, "please tell me what is going on with the economy in this country at the moment."

The Great One said, "We are going into a spiral inflation now which could lead us into double digits. The reason for this is that the economy is overheating, and there are too many dollars chasing too few goods."

"I thought you'd say that," I told the Exalted One. "What can we do about it?"

"We can do many things, but it has to get worse before it gets better."

"That's bad," I said.

"It could be good. If it gets worse before it gets better, it is better than if it gets better before it gets worse."

"I never thought of that," I said.

"That's why I'm an economist. When you live with a high employment rate, and a low productivity record, and the gross national product in real dollars does not increase, you are faced with a stagnant economy which makes everyone fearful and causes price hikes which lead to unrealistic wage demands."

"Of course," I said. "But surely there are other reasons for coffee costing $3.15 a pound."

"There are many reasons for that, not the least of which is that we are drinking more coffee from Brazil than we are selling coffee cups to the Brazilians. The American dollar is under attack and the weather has been lousy in São Paulo. That is why interest rates have gone up in Chicago."

"I feel like a rock has been lifted off my shoulders," I told him. "Tell me, Master, why does a shirt that cost me $7 two years ago now cost $11?"

"Government spending and OPEC must take equal blame for the rise in the cost of your shirt. While one is trying to take the shirt off your back, the other is squeezing you dry. Government drives the inflation engine, which is fueled by the oil we must import to pull the weight of our $60 billion deficit. At the moment the engine is going full steam while the average citizen is hanging on for dear life in the caboose."

"Blessed Guru, what is the answer?"

"The only solution is to bite the bullet."

"I like your solution. It seems much simpler than the others," I told him.

"But while biting the bullet we should not throw out the baby with the bathwater."

"Right," I said, trying to remember it all.

"We must hold our hand firmly on the rudder until the storm blows over, keeping all options open even if it means tightening our belts."

"I knew you would have the answer, Exalted One," I said with tears in my eyes.

He turned to go into his cave to broil his steak. The last words he said to me were, "Then again, I could be wrong."

The Tourists Are Coming

It has just been announced that for the first time more foreign tourists visited the United States than American tourists went abroad. These foreign tourists know a bargain when they see one—and the U.S. is now one of the cheapest countries in the Western world.

This may be hard for Americans to swallow, but it's a fact of life, and since our economy depends on such hard currencies as the Japanese yen, the German deutschemark, the French franc and the British pound, we all have to make a better effort to see that these tourists get their money's worth.

Here are some helpful hints to accommodate visitors from other countries.

Most of them have cameras, and they are dying to take pictures of the "natives" that they can show when they get back to Hamburg or wherever they came from. Don't get angry when they ask you to pose for a photo with your family on the front steps of your house or when you're taking out your trash in the morning. Don't ask them for money before you agree to allow them to shoot your picture. If they offer you a few Danish kroner or a Swiss franc you may accept it, but be sure to say thank you.

Foreign tourists are great shoppers. If you are a store owner or salesperson, always wait on them first, because the more money they spend, the better our foreign balance of payments will be.

The exchange rate on the dollar changes every day, so there may be some delay in the transaction as you try to figure out what their traveler's checks are worth. Be patient and keep your temper, even when they call you a thief and complain that they could get a higher rate at their hotel.

People from abroad have their own conceptions as to what the United States is like, mostly based on our movies and television shows. They expect to get mugged in New York, mowed down in Chicago, gouged in Miami, and scalped by Indians in Phoenix, Arizona. They will be very disappointed if their fantasies are not fulfilled, and will go back home and say the U.S. is not what it is cracked up to be.

If we want Austrian schillings and South African rand, we must all play the roles expected of us. For example, if you see a foreign tourist in Central Park, and he hasn't been mugged yet, you owe it to your country to push him down and say, "Your money or your life." Something like this could make his whole trip.

Foreign tourists are very insecure when traveling in America. It does no good to remind a Japanese visitor that if it weren't for the Americans they still might be making ricepaper fans instead of Toyota cars.

Above all, don't mention Pearl Harbor unless they want to bring it up. But it's perfectly all right to ask them, "Is Tokyo Rose still very popular in Japan?"

European tourists are particularly sensitive about the Marshall Plan, so I wouldn't say anything about it. If you happened to be in the Air Force during World War II, don't tell a German tourist how you enjoyed clobbering Stuttgart. They don't want to hear about it, and it really has nothing to do with the bargains they can get here in blue jeans.

The important thing to remember is that America's main interest in tourists is how much money they leave behind. As the poor relations of the Western world, we have to swallow our pride and get on our feet so that in the distant future we all may be able to travel again. I know it's hard to imagine, but someday Americans may have the wherewithal to go abroad, and it will be our turn, once again, to say to a French taxi driver, "Here's a dollar. Buy your family a good meal."

No Reprieve

The sun was just rising over the horizon when McNally heard the shuffle of feet. There were four men, including a minister who was reading the Bible.

"Okay, McNally, it's November 4th. It's time to vote."

"Any word from the governor?" McNally asked.

"No, there doesn't seem to be any chance of a pardon. You're going to have to go into the booth and pull the switch."

"I don't want to do it," McNally said. "I'm innocent. Why do I have to vote?"

"We're sorry. But we are only here to take you to the booth."

The minister came in. "McNally, it's God's will. We will all pray for you. Is there any last word of comfort I can offer you before you go into the polling station?"

"Why me, Father? I've been a good man. I worked hard. I never did anything to hurt anybody. Why do I have to vote?"

"Everyone has to vote sooner or later. Go bravely, my son. It won't take long to pull the lever, and then it will all be over."

"I'm scared, Father. I've never been so frightened in my life."

"We're all frightened of the unknown, my son. But try to think of it as taking a nice journey into a beautiful country that you have never seen before. Imagine that you will be reunited with all the loved ones who have voted before you. Pray with me."

One of the men said, "Come on, McNally. You're just stalling for time. We gave you what you wanted for dinner and let you order anything for breakfast. We have to get the show on the road."

"Can I see my wife before I vote?"

"It won't do any good. She can't help you now. Nobody can help you."

"I won't go. You can't make me go."

"McNally, you can either walk into the voting booth or we can drag you there kicking and screaming. Which way is it going to be?"

"Okay, I'll go, but someday you're going to find out you got the wrong man to vote and it will be on your conscience forever."

Two men walked on each side of McNally as the minister read from his Bible.

Other men along voters' row shouted at him.

"Good luck, McNally. We'll see you soon."

The group arrived at the green door.

By this time McNally was perspiring and shaking. One of the men opened the door and McNally saw the forbidding booth. A man was making the final adjustments on the voting machine.

A registrar was seated at a desk. He checked off McNally's name. "Maybe the governor has pardoned me," McNally said.

The man in charge said, "We've been in touch with his office and he says there is no reprieve. You're going to have to vote."

Two men took McNally by his arms and shoved him into the booth. They pulled the green curtain behind him. They could see his legs, which were quivering.

Suddenly there was a scream from behind the curtain.

McNally had pulled the lever for one of the three presidential candidates, and his scream would be remembered by everyone in the room for the rest of their lives.

My Bendix Problem

The big story this month has not been the presidential campaign or the war in Iran, but the saga of Mary Cunningham, the brilliant 29-year-old Harvard Business School graduate who climbed her way up the corporate ladder of the Bendix Corporation in 15 months to become an Executive Vice President, only to be forced to resign because she was too beautiful, too young and too close to the Chairman of the Board.

It has divided the country, turned families against each other, and raised so many questions that even the Moral Majority can't deal with it.

On one side are those who say Ms. Cunningham would never have reached her position had she not been young and beautiful. On the other are people who say no one would have cared if she succeeded in the executive suite if she hadn't been a beautiful woman.

The most interesting part of the story is that this is the first time people have been more interested in what went on in the private plane of a large corporation than what happened when Farrah Fawcett split up with Lee Majors, and Jackie Onassis had dinner alone at the Stage Delicatessen.

The country was riveted by Gail Sheehy's syndicated newspaper feature of the step-by-step rise and fall of this poor young lady and, based on readership interest, we may soon be reading countless other Mary Cunningham sagas from "*Fortune* magazine's 500 leading corporations list."

My worry is that most people will get a distorted view of the executive suite and how we operate.

As most people know, this column is a conglomerate. We're into books, lecturing, recycling of old columns, and TV and theatrical enterprises—too numerous to mention.

As Chairman of the Board, I was on the lookout some time ago for a smart, young, beautiful person who could be my secretary and handle my mail and crackpot calls. I found one at Georgetown University who fitted all the requirements and hired her.

There are only two of us. Jeannie Aiyer became my confidante and closest adviser. Since she also corrected my grammar, I realized she had great potential. But as soon as she started showing some talent, people in other offices on my floor started whispering that the only reason Jeannie had gotten where she was in my organization was because there was something going on between us.

Then she came in one day and asked for a raise. I told her I couldn't give her a raise but I would make her my Executive Assistant. All the other secretaries on the floor were outraged, and said to each other that if it hadn't been for her looks she would never have been made an Executive Assistant in such a short time. But I ignored the whispering because Jeannie was too valuable to me to replace.

Six months later, she came to me again and said she was desperate for more money. I said she had hit me at a bad time, and instead of a raise I would make her Vice President of the Column.

Once again there was shock and outrage on the floor. Jeannie had been with me less than a year and yet she was in on all my important business decisions. Evans and Novak said that if Jeannie were a man she would never have been made Vice President of the Column in so short a time.

The final blow came a month ago when Jeannie again asked for a raise. This time I had no choice but to make her Executive Vice President of Mergers and Acquisitions, which meant ordering my lunch for me in the office when I didn't go out.

This was too much for everyone on the floor to swallow and the pressure is on now for me to ask for her resignation.

But I'm hanging tough. If she couldn't do the job she wouldn't be here, and her beauty has nothing to do with her new title.

The lesson in all this is that some companies such as Bendix give women titles because they are better than men at what they're doing. Others such as mine hand them out in lieu of giving a person a raise.

The Trouble with the FBI

It is obvious that the FBI is not ready for prime-time television. I plan to discuss the ABSCAM tapes today, but not the moral and ethical questions of whether they should have been played or not. I will deal with the quality of the show as it pertains to show business.

The ABSCAM production values were the worst I've ever seen. The tapes in many cases were out of focus, and the sound made most people think they were hearing *Shogun*.

The acting, except for Congressman Myers, was way below professional standards. The FBI men who played the parts of those offering bribes were stiff and showed no emotion. The director, whoever he was, did nothing to encourage his cast to move around the room and bring some life to this listless drama.

As for the set in the hotel suite, it is evident that the FBI was scrimping on its budget, hoping that no one would notice how cheap the furniture was. Even the costumes were badly chosen; you couldn't tell the difference between the people who were pulling off the sting operation and the congressman who was being stung.

If this wasn't enough, the FBI went with a cliché-ridden script that we've seen on television time and time again. The lines sounded as if they had been written by someone in the fingerprint department, and it comes as no surprise that the writer chose to take his name off the credits.

As a hard-hitting who-done-it, ABSCAM was one of the biggest disappointments of the year, and the FBI better get its act together before the show is canceled from the air.

The first thing I believe the bureau will have to do is get in someone who knows television. If the FBI expects to stay in showbiz, they should appoint Freddie Silverman of NBC as the new director of the FBI.

Then they will have to move their headquarters to Hollywood, where all the studios are equipped to handle this kind of series.

They're going to have to cast their show with professional

actors. You can't risk putting amateur FBI agents in key roles when millions of dollars are at stake. You need a Peter Falk, Lloyd Nolan and Angie Dickinson to play the parts of the undercover agents. The congressmen can play themselves, since they seem to have their hearts in their work more than the FBI actors.

In order to keep up the interest of the audience, you can't stage the entire sting operation in a hotel room. You have to go outside and show shots of automobile chases and work in a few hot love scenes. That may not have anything to do with ABSCAM but will keep the people from turning the dial.

Lee Remick could play the frustrated wife of one of the FBI undercover men, who takes to drink because her husband keeps going out every night dressed as an Arab shiek and won't tell her what he's up to.

She could be having an affair with a labor leader who she doesn't know is also an FBI undercover agent. The possibilities are endless to make ABSCAM into another *Dallas*.

The American people deserve more for their tax money than scratchy tapes with unintelligible dialogue. You either produce a sting operation with class or you don't put it on the air. We can't have a law enforcement agency that thinks all it needs to get an Emmy award is a hand-held Sony camera and a cassette of half-inch tape. Anyone can catch a crooked congressman taking money, but it takes talent to put it on the screen and persuade the TV audience to tune in for next week's episode.

Take My Wife

I think I have a problem. Pope John Paul II has just offered a new sweeping definition of adultery. He said, "Adultery in your heart is not only when you look with concupiscence (strong or sexual desire) at a woman who is not your wife, but also if you look in the same manner at your wife. . . . The husband must not use his wife, or her femininity, to fulfill his instinctive desire," the Pope said. "Concupiscence diminishes the richness of the perennial attraction of persons for interpersonal communion. Through such a reduction, the other person becomes the mere object for satisfying a sexual need and touches the dignity of the person (wife)."

In other words, if you really want to have a good marriage, lust has to go.

I don't have any problem with adultery per se, but I do with concupiscence. I guess some people are born with concupiscence and some people are not. I can be at a party, look at a woman sitting on a sofa in a slit skirt and a low-cut bodice, and my thoughts will immediately go to the problems of the automobile industry in Detroit. Or I can sit in a disco, watching a woman swinging her hips from one end of the dance floor to the other, and wonder whether Iraq or Iran will win the war in the Middle East.

I am the type of person who can sit on a beach staring at bikini-clad women for hours, and ponder the effects of aerosol spray on the ozone.

A cardiologist once told me, "You don't have to jog, because you have no lust in your heart."

"Is that good or bad?" I asked him.

"Well, it saves the heart from pumping too fast," he said. "But it could produce hypertension."

Being without lust for another man's wife does present problems in my society. The word gets out fast that you have no concupiscence, and women avoid you like the plague. I find myself standing alone at cocktail parties, ignoring the whiff of perfume in the air, while all around me people are flirting with each other, and occasionally glancing at me in disdain.

But it doesn't bother me because when you don't have adultery in your heart, you can eat all the taco chips and cheese dip you want, without anybody taking notice.

So what's my problem?

I've never confessed this before to anyone, but I have concupiscence for my wife. Not just a little, but a lot. I can't look at her without having this instinctive urge to do something about it. I know it diminishes the richness of our marriage, and can cause great problems in our interpersonal relations, but I can't help myself. I've tried taking cold showers, and reading the *Congressional Record,* but nothing seems to help. What makes it worse is that she has concupiscence too.

Our family doctor knows about it, and he says it's rare these days for a husband and wife to have concupiscence for each other, but it isn't harmful as long as we take plenty of vitamins and eat a lot of fresh vegetables.

And we were just getting to accept our lust when Pope John Paul came out with his strong statement.

Then the roof fell in. I was reading the newspaper when my wife walked into the bedroom in her silk negligée. "Any news?" she asked.

"Nothing much," I said, trying not to look at her.

She put on a Henry Mancini record.

"Okay," I said, "knock it off."

"What did I do wrong?"

"Nothing, but we can't practice concupiscence anymore. It lowers the dignity of our marriage and brings out the worst in us."

She started to cry. "Is there somebody else?"

"If you must know, there is," I said.

"Who is it?"

"Pope John Paul the Second. And don't ask me to go into the sordid details."

I'll Drink to That

"Hi, my name is Congressman Narbitt and I'm running for reelection from your district. I know there are many questions you would like to ask me so I will start taking them from the floor."

"Congressman. You were arrested for making passes at a sixteen-year-old sheep dog and pleaded guilty to the charges. Why should we return you to office?"

"I have a drinking problem which I'm working on now, and I have confessed my wrongdoing to God. I don't think what I have done has anything to do with the issues of this campaign."

"Sir, you were also caught in an FBI sting operation and found guilty of taking $10,000 from an FBI undercover agent. Do you believe with that background we should vote for you?"

"At the time I took the money I had a drinking problem. I was drunk all the time and didn't know what I was doing. But I always served the people of this district well, even when I had a buzz on. My case is now up for appeal and I don't believe this is the place to discuss it."

"Mr. Congressman. Isn't it true that you charged an illegal immigrant $5,000 to get a private bill passed through Congress making him an American citizen?"

"I charged $3,000 and the money went to my law firm, not to me. My opponent has tried to make political hay with this story, but I would like to tell you exactly what happened. I was drunk at the time. The pressures of this job can drive anyone to take a nip once in a while. I took my first one when I got up in the morning. By eleven o'clock I was smashed. I didn't even remember putting the bill before Congress until some rotten reporter smeared it all over the front pages of the newspaper. This country is getting fed up with an irresponsible media that keeps prying into the lives of its citizens."

"Congressman, can we talk about the hit-and-run charges pending against you after an accident on Route 95?"

"I've discussed the accident in detail and never hid it from my constituents. I had been to a rally, and stopped off at a bar to relax with some good friends. We had ten or eleven vodkas apiece for the road. I don't know if I've mentioned this tonight or not, but I am an alcoholic, and as soon as the stuff touches my lips I'm a goner. But let me say this. I can be a better congressman now than I've ever been before because I'm aware of my problem and I'm willing to face up to it. Wouldn't you rather have someone represent you who knows he can't handle booze than someone who doesn't?"

"Mr. Narbitt, is it true that you took kickbacks from your staff and have been pinching your secretaries for the past four years?"

"A Congressional Ethics Committee is investigating those charges now. But I do not see what that has to do with my holding political office. I have served this district well. I stand for the American Flag, the family, and abolishing waste in government. You must choose between an acknowledged alcoholic and my opponent, who not only is a tri-lateralist, but a humanist and a closet SALT II supporter."

"Congressman, one last question. If you go to jail will you resign your office?"

"That is a ridiculous question. If the good people of this district elect me, I would serve out my full term no matter where I am. I owe it to everyone who votes for me."

"Sir, on behalf of everyone in this room, I would like to say we will support you in your election drive. It's obvious if you hadn't been doing a good job in Washington, the Justice Department would not have tried to get you. We're honored that with all your problems you would still choose to run. Sober or drunk, we need you in the nation's capital now more than ever."

Getting Through on the Phone

National Secretaries' Week has come and gone, and now we are celebrating National Rejection Week, dedicated to the people who are rejected by secretaries who won't let them through to speak to their bosses. Many secretaries are so protective of their bosses that it's impossible to break the phone barrier.

Oglethorpe has solved the problem and many people may be curious as to how he has done it.

"The thing that really tees me off is when a secretary says in a very intimidating voice, 'Mr. Golson is in a meeting. May I inquire what you're calling about?' I keep a list of responses on my wall which I refer to, depending on my mood."

"What are some of them?" I asked him.

"My favorite," he replied, "is, 'Yes, I'm at his house now with a truckload of pork bellies which he bought in the commodities market, and I wish to know whether he wants me to dump them on his lawn or put them in his cellar.' "

"This works?"

"It never fails. I'm put through right away. Another one I use with equal success is, 'Tell Mr. Golson we just got his tests back from the lab, and it could be good news or bad news depending on how he takes it."

Oglethorpe said, "When the secretary asks, 'Do you know Mr. Golson?' I say, 'No, but I'm from his insurance company and I just wanted to tell him the fire has been put out and the only real structural damage to his house was the roof.' "

"Beautiful," I said, "that would even get him out of a board of directors meeting."

"There are some secretaries who are very nosy and will ask, 'What is your business, please?' And then I say, 'Mr. Golson left his American Express card on the waterbed of the Silk Pussycat Motel the other afternoon and we were wondering if he wanted to pick it up or have it mailed to him.' "

"You really play hardball," I said.

"Sometimes you have to with guys who won't take your calls. I also reply to the same query, "This is his pharmacist.

Just tell him if he took any of the pills I gave him yesterday to have his stomach pumped out as my boy delivered Mrs. Klingle's prescription to him by mistake."

Oglethorpe told me he has an answer for every secretary. "If she says, 'Mr. Golson is tied up. Can you speak to somebody else?' I tell her, 'I don't think so. We're planning a *Time* magazine cover on solid waste, and we're thinking of doing it on Mr. Golson.' Or, 'He's just been cleared for the ambassadorship post and there are just a few more questions I have to ask him.'"

"What is your record on getting through with the last one?" I asked Oglethorpe.

"Three seconds. There's one I use when the secretary is pretty nosy about the nature of the call and it always works. I lower my voice to a whisper and say, 'I can't tell you what I'm calling about, and your life will be in danger if anyone in the Soviet Union finds out I made this call.'"

"Give me some more," I said, writing them all down.

"Well, sometimes I might say, 'I'm the manager of the Aknee Tow Truck Co., and one of my new drivers was towing your boss's car away and accidentally rammed it into a brick wall.' And then there's the salad oil ploy. 'If Mr. Golson had oil on his salad yesterday I think I better talk to him. Apparently the can it came in from Sicily was damaged in shipping.'"

"What if the secretary has heard them all?"

"Then I drop the bomb on her. I say angrily, 'I found Mr. Golson's private number in my wife's handbag and I want to know what the hell it was doing there.'"

How Could You, Playboy?

It's impossible to find a copy of the November issue of *Playboy* in Washington. The reason is that it is featuring a 10-page display of "The Women of the U.S. Government," *Playboy*-style.

What is Washington's reaction to the spread? Shock, outrage and horror. I haven't spoken to anyone in the capital who has studied the spread closely and come away thinking it had any redeeming quality.

One congressman told me, "I've never been so shaken up in my life. I can't believe that any U.S. government employee would look like the women portrayed in these photographs."

A high official in the Bureau of Statistics said, "What we're dealing with here is crude data, and it's impossible to assess what we've got until we can refine it and see how much margin is left for error."

An aide for a senator, up for re-election, said, "We feel that the photos were published at this time for political reasons. It is no accident that *Playboy* would spend so much time and effort on asking government women to pose for them if it wasn't an election year."

The fear in Washington is that, because of the 20 persons on display, the rest of the country might get the impression that *all* Washington women look like these do.

It is not true.

You can go from one end of the Department of Transportation to the other and not find one woman who bears resemblance to anyone in the November *Playboy*.

The truth is the women in our government are plain, hardworking and devoted to their jobs, devoid of any of the attributes so brazenly displayed in the magazine.

They think about their work all the time, and take pride in what they're doing to insure that the taxpayer is getting his money's worth.

When a woman goes into government, she takes a vow of chastity and promises she will devote all her working hours to see that the Constitution is upheld, and all federal regulations are carried out, regardless of race, creed or sex.

Women in Washington don't drink or smoke because they know it will interfere with their efficiency. Rather than waste their hours in some singles' bar or disco, they take their work home with them at night so they'll be prepared for their meetings the next morning.

I know countless female government employees who have turned down dinner dates because they would rather have a good night's sleep than sit around a candlelit restaurant table with some attractive man holding hands and wasting time talking about something that has nothing to do with their careers.

Washington women are a breed apart—dedicated and loyal to the federal bureaucracies they serve. They would no more think of posing in the buff than they would of misaddressing someone's Social Security check.

Playboy's outrageous portrayal of them will only play into the hands of those who want more government instead of less.

As one who comes into contact with Washington's women every day, all I can say is that I'm glad I'm not Hugh Hefner. He's going to have to live with this lie for the rest of his life.

The Redskins Blues

Something happens to a town when it has a losing football team. The people become embittered, irrational, and, in some cases, downright spiteful. Now, it isn't as serious if the team has a franchise in Green Bay or New Orleans—but when that team is located in Washington, D.C., and is called the Redskins, it could affect every man, woman and child in the country.

Monday morning is the most dangerous time of all because that is when most of us still have the bitter taste of defeat in our mouths. People wander around the government offices snapping and snarling at each other, and purposely spilling cooler water on each other's shoes. Anyone who is waiting for a decision from Washington could become an innocent victim of what psychiatrists call "The Washington Redskins Blues."

Here is how anyone could be affected:

"Sir, there is a letter here from a World War I veteran who says he hasn't received his check for four months."

"Isn't that just too bad. Let him wait like everybody else. If he had a job, he wouldn't be looking for his government handout every month."

Over at the EPA, they are about to make a multimillion-dollar decision on a project to be built in Philadelphia. The person who made the study reports, "Philadelphia has met all our standards and qualifications."

"Impossible. Everyone knows if they met all our standards and regulations, it would be impossible to build the thing. I say we don't give them the go-ahead."

"What will we tell them?"

"To appeal our decision like everybody else."

"But they'll be so disappointed in Philadelphia."

"They should have thought of that when they cheered the Eagles while they were trouncing us yesterday afternoon."

Over at the Federal Home Loan Bank.

"Would you like a cup of coffee, Mr. Zack?"

"Yes, Miss Thatcher, and you also might tell Higgins to

raise the home loan rate another point. I never saw so many holding penalties by an offensive line in my life."

"Pardon me, Mr. Zack."

"Never mind. I was just thinking out loud."

Over at the SEC, a Redskins fan picks up the phone.

"Merrill, I'm turning your company's file over to the Justice Department for criminal anti-trust violations. . . . No, I have no intention of telling you why. If you saw the game yesterday on television, you wouldn't be asking me a stupid question like that."

The Department of Agriculture takes its football hard too.

"The cotton farmers in Texas are still waiting for our decision on how much support we will give them this year because of the drought. If they don't get an answer soon they could go under."

"Tell them we'll give them 500 million dollars if the Dallas Cowboys will give us Tony Dorsett and the Houston Oilers trade us Earl Campbell."

"Is that legal?"

"Probably not. But we have to get some running backs if we ever hope to beat anybody this year."

The most dangerous place of all to be when the Redskins are losing is the Pentagon. They take their football very seriously over there.

"Sir, we've just received a report that a Danish fishing boat has been spotted in our territorial waters off Maine."

"Sink it."

"Did you say sink it?"

"You heard me, Commander. I said sink it."

"But why?"

"Because Mark Mosely can't kick a field goal. Do you need a better reason?"

"No, sir, that's good enough for me."

"Knock, Knock"

"Knock, knock."

"Who's there?"

"The police."

"The police who?"

"The police with a warrant to go through your files and notes and photos to see if you have any evidence that might help us catch a criminal."

"I don't believe it."

"Oh, you don't, huh? Well, just read the Supreme Court ruling written by Justice Byron White in a 5 to 3 decision. It says you newspaper people have no more protection than anyone else."

"What are you looking for?"

"A little of this, a little of that. You never know what you can find in a newspaper office."

"But if you can go through our files and notes, nobody will be willing to blow the whistle on crooked politicians, waste in government and violations of the Constitution."

"That's right. So open the door before we break it down."

"Wait. It goes deeper than that. Many of our sources are willing to talk to us about crimes that have been committed. If they realize their identities can be revealed, they'll clam up, and then you people will never be able to arrest the guilty parties."

"Maybe so. But you guys have been getting a free ride on the First Amendment for too long. This will stop you meddling in the government's business, once and for all."

"What are you throwing all those photos on the floor for?"

"We want to see if you have any pictures of cops beating up demonstrators."

"Why?"

"Because we want the pictures of the demonstrators. A lot of them got away when we were beating up the ones who didn't."

"But people are allowed to demonstrate. It's in the Constitution."

"Tell that to the Supreme Court. After we get through these photos we want every reporter to turn over his notebook. We want to know who he or she talked to and when."

"But that's a fishing expedition. Tell us what you're looking for."

"We must know who told you people that the judge was taking bribes from the mob."

"What judge?"

"The judge who issued this warrant, dummy. Once we find the guy who was singing he'll be held in contempt of court."

"But that judge is part of the political machine in this town."

"That's right, and we want to see everything you have on the machine. We want names of people who have been trying to get the machine, and addresses, too."

"What else do you want?"

"You know the bridge that collapsed last week? Somebody told your paper that the contractor had put in cheap cement which made it collapse."

"You want the name of the contractor?"

"No, we want the name of the guy who ratted on the company that built the bridge."

"Why don't you find out for yourselves?"

"We don't have to, when we can come here."

"Knock, knock."

"Who's there?"

"The FBI."

"What do *you* guys want?"

"What have you got?"

The Customer Is Always Right

"Hello, Mr. Carter? This is Madame Gandhi. I'd like to call in my order. Have your deliveries gone out today?"

"No, ma'am. Our driver hasn't left yet."

"Well, I'd like a quart of milk, a dozen eggs, a box of steel wool and 38 tons of enriched uranium."

"Yes, ma'am. It sounds like you're planning a big party."

"Never mind what I'm planning. Just send over the order."

"I'm not sure we have 38 tons of enriched uranium in stock. You wouldn't care to take 38 tons of wheat instead?"

"I would not. Every time I call, you say you're out of enriched uranium. If you can't stock what your customers want, I will have no choice but to go across the street."

"Please don't get upset, Madame Gandhi. As you know, the motto of our store is 'Give Everyone a Bang for Their Buck.' Did you want the instant enriched uranium or the type you cook from scratch?"

"I don't know the difference."

"Why don't you look on your atomic reactor and see what it calls for?"

"How did you know I cook on an atomic reactor?"

"I just assumed it. Most people who order enriched uranium have atomic stoves."

"Send over the instant uranium. I'm in a hurry."

"All right. Just follow the instructions on the box. There are all sorts of delicious recipes on the back."

"I know what I want to make with the enriched uranium, and I'm certain the instructions are not on the box."

"Madame Gandhi, I'm obligated to tell you that under the Food and Drug Administration Act of 1962, enriched uranium, if not correctly used, could be dangerous to your health."

"Mr. Carter, I don't need someone telling me how to make uranium curry."

"There's no reason to get upset. I'm just following the law. If I sold the uranium and people got sick to their stomachs, I would be responsible."

"That does it. Please cancel my order. I'll get my uranium elsewhere."

"Don't hang up, Madame Gandhi. I'm sure you won't do anything stupid, and I won't pursue the subject any further. Did you want any heavy water to go with the uranium?"

"Why? Do I need some?"

"Oh, yes. You have to mix the uranium with heavy water or the uranium will stick to the bottom of the pan."

"How much heavy water will I need to cook 38 tons?"

"Offhand, I would say 25 gallons to a ton. You don't want it to get too thin or it will boil over and contaminate the entire Vale of Kashmir."

"All right, include the heavy water."

"Right, Madame Gandhi. I've written it down. Anything else I can help you with?"

"Do you have any plastic garbage bags I can put the waste in?"

"Certainly. Would a dozen be sufficient?"

"Not for what I've got in mind. You'd better send me a gross."

"I agree with you. There's nothing like stockpiling up for a rainy day. Heh, heh, heh."

"Don't get chummy with me, Mr. Carter. You're just lucky I'm giving you my business."

"And don't think we aren't grateful, Madame Gandhi. Your account means a lot to us."

"I should hope so, and you better remember it if you want me to keep buying your uranium."

"Don't worry about that. Your order will be on the truck this afternoon. And, on behalf of everyone in the store, we sincerely hope that you have a bang-up time."

No Reading for Johnny

If Johnny couldn't read before, he's really in trouble now that there is a taxpayers' revolt in this country.

In a couple of years this scene could be played all over the country.

"Hey, Johnny, what are you doing throwing that rock through the window?"

"Nothing."

"Why aren't you in school?"

"School's closed."

"Then why don't you go and play in the park?"

"Can't. The park's closed."

"Well, go to the library and read a book."

"No way. All the libraries are closed."

"Then go play in the streets."

"The streets are full of garbage. No one's picked it up for over a week."

"Surely you can find something constructive for an 11-year-old boy to do."

"I could set fire to a building. But that's no fun because the fire engines won't come anymore."

"That's a bad bruise on your leg. Have you been to see a doctor?"

"I tried to but the emergency room at the hospital is closed. They said they don't have any money."

"Where's your mother?"

"Working."

"Then you should be in a day-care center."

"I was until they closed it."

"Who gets your lunch for you?"

"Don't have lunch since they closed the school."

"I guess you're too young to get a job."

"Yup. Nobody wants to give me a job because they say I should be in school."

"What do you intend to do after you've broken all the windows?"

"I don't know. Maybe steal a bicycle, if I can find one."

"I don't like that kind of talk, Johnny. You should set your sights on higher goals than that."

"Like what?"

"Getting a good education, for one."

"How can I do that if the schools are closed?"

"They won't be closed *forever*."

"They'll be closed long enough for me to steal a bike."

"Why don't you educate yourself?"

"Don't have no books."

"There has to be something you could do that isn't against the law. What do you want to be when you grow up?"

"Don't care."

"Why not?"

"Nobody cares about me."

"That's a terrible thing to say. What makes this country great is that you can be anything you want to be when you grow up, including President of the United States."

"What's the President of the United States?"

"You mean to say you're 11 years old and you don't even know about the President of the United States?"

"I guess they closed the schools before I had a chance to find out."

"Well, if you don't stop breaking those windows I'm going to have to call the police."

"Won't do no good. Those windows is the police station. They closed it eight months ago."

The Walking Wounded

You see them all over Washington these days. Bright young men and women in their best clothes, carrying their résumés in their briefcases, going from one private office to another hoping to land a job.

They are the walking wounded of the Carter defeat, which not only brought down a President but a Democratic Senate. There are thousands of them, hired without the protection of the Civil Service, and now bright Republicans are going to get their jobs. Some of the wounded are qualified for the private sector and others, unfortunately, are not.

"Mr. Walcott, I've been reading your résumé. But I'm not too clear on exactly what you did for the government."

"I was in planning and statistics and dealt mostly with credibility discrepancies and shortfalls in the oversight department."

"I see. Could you be a little more specific?"

"My department made reports and studies involving budgetary problems that were outside long-term outlay ratios. We would assess the impact of these problems and then make recommendations on whether to pass them up the line to the seventh floor or send them back to the third floor for future clarification."

"Then your office was above the third floor?"

"Yes, sir, I was on the fifth floor with windows overlooking the Washington Monument. The people on the third floor reported to me and I reported to my superior who reported to the people on the seventh floor."

"That's very interesting. Could you tell me exactly what your day was like?"

"The first thing we did in the morning was to have a meeting on the fifth floor to discuss discretionary input policy. Then we broke up, and I went to my office and wrote a memorandum concerning the meeting, which I classified and then submitted to all those concerned, keeping a copy for myself just in case someone called me on it at a later date."

"Could you give a more specific example of exactly the service you rendered?"

"Of course. Let's say that at the meeting we discussed a restructuring of the infrastructure of the department. My superior wanted to know what grievance response mechanisms had to be built into the program for it to succeed, and how we could move the staff around without endangering the efficiency of his department by adopting the reforms. We didn't want to send a rocket up in the building that would crash down on our heads."

"Correct me if I'm wrong, but it seems to me that one of your many functions was to protect your superior's job."

"I never thought of it that way, but now that you mention it I guess that was what I was doing. You have to understand how the department worked. The seventh floor kept sending down memos that they were getting flak from the eighth floor to cut out the fat in the agency. The seventh floor said they had no fat to cut, and it was up to the fifth floor to enact a cost-saving program. We passed on their demands to the third floor for suggestions. But the third floor was very uncooperative and kept sending back memos insisting that any major savings in running the department could only be made on the upper floors. Obviously, we had to protect our own turf."

"How did you do this?"

"By increasing the staff on the fifth floor, so that in case we were forced to cut back we would have the same number of people we started with."

"I seem to be very thick, Mr. Walcott, but I'm perplexed as to how your job served the people."

"I don't understand the question."

"What contribution did you make to the taxpayer to justify your salary?"

"I believe that if you read the reports I've written over the past four years you'll see that I earned every nickel I got."

"What happened to those reports?"

"Twenty-six of them got to the seventh floor, and six, I was told, got to the eighth floor. I don't think that's a bad record."

"One more question. Given your background, why do you want to be a steward on the Eastern Airlines shuttle?"

"I've always been good with people."

The Home Appraiser

In all the fuss about homeowner taxes, no one has mentioned the official tax appraiser who decides how much your house is really worth. I myself hadn't given him any thought until the other day when I saw a nicely dressed man with a pad and pencil standing on a street corner studying a house.

"You thinking of buying?" I asked him.

"No," he said, "I'm just appraising. How much do you think that house is worth?"

"I know they paid $34,000 with a GI loan in 1947."

He wrote down $34,000.

"But it's in great shape. They put a new roof on it two years ago," I told him.

He added $10,000 to his pad.

"They make any other improvements?" he asked.

"They put in air conditioning in 1962," I said, trying to be helpful.

He wrote "A.C., $5,000."

"But they're really neat people. They take care of their lawn, and they have the most beautiful rosebushes in the back."

He scribbled "Rose Bushes, $16,000."

"When was the last time they painted the house?"

"Oh, they don't have to paint. All they do is wash down the brick every four or five years."

He wrote "No painting" and next to it "$7,500."

"What's that shack back there?" he asked.

"That's where they keep their electric lawnmower. The old man's getting on in years and can no longer mow his grass manually."

The appraiser wrote down $6,000 for "lawn improvement."

"They give many parties?" he wanted to know.

"Not many, but they have a lovely patio in the back and they bought a new awning for it last year."

Another $5,000 was added for the awning.

"You're really writing fast," I said.

"The law says any home improvement has to be added to the tax appraisal."

"I feel as if I'm ratting on those nice people," I said.

"Look at it this way. You're just making sure that they're paying their fair share of their property taxes. If they don't, then you'll be burdened with more than you should pay."

"That's true. I guess you know about the barbecue pit they built. The old man laid every brick of it himself."

The appraiser wrote down "Home-built barbecue pit, $25,000."

"Isn't that a bit much for a barbecue pit?" I asked.

"Since it's home-built it's one of a kind. These things have a lot of value. Their curb seems kind of new."

"They repaired it this spring. The winter wrecked it."

He appraised the new curb for $2,000.

"I see the house next door is up for sale."

"Yes, it's the best house in the neighborhood. Has a wet bar in the cellar, an automatic sprinkling system, a chime doorbell and a gazebo in the backyard."

"How much they asking for it?" he said.

"Two hundred and eighty thousand dollars."

"Well, why didn't you say so in the first place?" the appraiser said angrily, tearing up his notes.

"Why?"

"If that house is going for $280,000, then every house on the block is worth that."

"Oh," I said. "There goes the neighborhood."

Arrivederci, Arkansas

We almost lost Arkansas a little while ago. Some smart aleck threw a wrench into a Titan missile silo. It hit the fuel tank and set it off.

The only thing that saved the state was that the nuclear warhead, which was sitting on the top of it, didn't blow up.

The incident raised a lot of questions in the minds of the American people.

Q. Why Arkansas?

A. When the first Titan missiles were built, the experts in charge of selecting sites for them chose Arkansas because they were quite sure the Soviets didn't know where it was.

Many people in the Pentagon didn't know where it was either, and that was the reason for the delay by the Air Force in doing anything about it when the accident occurred.

Q. Now that the Soviets know where Arkansas is, will we have to move the Titan silos to another state?

A. No. They are too fragile to move, and because of the adverse publicity it's doubtful that any other state would take them.

Q. What effect will this have on the University of Arkansas football team, which is usually in the top ten at the end of each season?

A. It will be very difficult now to recruit out-of-state high school football stars, and the school may have to give up its entire athletic program.

Q. What are we to make of the accident in terms of all the fail-safe systems that were built into the Titan?

A. It depends on which side you're on. If you're on the military's side, you can claim that the system worked because the nuclear warhead didn't go off in spite of the beating the Titan took. If you live in the area you may find it hard to sell your house.

Q. What is the Soviet reaction to seeing one of our Titans come flying out of the ground without prior warning?

A. They are probably frightened silly. They always thought that we needed tremendous amounts of sophisticated electronic gear and computers to launch a Titan. But now they know we can set one off just by throwing a monkey wrench down into the hole, and they have no answer for this. If the SALT II talks ever start up again, the first order of business may be the banning of wrenches anywhere near a missile site.

Q. Do the Soviets have anything comparable to the Titan II?

A. As far as we know they don't. We do know they've been dropping wrenches on their MIRV missiles for 20 years, but they've never been able to breach their fuel tanks with them. When it comes to wrench-penetration capability, we're at least 10 years ahead of them.

Q. Then most American people can take pride in the fact that the Titan II missile is our greatest deterrent against the Soviets?

A. You could say that. But don't if you live in Arkansas.

Q. Did the accident breach any security secrets that might impair our defense posture?

A. Only one. As many people know, there is a man with a black box who follows the President everywhere he goes. The black box is at the President's disposal in case of a nuclear attack. Up until now no one but the President and his National Security Adviser knew what was in the box. Now the secret is out of the bag.

Q. What is in the black box?

A. A three-pound monkey wrench.

No Close Shave for Arafat

A reader has asked me to help him with a problem he has. The question he posed is, "I notice that PLO leader Yassar Arafat and the now Iranian Prime Minister Rajai manage to appear with a four- to six-day growth of beard, which never grows any longer. How do they manage to do it?"

In order to get the answer I called a friend of mine at the CIA who was very upset that I was on to something. He agreed to meet me in a safe house in McLean, Virginia. He told me to take a taxi to National Airport, buy a ticket to Bangor, Maine, and then at the last moment rent a car and drive to the address.

When I met him at the house there were three CIA agents in the living room who refused to give their names, including my friend.

"Why are you interested in Arafat and Rajai's shaving problems?" one of them wanted to know.

I played dumb. "Just curiosity. A reader asked me and I thought he deserved an answer."

"A likely story," one of the others sneered. "You were tipped off by someone in the agency, weren't you?"

"I don't think I have to answer that."

"We've been working on this problem for months now. There are only six people in the Company, not including the CIA barber, who know what we've been up to. Now it looks as if one of them is a mole."

"You mean he's working for both sides?"

"It's obvious he is. To get to the bottom of this we'll tell you what we know if you tell us what you know."

"It sounds good to me," I said. "There seem to be a lot of leaders in the Middle East who don't shave every day. By the same token they refuse to grow beards. They prefer a four- to six-day growth, but no more. My source believes they're all using the same razor blade."

One of the CIA men was taking notes. "He's on the right track," he said.

"Did your source tell you how they manage to get the razor back and forth?"

"Arafat seems to be the bag man. He's always traveling somewhere and my man believes he has the razor blade hidden in his turban. We've never seen a picture of Yassar without his headdress. It would be the obvious place to keep it."

The men looked at each other before one spoke.

"Suppose we told you it wasn't a razor blade, but a Soviet electric razor."

I hit my head with the palm of my hand. "An electric razor. I never thought of that. But wouldn't an electric razor give them all a clean shave?"

"You would think so," my friend said. "But we have evidence that the Soviets have been unloading bum electric razors on their clients in the Middle East. No one in Russia will buy them because they hardly will cut any kind of beard, so every time a leftist leader comes to Moscow they give him one as a gift. Arafat shaves every day with one, and so does Rajai, and a lot of the other people in that part of the world. But even on the adjustable high setting it's the best they can do."

"Why do you people want to keep this a secret?" I asked. "I should think it would be to our advantage to publicize the fact that the Soviets were unloading rejected electric razors on their friends."

"Because every morning Arafat and his cronies shave, it causes them excruciating pain, and for the moment we want to keep it that way."

Kooks Make the News

"Kooks Incorporated, Smiley speaking."

"Mr. Smiley, I saw your advertisement in the newspaper where you said you could get me on the evening news."

"That's correct. We can get you on the local news for $200 and national news for $2,000."

"Could you tell me a little about your operation?"

"Well, as you know, the stations are fighting for ratings and the kookier you are, the more chance you have of making the news. For example, if you made a statement that God doesn't hear the prayers of Jews, we could get you on all three networks."

"I'm willing to say it."

"It's too late. Someone already said it."

"Suppose I said that God *does* listen to Jewish prayers?"

"That would make you sane, and no one would want to put you on the air. You're going to have to come up with something that no other kook has thought of."

"What if I organize a paramilitary organization with some friends and we hold maneuvers in the woods, to prepare for a Russian invasion?"

"That's already been done by one of our KKK clients. We got three minutes on a national network with that story."

"Suppose I jump off the World Trade Center wearing a parachute?"

"It's too late. A guy already did it. Of course, if your parachute didn't open it would make a good film sequence."

"But then I wouldn't be around to see myself on the evening news."

"Yes, that would be the drawback. Can you drive a motorcycle?"

"No."

"Good. How would you like to take a flying leap over 12 Greyhound buses?"

"I don't think I'd like that."

"The Greyhound Bus Co. isn't too thrilled about the idea either. Our problem is that so many kooks have been getting on

television lately that you really have to be outrageous to get
them to send out a crew. Why don't you start a movement to
ban the teaching of Darwin's theory of evolution in the
schools? That would get you on the air."

"National or local?"

"Local at first, but it's the kind of story that the national
news organizations like to pick up. The thing to do is call for
the banning of all textbooks that mention Darwin and the firing
of any teacher who refers to him in the classroom."

"How big does my movement have to be?"

"You can start with your own family. When the reporter
asks you how many people support you, you can tell him
thousands. They never check on a kook's figures as long as
they get good film out of it."

"That doesn't sound too bad. I'll bet after I appeared on
television I could get a lot of people to join the anti-Darwin
movement. Maybe I could even make money on the side."

"Kooks Inc. will help you do it. We had a client who
demanded every copy of *Catcher in the Rye* be burned in his
district's libraries and we not only got him on TV, but he raised
$100,000 to censor every book that was bought by the county.
He now publishes his own blacklist and he's pushing book-
censoring kits all over the country."

"You sold me. What's my next step?"

"We'll send you a speech you can read at the next school
board meeting attacking Darwin. Then we'll tip off your TV
station that a religious fanatic is going to disrupt the proceed-
ings."

"Will the TV people show up?"

"Of course they'll show up. They have to cover the news."

You Have to Talk Business

The Internal Revenue Service is everywhere. An item in the newspaper the other day revealed that IRS agents had their field glasses focused on the VIP boxes in Philadelphia Veterans Stadium for the World Series. The boxes are, for the most part, owned by corporations who use them to entertain their customers.

The reason the IRS was watching so carefully was that in order to make the boxes a deductible business expense, "Businessmen entertaining clients must engage in the active conduct of business during the entertainment."

This has made many businessmen who take their customers to sports events very nervous.

I was at the Meadowlands watching a New York Giants football game a week after the IRS ruling was publicized, and I happened to be sitting in a box next to two men who apparently were in the dress business. I overheard their conversation.

"Now, Sam, the reason I brought you here today is I wanted you to see my new spring line."

"I'd like to watch the game, Irving, if it's all the same to you."

"You see the green jerseys the Giants are wearing? That's the green we're using in our pullover sequin disco dresses. The jerseys will be cut a little lower at the neck than what the tackles are wearing, but the sleeves will be the same length and you can roll them up like the guards have done."

"Irving, it's third down and inches to go. Will you please shut up."

"You're probably wondering what I've done with my pantsuits. Would you believe we've designed a knicker just like the center is wearing? You can wear them with bright wool socks. The women will go crazy for them. We're offering them in Redskin Maroon, Oiler Blue, Steeler Black or Cleveland Brown."

"They missed the first down! They're going to have to kick."

"You won't have any kick coming, Sam, if you take the whole line, I guarantee you'll be sorry you didn't order more.

We also have a teen-age look this year with leather belts in goal-line stripes."

"Look, Irving, the left end hurt his shoulder."

"I'm glad you mentioned that. We have a lace off-the-shoulder gown that Dior couldn't duplicate for $1,000."

"The trainer is taking off the end's shoulder pads."

"Sam, this model doesn't have shoulder pads. We put a feather where the trainer is wrapping a bandage on the end's arm. You want an organdy flower there, we'll make it with organdy."

"Irving, for heaven's sake, I want to watch the game. Will you shut up?"

"Of course, that's why I brought you here today. You see the cheerleaders with the pompons? I'll tell you a secret, Sam. Pompons are going to be very, very big this spring. We're putting them on all our jumpsuits, and we're backing them with full-page ads in all the newspapers."

"What a runback! Oh, oh, there's a clipping penalty."

"If you don't breathe a word to our competitors we're clipping two inches off our culottes. And we're adding ruffles. It's going to be a big year for ruffles. We're making them in cotton/acrylic so all a woman has to do is put them in the washer and hang them up."

"This is turning into a tightknit game."

"I'm glad you mentioned knits. Picture this, Sam. A sleeveless knit canary yellow dress with light matching jacket in cotton voile and scalloped-edged sleeves and collar. The buyers are flipping over it."

"Irving, will you stop discussing business for just a few minutes?"

"I can't, Sam. You see the guy with the binoculars over there? He's from the IRS and someone told me the s.o.b. reads lips."

Torture in Moderation

The Reagan administration has a new approach to human rights which, while it won't affect anyone in the United States, may have some important ramifications for political prisoners around the world. The philosophy of the new approach was expressed recently by Prof. Jeane Kirkpatrick of Georgetown University, who is a very influential Reagan adviser.

"If we are confronted with the choice between offering assistance to a moderately repressive autocratic government which is also friendly to the United States, and permitting it to be overrun by a Cuban-trained, Cuban-armed, Cuban-sponsored insurgency," Ms. Kirkpatrick was quoted as saying.

Nobody in her right mind would argue with that. The big question is how far a moderately repressive autocratic government can go to keep the opposition down. New human rights guidelines will have to be written for the MRAG countries.

Right now the ambassadors of Moderately Repressive Autocratic Governments are being called home for Christmas to advise their juntas on what the new American government will expect of them in the human rights field.

"Colonels, I am happy to report we can expect all the support we need from the United States to put down the political opposition, providing we can prove our repressive government is being threatened by Cuban intervention."

"Suppose we can't prove it?"

"They'll take our word for it if we can produce confessions from our political opponents."

"Does that mean we can still resort to torture to exact the confessions?"

"In moderation. Obviously, a certain amount of torture has to be used, but we can't overdo it."

"Can we still beat political prisoners with truncheons?"

"Of course that is acceptable. But attaching electric wires to a person's intimate parts can only be done under the supervision of a doctor."

"What about dunking them in water until they almost drown?"

"If it's done with compassion. But I think we better stay away from pulling out fingernails at least at the beginning of the Reagan term."

"Can we continue summary executions without trials?"

"Nobody in the Reagan transition team has spoken out against them. From all I can gather, the U.S. will no longer interfere in our justice system."

"Thank God. Does that mean we can still throw writers, editors and students into prison without having our military aid cut off?"

"I believe that the U.S. would encourage it, as long as we can prove they are a threat to the regime."

"Will the secret police be able to get the latest equipment to put down terrorism in our country?"

"That goes without saying. If the United States wants to keep us as a friend, they're going to give us the tools to keep another regime from taking over."

"They're finally making some sense in Washington. As I see it, as long as we torture our opponents in moderation, and repress our people for their own good, and only shoot the people who deserve it, we can have good relations with the United States again."

"Colonels, I don't know about the rest of you. But as head of the Moderate Repressive Junta, I recommend we give human rights a try."

A Shot in the Dark

It was midnight in Joe's Gun and Tackle Shop.

"Hi, baby, you're a cute little .38 snub-nosed, pocket-sized revolver. Where are you from?"

"Connecticut. You're not bad looking yourself, handsome. What's your name?"

"Saturday Night Special. I'm a .32 caliber Bulldog. They call me Bulldog because of my grip."

"I hear there's a big hue and cry about registering us because of John Lennon."

"Don't worry about it, baby. It'll never happen. The do-gooders always start yelling about handgun controls when someone famous gets shot. But once the noise dies down, it never happens."

"How can you be so sure?"

"We have the National Rifle Association on our side. They're the most powerful lobby in the country. They're pledged to see that no laws are passed to take guns out of the hands of people who want to buy them."

"But we're not rifles—we're handguns."

"It's all the same to the NRA. A gun's a gun—whether it's a rifle, a shotgun or a pistol. The lobby has a million members and an unlimited war chest. They get pro-gun congressmen and senators elected and defeat anyone who wants to put controls on us. When it comes to the right to bear arms, no one is safe from the wrath of gun-lovers."

"I'm still scared. I'd hate to be confiscated or thrown into the ocean."

"Relax, kid. The bleeding hearts don't have the stamina to hurt us. Besides, the Constitution is on our side. Nobody in his right mind is going to tell the American people they can't own a handgun."

"You sound so reassuring. But I heard from a .44 Magnum that more and more states are passing tough handgun laws."

"So one state passes a tough handgun law and the next state doesn't have any laws at all. They can't stop somebody from buying us."

"What about the federal gun laws?"

"The Federal Handgun Law is dead. Republican Senator McClure of Idaho has a bill in Congress right now that would rescind the law and take the government out of the gun control business, which it should never have been in, in the first place. Even Reagan is against gun control."

"You seem to know a lot about it."

"When you're a Saturday Night Special, you have to. If they really wanted to get tough on handguns, we'd be the first to go. There are a lot of creeps in this country who would deep-six us if they had half a chance. But the gun people know that if they start with us, they'll only be encouraged, and no handgun would be safe in America."

"How much do you sell for?"

"Well, I wasn't made in this country, so I can be had for $50."

"How much do you think they'll ask for me?"

"A pretty little thing like you? I'll bet with that blue steel body and smooth walnut stock, somebody would pay over $200 to have you under his pillow."

"You're really a smooth talker. Have you ever shot anybody?"

"Not yet, but I'm primed and ready."

"Do you think I can shoot somebody soon?"

"You've got as good a chance as the next handgun."

"I hope somebody doesn't just buy me and stick me in a drawer."

"If he does, the kids in the house will probably find you and shoot you off for kicks. It happens all the time."

"I don't want to kill anybody."

"You won't. Don't forget what the NRA says. Guns don't kill people—people kill people."

"That makes me feel better."

"I wouldn't be surprised if you're out of this glass case and on the streets by Christmas."

"You make a handgun feel real good. It's been nice talking to you."

"Don't mention it, baby. Maybe we'll be meeting in a dark alley one of these nights."

The Good Old Days

Those of us who have been yearning for the good old days of the late Forties and early Fifties got a shot in the arm the other day when it was announced by Senator Strom Thurmond, the new chairman of the Senate Judiciary Committee, that he was reviving the Subcommittee on Internal Security.

The committee, which had seen its best days under Senator James Eastland of Mississippi, was abolished four years ago because the country seemed to have run out of Communists.

But, as a member of the ultra-right, I never believed it. And when I heard that Thurmond assigned Senator Jeremiah Denton of Alabama, one of the Moral Majority's favorite sons, to head up the committee, I knew the country was back in safe hands.

I wanted to see the expression on the faces of some of my liberal friends when they heard the news, so I went to a meeting of the Georgetown Tri-Lateral Club to chortle.

"Well," I said, "you left-wingers have had it. The Internal Security Subcommittee is back in business, and they're going to be watching every move you make."

"We have nothing to worry about," said Mortimer. "We're not Communists."

"Boy," I said, "do *you* have a short memory. You don't have to be a Communist to be investigated by the Internal Security Subcommittee. You just have to *think* like one or attend a meeting with people who *might* be fellow travelers."

"That's old hat," Mortimer said, "The reason the Senate Internal Security Subcommittee went out of business was because they couldn't find any Communists. Every time they thought they had a biggie, he turned out to be an informer for the FBI. The only way the Communist Party survived as long as it did in this country was that J. Edgar Hoover paid all the membership dues."

"That's a lie and you know it," I said angrily. "There were millions of pinkos in this country when Hoover and Joe McCarthy were alive. Hollywood was loaded with them. How do you think we lost China? Well, I want to tell you something. The liberals had us believing that the red menace had abated. But there were many of us who thought differently, and we also knew that if Strom Thurmond ever got the Judiciary Chairmanship, commie-hunting would come back."

"What are they going to do? Most of the people on the old committee's list of subversive organizations are either dead or on Social Security."

"We'll make a new list," I retorted. "We can start with the Moral Majority's hit list and go from there. If you don't think the pro-abortion, pro-ERA, anti-school prayer groups are being financed by the Kremlin, then you're a bigger dupe than I thought you were. I have a good mind to turn in your name."

"For what?"

"We know all about you, Mortimer. You're pro-consumer, anti-nuke, for gun control, and a closet environmentalist."

"That doesn't make me a Communist."

"Where there's smoke, there's fire."

"What the hell does that mean?" Mortimer yelled.

"All we want you to do is tell us who is behind the Save the California Redwoods campaign?"

"You're crazy," Mortimer said. "This country went through its witch-hunting period once. The people are not going to buy it again."

"Don't you believe it. Americans will buy a red menace any time you offer them one. It makes life a lot simpler for everybody. Mortimer, if you just give me the names of the people on the Tri-Lateral Commission, I'll see that the Sub-committee goes easy on you."

Dear Diary

"Mr. McCall, Mrs. Wesley Heights, the wife of Congressman Heights, is here to talk to you about publishing her book."

"Send her in. Ah, Mrs. Heights, this is indeed a pleasure. I'm terribly sorry about your husband being found guilty in the ABSCAM trial. I definitely believe his constitutional rights were violated."

"You know he was a lush, don't you?"

"It seems to me I did read something about that in the papers."

"They didn't really go into the sordid details. It's all here in the book. He was smashed from morning till night. I used to have to pour a pot of coffee over his head to sober him up enough to attend his Congressional Prayer breakfasts."

"I'm sure you don't want to talk about it, Mrs. Heights."

"Are you kidding? It's all here in Chapter One. He was a mess."

"It must have been very tough on you."

"It wasn't as tough as him playing around—that's in Chapter Two. I swear you wouldn't believe the type of women he would drag home with him at night. They were old enough to be his mother."

"How did you put up with it?"

"That's in Chapter Three. I was determined to be a good congressional wife and pretend that nothing was wrong. It was a role the people in Wesley's district expected me to play. So I just closed my eyes when Wesley came into the house with a paramour and closed them again when she left."

"This is all in the book?"

"You bet your life. There was this one night when I woke up and . . ."

"That's all right, Mrs. Heights, I'll read the manuscript. Does your book tell anything about how Washington works socially?"

"Of course. That's in Chapter Four. I went to this fund-raising party and someone offered me coke—and I said I didn't do coke, and he said everyone in Washington did coke and I wasn't a team player. So I got mad, and we went for a drive along the Potomac and when we got back in the morning, the party was still going and everyone was stoned."

"You paint a different picture of Washington than, let's say Arthur Schlesinger, Jr., does."

"He's never been a congressman's wife. Now, in Chapter Five, I talk to other politicians' wives and they tell me what they've been through. This chapter tells how they have to beat off every woman in a skirt who thinks the hunting season on congressmen is twelve months long. The wives really have been through the mill and, boy, do they have stories to tell! It makes my life sound like *The Waltons*."

"You've done a lot of work in a short time."

"I kept a diary and I'm a fast writer. Besides, my husband helped me fill in the gaps that he could remember."

"Then your husband knows about the book."

"Of course. He has no objection to me writing it. He voted against ERA but he thinks a woman should do anything she wants to as long as it makes her happy. He made a big contribution to Chapter Six, when I tell how he took money from the phony Arab sheiks."

"He didn't mind you writing that?"

"Au contraire, he gave me lots of good stories that aren't on the tapes about how he stuffed the 100-dollar bills into his socks and stole the sheik's gold cigarette lighter when he wasn't looking."

"I must say, Mrs. Heights, this is not your ordinary Washington memoir. But it may have some interest for the reading public, particularly since it's told from a woman's point of view. I'm sure we can make a very generous offer. But I'm curious about one thing. Why did you write this book in the first place?"

"I was bored just being a congressman's wife—and it was either this or getting a job selling real estate."

Mail Call

You really have to know your stuff to work in the mailroom at the Pentagon these days.

"Sarge, where do these boxes of anti-aircraft missiles go?"

"Let's see. I think they're supposed to be sent to Jordan. No, wait a minute . . . the anti-aircraft missiles go to Saudi Arabia —the anti-tank missiles go to Jordan. Actually, it doesn't make any difference, because they're probably all being shipped to Iraq anyway."

"Why don't we send them directly to Iraq and save the postage?"

"Because we're not supposed to send anything to Iraq while they're at war with Iran."

"There's a box of aviation spare parts over here for Iran. Should we ship them off to Tehran?"

"No. Don't send anything to Iran until they release the hostages. Then we'll mail all the boxes over there so they can fight their war against Iraq."

"How come we're shipping stuff to both Iraq and Iran to fight each other?"

"We're not shipping anything to Iraq or Iran. We're shipping it to Jordan and Saudi Arabia, and they're shipping it to Iraq. When we get our hostages back from Iran, we have to give the Iranians the stuff they ordered before they took them."

"What about these large crates of 155-millimeter guns?"

"They go to Israel to defend themselves against Jordan —though don't be surprised if they wind up in Iran. The skinny is that Israel is helping Iran because Saudi Arabia is helping Iraq."

"I gotcha. Sarge, are you sure these laser-guided bazookas go to Egypt?"

"If it says so on the box, that's where they go. They're supposed to shoot down Libyan airplanes."

"I don't see anything here for Libya."

"They're off our list because they're buying all their stuff from France and the Soviet Union. Also, don't send anything to Syria. They just made a friendship treaty with the Russians."

"Is it okay to ship these flamethrowers to Oman?"

"Let me check. Yeah, Oman is okay. But don't send them to Yemen by mistake."

"I'm not a dummy, Sarge."

"Give me a hand with these F-4 fighter planes. We have to airmail them to Amman."

"What's the big rush?"

"Hussein wants them in case he's attacked by Damascus."

"What's he giving all his stuff to Iraq for if he's afraid of being invaded by the Syrians?"

"Because he's being supported by Saudi Arabia and they hate the Iranians."

"It makes sense when you explain it."

"Okay, now these crates of F-5s go to Pakistan at the same time we mail this plutonium to India."

"Slow down. I've only got two hands, Sarge."

"I know, but we don't want Pakistan to get nervous about their defenses and attack Kashmir."

"We could use another guy in this mailroom—my back is killing me. Where do these radar-guided bombs go?"

"Send them to Kuwait or they'll be sitting around here for days."

"We're almost cleaned up, Sarge. All we have left are these torpedo boats."

"Are they tagged?"

"Yeah. They say, 'Ship to U.S. Navy, care of the Straits of Hormuz.' "

"There must be some mistake. We wouldn't be sending any equipment to our own navy. Hold off that one until I check with the brass upstairs."

Where Have All the Consumers Gone?

It appears that the fortunes, hopes and dreams of everyone in this country this Christmas are based on only one person—"the Consumer." For better or for worse, he or she controls the destiny of multibillion-dollar corporations, whose fourth-quarter earnings will depend on what the consumer does between now and December 24th. If the consumer decides to sit this Christmas out, the country will continue to be in a recession, unemployment will increase, managerial heads will roll, and Ronald Reagan will walk in as President with one helluva mess on his hands.

Millions of dollars are being spent every day to get the consumer off his butt and into the stores. But so far it doesn't seem to be working.

I went to visit a consumer the other day. "Why aren't you jamming the stores and helping them ring up record sales so the economists can announce that the recession is over?"

"I can't afford it," Harvey said. "The prices are out of sight."

"But, Harvey," I protested. "Everyone is counting on you to get them healthy again. The stores are staying open until 10 every night, just for you—they're not even closing on Sundays. You can make or break everyone's Christmas."

"I'd rather watch this football game."

"Do you know why you can watch a football game, Harvey? Because it's brought to you by the people who make blue jeans and electric shavers, light beer, and popcorn machines. The only reason they're bringing it to you is because they feel you'll show your gratitude by going out and buying their products. If you just sit here, they won't be able to sponsor any more sports events. There is no such thing as a free lunch."

"You can say that again. Do you know what these potato chips cost? I'm lucky I don't eat M & M's during a game."

"You mustn't think of yourself during Christmas, Harvey. You have to think of the economy. The stores are depending on you for 50 percent of their annual sales in the next two weeks. If you don't go into debt this year, everyone's going to think you're a rotten person."

The phone rang. Harvey picked it up. "Yeah," he said, "I

know you've been waiting for me out in the parking lot since nine, but I'm busy now. I'm watching a football game. No, I have nothing against you personally. It's just that I'm not sure I'm going to buy too much this year . . . What with inflation and everything, we thought we'd cool it. No, it won't help to keep the store open all night long . . . Yeah, thanks for calling and the same to you."

Harvey handed me back the phone. "It was J.C. Penney. He wanted to know why I hadn't responded to the ad he ran in the newspaper yesterday for an auto racing set. He said if I couldn't come in he'd take my order over the phone."

"Call him back, Harvey," I said. "Tell him you'll borrow the money if you have to. But don't spoil the man's Christmas."

"He's not the only one who has called me. I've heard from Sears of Sears Roebuck, Mart of K-Mart, Shack of Radio Shack, and Mrs. Tiffany. Everyone thinks I'm loaded."

"Harvey, you live in the greatest country in the world. But it won't remain that way if you sit at home during the Christmas Shopping Days watching football. That doesn't put bread on anyone's table. The only way you can repay America for all its blessings is to blow your savings on gifts for everyone you know."

The phone rang again. Harvey didn't want to pick it up, so I did. I was surprised to hear the voice on the other end.

"Harvey," I said, "it's Lee Iacocca of the Chrysler Corporation. It sounds like he's been crying."

Harvey grabbed the phone. "Yeah, Lee, what do you want now? . . . I told you if I decided to buy a car for my kid, I'd consider a new K-Model . . . But I'm flat busted . . . The interest rates on my house are killing me . . . No, I don't want to speak to Frank Sinatra . . . Okay, I'll speak to Sinatra . . . Yeah, Frank, I've seen your commercials for Chrysler. They're great . . . You're doing a fine job . . . No, Frank, don't come over now. I'm tied up . . . Look, give me your phone number and if I change my mind I'll call you . . . Nice talking to you again."

Harvey hung up and sighed, "It's not easy being a consumer these days. If it wasn't for these TV football games I don't know how I'd make it through the holidays."

Everyone Is Helpful

According to the reports I hear, the Carter appointees and the new Reagan people are working smoothly to make the transition. You don't find the bitterness which has been present during the changeovers of other administrations. In many cases, the Carter people even seem *happy* to turn over the reins of government to the Reaganites.

I dropped in on one of the departments where a Carter appointee was briefing a Reagan lieutenant on what to expect.

The Carter person said, "Now, in this blue metal file cabinet are all the plans for improving mass transportation in the country."

"Good, I'll go through them this afternoon."

"They cover everything from buses, to subways, to railroads, to movable sidewalks. If it transports people—we've made a study of it."

"Excellent. What are in those six green cabinets over there?"

"The reasons why we can't build them. Let me show you how the system works. Let's say you were planning to build a 165-mile-an-hour train for the northeast corridor of the United States. You would look up 'Super train' in the blue cabinet. We have photos of Japanese trains, French trains, German trains and Swiss trains, as well as plans for each of these systems."

"They all look beautiful," the Reagan man said.

"Now we go over to this green file cabinet and look up 'Super train.' This photo shows you what would happen if you tried to go 165 miles an hour on an American track bed."

The Reagan man said, "It looks like the train has crashed into a garbage dump somewhere in Philadelphia."

"It's actually Baltimore. Our engineers have figured out that at 165 miles an hour, the Super train would fly off the tracks in Philadelphia and land just about here in Maryland, unless it smashed into a freight train in Washington first."

"How would I find the answer to that problem?"

"You go to this green file cabinet here and look up 'Cost of laying new tracks for Super train.'"

"Twelve billion dollars?!" the Reagan man said.

"That doesn't include switching equipment and computers. When you have a train going that fast, you have to keep the tracks clear at all times, because it can't stop if it sees something ahead. In order to make sure that it is safe, you would have to build electric gates at all the railroad crossings, which we figure will cost another six billion."

"I guess we better forget about the Super train. What other ideas are in the files?"

"We have an excellent plan for busing."

"Governor Reagan is against busing."

"This would not be used for busing schoolchildren; it would be to bus people to work. Here is a prototype of a new air-conditioned vehicle which would seat 80 people and have room for 60 standees."

"That makes a lot of sense. What's wrong with it?"

"To make it pay for itself, it would cost $4 per person for a two-mile ride. The cities won't buy them unless we give them one billion dollars in supplemental payments."

"That's ridiculous. What about monorails? Governor Reagan was very impressed with the monorail he saw at Disneyland."

"I think the monorail folder is over here. Yes, here it is. A monorail, at present construction estimates, would cost four million dollars a foot—without stairways for the stations."

"Do you people have any mass transportation ideas the new President could implement?"

The Carter man went through the files.

"Here's one our Research and Development people have been working on. It's a dog sled that can pull six people at one time and only costs $900."

"Now you're talking. What's wrong with it?"

"You need artificial snow machines every block along the route or the dogs will refuse to pull the sleds."

"You Carter people aren't leaving us much to work with."

"That isn't true. We've ordered fourteen new green file cabinets for the office, and here's the number of the General Services Administration in case you need any more."

Now for a Test

I hate to be critical of the medical profession, but have you noticed that doctors are ordering up more tests all the time? Gone are the days when MDs used stethoscopes and wore reflecting mirrors over their eyes. Now they sit behind their desks and, no matter what your complaint is, they say, "We better do a test on that." So you give the nurse your blood, and they tell you to call back in a few days, and they'll let you know if "you have it" or "you don't."

Now, there is absolutely nothing wrong with this, because medical science has become so sophisticated that they can now look at a cell in a lab and tell more about you than if they make you breathe in and out all day long.

The only problem is that while we are putting ourselves in the hands of trained people who have devoted their lives to medicine, they are now basing their diagnoses on the results of laboratory tests done, in many cases, by people barely out of high school.

I don't know if Washington is typical of the rest of the country, but I hear more and more stories about labs messing up on medical tests. The following ones are all true, and took place during the last six months.

A lady friend of mine had a blood count done while she was in a hospital in the nation's capital. The results were so perplexing that her internist called a hematologist and checked it out with him. The hematologist said, "You have nothing to worry about. If that blood count is correct, your patient is dead."

A neighbor returned from the Middle East and wound up with an exotic bug that mystified the doctors at another Washington hospital. They were going to call in a tropical disease man when the neighbor's blood report revealed he had hepatitis. Everyone breathed a sigh of relief that they finally had a diagnosis, until it was discovered the patient's blood sample had inadvertently been switched with another man's. The other man's doctor was so confused by my neighbor's blood sample that he ordered it sent to the Center for Disease Control in Atlanta.

I am not making these up. A friend was being tested for a neurological problem. He was told that the test results would take about three weeks. He waited patiently (actually, he sweated it out, and was a nervous wreck). When he didn't hear from the doctor, he expected the worst. He called. The doctor was surprised he hadn't heard from the lab. The doctor called. The lab people checked around. Somehow they had lost the sample and couldn't locate it. The test would have to be done over again.

I do have a lot more stories that I've collected—but so does everyone else. The system is breaking down. How can an MD diagnose an illness and prescribe the treatment when he has no assurance that the tests he's asked for are accurate? No one knows anymore who is down in the basement mixing up test tubes and putting the wrong labels on microscopic slides.

The obvious solution would be to up the standards required of lab technicians and pay them a lot more money. Nobody would agree to this, so the second-best answer is for the doctors to work in the labs and the lab technicians to work in the doctors' offices.

Since all of the important work in diagnosing an illness is now done in the laboratories—that is where the MDs should be. Anyone can man a desk in a doctor's office and listen to someone's complaint. It doesn't take much to ask someone to say, "Cough when I say cough," or "When I do this, tell me if it hurts."

Nobody needs in-depth training to say, "Take off your clothes and stand on the scale over there." But it does take a lot of education and experience to look into a microscope and know whether a person "has it" or "doesn't have it."

My dream is to some day walk into a lab of one of our hospitals in Washington and see MDs hunched over microscopes solving the mysteries of their patients' illnesses, while up in their offices are seated fresh young lab technicians saying to the nurse, "I don't like the sound of that elbow. I think we had better order some tests."

The Washington Media Mafia

Memo to Reagan Appointees
Subject: The Washington Media Mafia

During the course of your stay in Washington, you will have dealings with the Washington media. Although you may run a multimillion-dollar corporation or a billion-dollar law firm, do not be under the misapprehension that you can handle a reporter making $250 a week.

The Washington Press Corps is a type of Mafia. The head of the families are publishers, network bureau chiefs, star political reporters and syndicated columnists. They usually can be snowed if you pretend to take them into your confidence and throw them a piece of red meat every once in a while. They are duck soup to manipulate and since they are part of the establishment, you can always make them an offer they can't refuse.

What you have to worry about are the foot soldiers in the families who wear turtle-neck sweaters, socks that don't match and thick rubber soles on their shoes. Every one of them has a contract out on you.

These soldiers, both male and female, are the ones who stand out shivering in the cold for hours and wait for one morsel of information while you are inside having lunch with a noted pundit on his expense account.

They have nothing to lose and everything to gain by putting your ham hocks in the frying pan.

Underpaid and overworked, the soldiers of the media mafia all have fantasies of becoming another Woodward, Bernstein, or Barbara Walters. They know the only way they can do it is over your dead body. Since they are never invited to swank parties or intimate breakfasts, they have all the time in the world to find out what you're really up to. You would do well not to underestimate them just because they eat their lunch at McDonalds and take notes with a 49-cent Bic pen.

Surly and unresponsive to flattery, the soldiers are not impressed with titles or bloodlines or your old school tie. Most

of them have never worn a tie in their lives. They live in a
jungle and are constantly scrounging for food for their stories.
They have the killer instinct and would just as soon dine on
your carcass as the next public official's.

The most dangerous of all the soldiers are the females
assigned to cover social functions. Most of them appear to be
younger than your daughter, and are selected for their innocent
looks and helpless demeanor.

Although they always appear flustered and about to cry, they
have mastered the art of taking notes with one hand while
putting on lipstick with the other. Women assigned to cover the
social scene are trained to hover near their quarry and overhear
conversations not meant for their ears. Many of them have
taken lip-reading courses and can pick up your remarks at 30
feet.

The big news in Washington is usually made at parties, and
while most readers of papers are skeptical of what appears on
the front pages, no one questions the facts about what actually
took place at a party, when reported in a gossip column.

The electronic mafia is something else again. You have to
keep in mind that every TV reporter sent out on a story has
only one goal in mind, and that is to get on the air that night. In
order to do that, they have to provoke you into saying
something newsworthy, and if you don't say anything of
importance, they'll be satisfied with 30 seconds of you
bumping your head on your car.

The main difference between the printed press mafia and the
electronic soldiers is that when a story appears in a newspaper
about something you said, you can always deny it. But if you
deny something attributed to you on television, they will show
you denying it and then replay the tape of you saying it.

Now that you understand how the Washington media mafia
works, it is up to you to decide how to handle it. But don't
make the mistake of threatening the soldiers, after they have
written something you don't like, by saying *you* know Bill
Paley, or Katharine Graham, or Arthur Sulzberger or Otis
Chandler—because in almost all cases, *they* don't.

Part VII

Four Years in the Think Tank

What makes the United States system of government different from others is that when you're thrown out of high political office you are not sent to a labor camp or put under house arrest. In this country, you are condemned to a tax-free think tank until your party comes back to power.

When the Republicans went into exile, they were sentenced to the Hoover Institution at Stanford, the Georgetown Center for Strategic Studies and the American Enterprise Institute. Now it's the Democrats' turn to do time in Academia.

The other day two Republican transition men in trenchcoats showed up at Carter appointee Doolittle's office to take him away. Doolittle, who had been making $50,000 a year, was reluctant to go.

"You can leave with us quietly," one of the trenchcoats said, "or we can drag you out by your feet."

"Where are you taking me?" Doolittle asked.

"To the Brookings Institution on Mass. Avenue."

"But that's a maximum-security think tank!" Doolittle cried.

"If you keep your nose clean and stay out of trouble, in time you might work a transfer to the Aspen Institute or the John F. Kennedy School of Government in Cambridge."

"Do they give you a parking place at Brookings?" Doolittle asked.

"How do we know?" said the other trenchcoat. "We're Republicans—we've never been inside the walls."

Doolittle packed a toothbrush and an autographed picture of
Carter in his briefcase. No one in the outer office dared talk to
him. He was placed in a car between the two men and driven to
Brookings, a forbidding building with an armed guard at the
gate.

"Here's another one for you," one of the trenchcoats said as
they dumped Doolittle out of the car.

The guard took him into the warden's office. The warden
said, "I've been reading your record, Doolittle. You're a tough
nut. You predicted a seven percent inflation rate for 1978, four
percent unemployment in 1979, and said the Gross National
Product would double in 1980. That makes you a three-time
loser. If you don't walk the line here, we'll send you to the
Lyndon B. Johnson School in Austin, Texas."

"Not Austin," Doolittle pleaded. "I couldn't do four years in
Austin."

"Keep that in mind if you get any smart ideas of breaking
out of this think tank," the warden said. "Guard, take this man
to his cell."

The guard took Doolittle down a long, dark hallway and
finally unlocked a cubbyhole. All that was in there was a desk,
a chair and a small couch filled with straw. On the wall was a
blackboard with a piece of chalk.

"Is this it?" Doolittle said.

"This is your home, buster. Now start thinking."

"What about?"

"We don't care. You're expected to turn in a progress report
once a week on what you're working on, but no one pays
attention to it. Lunch is at noon. You're entitled to two visitors
a week and you can write one 'Letter to the Editor' a month to
the *New Republic*. Lights out by five o'clock."

The guard slammed the door shut and locked it. Doolittle
walked over to the desk and sat down. He started writing on a
yellow legal pad, "Human Rights and Its Effect on Killer Bees
in Brazil."

The Crystal Ball

Gleam, the neighborhood soothsayer, was sitting in front of his crystal ball when I was ushered into his dark room.

"What do you see?" I asked him.

"Fifty dollars," he said.

"You see $50 in the ball?"

"No, that is what it will cost you before I tell you what 1981 holds in store for us."

"But last year you only charged me $25."

"That was before I saw a double-digit inflation figure in my ball."

I handed him $50 and waited.

"I see Dunkirk," he said.

"Dunkirk! That was in World War II!"

"I see an economic Dunkirk. I see economists fighting to get into lifeboats and retreat from their forecasts of 1980."

"Do you see a tax cut?"

"I see a tax cut."

"That's good."

"I also see a rise in Social Security, real estate assessments and gasoline prices. Now I don't see the tax cut anymore."

"What do you see now?"

"I see Lee Iacocca."

"What is he doing?"

"A TV commercial for American Express cards."

"That's bad."

"I see Richard Nixon dancing at the White House."

"Who is he dancing with?"

"Mrs. Spiro Agnew."

"I was afraid of that. What else do you see?"

"I see President Reagan."

"Who is he dancing with?"

"He isn't dancing. He's on a horse, taking a ride through the Rose Garden."

"Where is the First Lady?"

"She's upstairs, sewing drapes for the bedroom."

"That isn't worth $50."

"Wait, there is a lot more. I see a network sit-com which takes place in a bordello, but it will be done with taste and good humor."

"You don't need a crystal ball for that one."

"Now I see the bordello show being canceled and replaced by a divorced father trying to raise a son in a nudist colony."

"It sounds like it's going to be a very dull year."

"I am now in a supermarket. A lady is trading in her diamond wedding ring for a piece of roast beef. A man is exchanging his new car for a pound of butter. The manager is refusing to take a woman's sofa for a box of Jell-O."

"Good Heavens, Gleam, don't you see anything upbeat in the ball?"

"I see a banker announcing that he is reducing the prime rate to six percent."

"That's good. What else?"

"I see two men in white coats putting him into an ambulance and taking him away."

"Is that it?"

"That's it for $50. If you want to give me another $50, I'll tell you what your new nine-digit postal ZIP code number will be."

Transition Time

Nobody knows how many there are. There could be hundreds—even thousands. They are members of Reagan's transition team, and they are sweeping through government buildings, trying to find ways to cut out waste and sloth in the bureaucracy. It isn't an easy job, but it has to be done.

As soon as word is passed that a transition team is on the premises, every bureaucrat rushes to his or her desk and gets to work. Bureaucrats have been through it all before, and the transition people are, in most cases, babes in the woods.

This is how it goes:

A transition team member stops by a desk.

"What are you doing?" he asks the bureaucrat.

"I'm working on these authorization papers for my supervisor."

"Where is your supervisor?"

"He took holiday leave and I believe he is in New Hampshire skiing with his family."

"May I see these authorization papers?"

"Of course, sir. As you will note, in the first 40 pages, the authority concurs with the regulations as laid down by the Secretary. The next 32 pages deal with the impact study, and this bound report, which is attached, was done by an outside consulting firm.

"We still have one more study to come in, which was done by another consulting team, checking out the findings of the first consulting firm. By the way, I voted for Reagan."

"What exactly are you authorizing?"

"Funds for deregulation of the clam-digging business."

"Why do you need money to deregulate an industry?"

"If you read the report, you'll see that it takes as much money to deregulate an industry as it does to regulate one. My father and mother are both Republicans."

"We're looking for ways to cut out waste and sloth in government. Do you have any ideas?"

"Can I speak frankly, sir? I've been working on this problem secretly for seven years, but no one will listen to me. That's why my wife also voted for Reagan. First, we have to set up an ad-hoc committee on waste and sloth, which would create a department independent of the inspector general's office. This department would be staffed and housed in its own building so that it would not be contaminated by the people who are throwing the taxpayers' money down the drain. I have the plans here for the new building if you would like to see them."

"It's a very large building."

"When you're looking for waste and sloth in the government, you can't operate on a shoestring. Once we get the department in shape, I suggest we turn it into an independent agency which would report directly to you."

"But I'm only on the transition team. I don't believe I'll be around after January 20th."

"That's a pity. It was your idea, and you can't see it consummated. Can I have your name, sir? I'd like to tell the President-elect you're the most valuable transition team person I've talked to."

"It's Elrod. Melvin Elrod, of Tulsa, Oklahoma."

"It's an honor to meet you, Mr. Elrod. My name is Duval, Harvey Duval. My supervisor's name—the one who is skiing in New Hampshire—is Garfield Flieger."

"What kind of supervisor is he?"

"A very fine person. You can go into his office. It's the one that has a personally autographed photo of President Carter on the wall."

Remember El Salvador!

"What are you doing, Paw?"

"I'm getting out my old Marine Corps boots."

"What for, Paw?"

"The United States may have to go fight El Salvador."

"El Salvador. What's that?"

"It's a country in Central America, and the Soviets and Cubans have been supplying their guerrillas with arms so they can overthrow the military junta."

"You mean to say, Paw, the United States is seriously thinking of getting us into a war over El Salvador?"

"It ain't El Salvador, Maw. The Reagan administration has been looking for a place to show the Soviets that we mean business. El Salvador just happened to be in the right place at the right time."

"That's what they said about Vietnam, Paw."

"This is different, Maw. This is in our hemisphere. We can't let the commies just ship in arms and equipment to guerrillas who don't like their government."

"What's the guerrillas' beef in El Salvador got to do with the junta?"

"No one is quite sure, Maw. I think it has something to do with them wanting land reform. It seems the powerful families in El Salvador are against it and the military is killing the peasants, and the government is trying to find a solution in between."

"And we're going to go to war to solve that one?"

"We ain't going to go to war yet, but I'm getting out my boots just in case, because Secretary of State Haig is taking a hard line against anyone who accepts arms from the commies."

"I ain't against stopping the commies, Paw, but I wish it was something more important than El Salvador."

"Haig's got no choice. They found Captured Enemy Documents on the bodies of the guerrillas."

"I ain't heard anyone use 'Captured Enemy Documents' since Vietnam. You got any idea how Haig hopes to stop the commies from giving the guerrillas arms?"

"Wal, I don't want it bandied about, but I saw on television that Haig was thinking about blockading Cuba if they kept it up."

"That's big stuff, Paw. We could get us in a war with Russia at the same time."

"You got to call their bluff sooner or later. That's why I'm getting my boots ready. If it really gets big, we ain't got enough boys in the service to handle it. They're going to need us old-timers to pitch in and fight."

"But you were in World War II. Won't they ask the younger boys to go first?"

"Ain't going to get no young kids to go into the service to fight for El Salvador. It's only old-timers like myself who understand if you don't stop them in El Salvador, you'll be fighting them on the beaches of Santa Monica."

"I thought Reagan said he wasn't going to get us into no wars."

"This ain't a real war. It's just a test of our credibility, Maw. Nobody's going to ever believe us if we don't have a showdown soon."

"The whole thing smells more and more like Vietnam, Paw."

"That's not for you to say, Maw. El Salvador has a lot going for it when it comes to seeing who blinks first. It's small, has plenty of jungles, and if we win the hearts and minds of the people there we can scare the hell out of Nicaragua."

"Nicaragua! What have they got to do with this?"

"That's how the guerrillas are getting their arms. Believe me, Maw, if this thing keeps up, we're going to be up to our necks in old muddy."

"When do you think they'll call you, Paw?"

"As soon as all the young kids in this country realize what's going on and take off for Canada."

Appropriations Is Hell

There is no doubt in anyone's mind that the military is going to get everything it asks for in the new Reagan Budget. But it's easier to give money to the Pentagon than it is to spend it. All the services want their mitts on the new funds, and once it's been okayed, we may see internecine battles between the armed forces, the likes of which this country has never witnessed before.

As soon as Congress appropriates the money, it will be delivered in a Brink's Truck to the doorstep of the Pentagon, where high-ranking officers of the four branches of services will be waiting for it.

An admiral will say to the Brink's employees, "Okay, men, bring the money up to the safe in the Navy Procurement office."

"The hell you say," an Air Force general will shout. "That money is going for our MX missile program. The Air Force needs every penny of it, and more."

An Army four-star general will chip in, "Keep your hands off those bags. They've been set aside to build up our conventional forces."

"In a pig's ear," the admiral says. "Every cent has been allotted for new nuclear carriers and anti-submarine ships."

"What about me?" a Marine Corps general says.

"Oh, shut up," the Army general says.

The Brink's driver is annoyed. "Will you guys make up your minds? We have to go to lunch."

"I talked to the Senate Armed Services Committee and they said we could build a new bomber with this money," the Air Force general says, trying to grab one of the bags.

The Army general pushes him. "Keep your hands off that bag. That's going for our M-60 tank."

"President Reagan says he wants a Rapid Deployment Force," the Marine Corps general says, "and the Marines are the only ones who can do the job."

"You stay out of this," the admiral warns. "We'll give you what's left over once we build our missile cruiser ships."

The Air Force general says to the Army general, "Don't ever push me again or we'll bomb Fort Bragg back to the stone age."

"Oh, yeah?" the Army general says. "How would you like to see SAC headquarters filled with nerve gas?"

While the two are arguing, the admiral is heaving bags of money behind a bush. The Air Force general and Army general start beating up on him. The admiral shouts to the Marine general for help and the Marine says, "Not until you promise me enough funds for 1,000 helicopters."

The Brink's guards separate the officers. The admiral, dusting himself off, says, "That does it. We attack Langley Air Force Base tomorrow morning."

"Listen," a Brink's guard says, "if you guys don't want the money, I know a lot of people in the government who do."

By this time, someone has notified Secretary of Defense Casper Weinberger, who rushes down.

"What's going on?" he says angrily.

"Did you promise the Air Force this money for an MX system and a new bomber?"

"Yes, I did," Weinberger says.

"And did you give me your solemn word it would go for new aircraft carriers and submarines?" the admiral asks.

"Of course."

"And didn't you swear," the Army general says, "that we would get the bulk of the new appropriations to modernize our equipment?"

"I recall saying that."

"So which service gets the money?"

"None of you," Weinberger replies. "I just got a call from Al Haig and he says the eight billion dollars has to go for military equipment we're giving to El Salvador."

Setback for Earth

The Grumman Co., which built vehicles for the moon and is one of the leaders in space technology, has been having trouble building a bus that won't collapse when it is trying to get from 23rd Street to 57th Street on Madison Avenue in New York City.

This has caused tremendous consternation in engineering circles. How can someone develop a lunar lander for the moon without any difficulty, and not be able to build a bus for New York and other cities?

I discussed this with an urban transportation expert, and he said the Grumman people were not at fault.

"Building a bus for New York City is not the same as developing a moon vehicle. There were so many unknown factors that Grumman had to deal with. New York streets have a far harsher atmosphere than the moon. For one thing, New York's craters are much larger than anything they have up there. For another, the environment in Manhattan is so unpredictable that no one can be sure what pressures a bus will encounter when it tries to crawl across town."

"But surely the Grumman people must have tested its Flxible Bus before they delivered it."

"Of course they did, but all they had to go on were aerial maps of Manhattan taken from five miles up.

"They had no idea what they would face once the Flxible model was actually put on a street. Everything worked perfectly in the lab, and Grumman scientists were certain their bus could hold up under the toughest jobs it would have to perform on earth. But unfortunately when you're dealing with an unknown crust such as New York City, you have to expect setbacks.

"We now think we know what the problem is."

"What's that?"

"Grumman didn't realize that the buses would carry people. So they failed to make the trunnion strong enough to support the frame. After four blocks the frame developed cracks, the trunnion collapsed against the wheel, and the bus couldn't move. Urban Mass Transportation is still not an exact science, and it could have happened to anybody."

"Does this mean New Yorkers will never be able to have buses they can count on?"

"Not necessarily. But a lot more work has to be done in bus research. First of all we must devise a way of mapping New York City's potholes. No bus can be expected to hit one and not collapse, no matter how strong you build the trunnion. For another we have to test these buses under the worst-situation conditions. This means that we have to load them with twice their capacity and drive them for days through Queens, the Bronx, and Brooklyn, where the streets are almost impassable.

"If the trunnions hold up in these rugged tests they should be able to survive anything that could happen to them in Manhattan."

"Does the failure of the Grumman Flxible Bus mean that our entire space program on earth will be delayed?"

"No, it only means that New Yorkers will have to do their exploration on foot until the engineering mistakes have been ironed out. We can't afford to send another bus to New York City until we're sure it will work. Actually the failure of the Grumman Flxible could be considered a plus for the earth space program. We know that many cities were going to order them, and if something terrible had to happen, better it be New York, which is used to its public transportation breaking down, than Boston."

With a Chop, Chop Here

When David Stockman, the head of the Office of Management and Budget, was a little boy, his father gave him an ax. The next morning, the father went out in the backyard and saw his favorite tree chopped down.

He called his son and said, "David, did you chop down this cherry tree?"

David replied, "Yes, Father, I did it and it's only the beginning."

"You can't go around chopping every cherry tree just because I gave you an ax," David's father said.

"Yes, I can. Uncle Ronnie says anytime I see a cherry tree I should chop it down."

"But there are good cherry trees and bad cherry trees. You have to use some discrimination in the ones you ax."

"That isn't what Uncle Ronnie told me. He said he wants the trees cleared out, across the board."

"David, you have to understand something about cherry trees. Some cherry trees give off beautiful blossoms but don't bear any fruit. If you chop them down you lose nothing. But other trees produce cherries and we need them or we won't have anything to eat."

"I don't have time to figure out which are the good cherry trees and which are the bad ones. Uncle Ronnie says he promised to cut all the cherry trees in Washington except for those around the Pentagon. He said under no conditions could I touch them. Well, back to work."

"Wait, David. Are you sure you know what you're doing?"

"Look, Father, I'm not chopping down the entire cherry tree. I'm just lopping off the branches and part of the trunk."

"That's good for some trees, but it's very bad for others. Once you sink an ax into the trunk, the cherry tree will die."

"Well, we've got to get rid of the cherry trees, and this is the only way I know how to do it."

"Do you realize that every tree in Washington is a favorite of somebody's? They don't mind you cutting down the other fellow's cherry tree, but they're going to get awfully mad when they find out you're going to knock down theirs."

"Uncle Ronnie knows that and he's willing to back me up if anyone gets mad when I cut his tree. He says we can't afford all these trees and the only way he can get our yard in order is to knock down as many as we can, even if it means people are going to have to go without cherries."

David starting swinging his ax and singing, "With a chop, chop here and a chop, chop there, ee yi ee yi oh."

A neighbor stopped by and said to David's father, "That son of yours swings a mean ax. What's he doing?"

"I'm not quite sure," the father said. "I gave him this ax and his Uncle Ronnie told him to chop down every cherry tree in Washington except the ones around the Pentagon."

"He's not going to chop down my cherry trees, is he?" the neighbor asked.

"He chopped down *mine,* and I'm his father."

"That's some kid you've got there. I wonder what he's going to do when he grows up?"

David's father said, "Your guess is as good as mine."

J.R. and Deregulation

The only people I know in the oil business are the Ewing family, which I watch on the TV hit show *Dallas* every Friday night. As soon as I heard the news that President Reagan had deregulated oil and was going to deregulate natural gas, I called J.R., the president of Ewing Oil Company, to congratulate him.

"I know I'm going to have to tighten my belt," I told J.R. "But I'm happy for you. This could mean millions of dollars for Ewing Oil."

"Let's say we won't have to apply for food stamps."

"Are you going to use the profits to drill for new oil?" I asked him.

"No, we're just going to start selling oil that we had capped until the deregulations went into effect. There was no sense selling it while the controls were on."

"I thought the idea of deregulating oil was to encourage new drilling so we would become independent of overseas imports."

"That might have been the idea, but we don't want to glut the market or the price of oil will come down. We can't have that."

"I should hope not," I said. "How much do you think it's going to cost us at the pump?"

"Maybe ten or twenty cents a gallon more. I have to talk it over with the boys at the Petroleum Club. We don't want to get into a price war or we'll cut each other's throats."

"Americans would hate to see you people do that," I said. "Do you think the deregulations will encourage more people to look for oil?"

"It's hard to say. Daddy is going into real estate, and my brother Bobby wants to invest into solar energy. I need money to keep all the women I've been chasing happy. So I don't know how much we'll have left for drilling."

"You'll have plenty. We've been paying through the nose for oil ever since they deregulated it. You should see our fuel bills here in the East."

"The Ewing family is aware of the burden the average person is facing. We talked about it last night at dinner."

"What conclusion did you come to?"

"It was none of our business."

"I guess with natural gas deregulation you people will really make a potful of money."

"It will help get us through the winter," J.R. said. "But don't forget President Reagan said our 1960 dollar is only worth 36 cents now, so Ewing Oil can't just sit back and rake in the money. We have to think what we're going to do about inflation."

"Have you come up with any good ideas?"

"We're going to live within our means."

"You're not going to give up your helicopter are you?"

"No, we don't have to do *that*. But I told my brother Bobby, he can only have one Mercedes-Benz at a time."

"I'll bet he didn't like it."

"Well, as President Reagan said on television, you don't tell a kid you don't have any money—you just cut his allowance."

"What I don't understand, J.R., is, if you people can charge anything you want for oil and gas, how is that going to cure inflation?"

"It will cause people to conserve and that should bring the cost of fuel down because it will make the marketplace more competitive."

"That would be terrible. How can you avoid that?" I asked him.

"We'll just put caps on our wells until the price goes up again."

TV in the Courts

The Supreme Court just voted to allow television cameras into the courtroom. It might be one of the most far-reaching decisions the Burger Court has ever made, and possibly the most frightening as far as protecting the innocent goes.

Let me explain. Anyone who has had any exposure on television knows that everyone who has seen you recognizes you, but no one can remember what you said or did. For 15 years people who watched them every night didn't know Huntley from Brinkley. I had the good fortune to be on *60 Minutes* in a friendly piece done by Mike Wallace—but to this day people can't remember if I was the scheming real estate developer in Arizona or the guy who was smuggling in illegal aliens from Mexico.

With the advent of cable television and its eventual choice of 50 channels, we have to assume that the courtroom trials will provide some of the best entertainment on television. Therefore some smart cable-TV operator will plug into the courts and get an entire channel of free-time shows.

Let us assume that a defendant, Arnold Gullible, is being tried by a jury in New York for refusing to pay for an Amtrak train ride because there was no heat in the car and the train was two hours late.

After three days, Arnold is found innocent of the charges and freed. All this has been on television.

The next day Arnold is walking to his office and one lady on the street says to her companion, "Look, there's the man we saw on television who held up the liquor store in the Bronx."

"No, that's not the man who held up the liquor store. He's the one who mugged the old man in the park."

Arnold keeps walking.

He stops off at his bank to cash a check. The guard immediately recognizes him and draws his gun. "You're not going to pull another bank robbery here," the guard tells him. "I saw you on TV and I couldn't believe the judge would give you a suspended sentence."

"I'm not a bank robber," Arnold protests. "You saw me on television in a case where I refused to pay a train ticket."

"Don't tell me what I saw on television. You were on Monday night."

"That was another trial."

"Get out of the bank. I don't ever want to see you here again," the guard tells him.

Arnold leaves in a daze. He's stopped on the street by a man. "Hey, Arnold. I'm a big fan of yours. Anyone who could embezzle $7,000,000 from his company and wind up with a hung jury is my kind of guy. How about your autograph?"

"I didn't embezzle $7,000,000 from my company."

"Okay, so it was more. I bet 5 to 2 you'd beat the rap. Just put your John Hancock here on my business card and sign it to my son, 'Billy.'"

Arnold signs it. A crowd gathers and asks for autographs. "Who is it?" a lady wants to know.

"It's the 'Son of Sam,'" someone else says. "They just let him out."

Arnold manages to break through the crowd and make it to his office where all his friends are shaking his hand. One says, "Arnold, I don't want to be critical, but you should look at the camera more when you're talking." Another says, "You looked awfully nervous. Were you nervous?" A third says, "I didn't see the show but my wife said your lawyer was a dummy and if she'd been on the jury she would have given you the maximum."

The boss calls Arnold in. "We're going to have to let you go. I've had calls from three customers who said they don't want to do business with a company that hires wife beaters."

"I'm not a wife beater," Arnold protests. "I just refused to pay a train ticket."

"I know it and you know it. But the TV audiences don't know it. They got you mixed up with a fellow who was tried right after you. We can't afford to have a bad image. You're going to have to pack it in."

Arnold winds up driving a bus, but his superior warns him, "We know you're an ex-con but we're going to give you a break. But one false move and I call your parole officer and you'll go back to the slammer where you belong."

The New Hostages

A dissident poet and a journalist were sharing the same cell in a small totalitarian country in the "free world" when the guards threw in a beaten-up leader of the political opposition.

"Maybe that will teach you a lesson in opposing General Caesar's martial law government," the guard said.

"What news from the outside world?" the journalist asked.

"The United States has a new foreign policy," the opposition leader said. "Human rights will no longer have a high priority."

"No kidding?" the poet said. "What does?"

"International terrorism is going to take the place of human rights as America's first concern."

"I guess that leaves us out," the journalist said. "Or rather in."

The poet said, "I always suspected the United States wouldn't stick with human rights for too long. It never did play in Peoria."

The opposition leader agreed. "I was arrested two hours after Haig made his declaration about the new American policy. General Caesar would never have dared to do it if he thought human rights was still a U.S. concern."

The journalist said, "I can see putting human rights on the back burner, but why replace it with a war on international terrorism? What's he going to do—bomb Rome if the Red Brigade kidnaps a judge, or waste Belfast if the IRA blows up a department store?"

"He didn't spell it out," the opposition leader said, "but I think it has something to do with the hostage fever in the United States. He was enunciating the new 'get tough' policy of the Reagan administration. Haig probably believes protecting human rights is a sign of American weakness. But showing that you're going to be tough on terrorists proves you're a hardliner."

"It makes sense to me," the poet said. "Besides, as long as Caesar swears fidelity to Washington, Haig feels it's nobody's business who the general throws in jail."

"I wish you would look at it from our point of view and not his. Caesar plays rough with anyone who opposes him."

"I just had a thought," the poet said. "Since we're not going to get the Reagan administration too excited about our plight as political prisoners, why don't we send out word that we're being held hostage?"

The opposition leader said, "That's not bad. Americans get very upset these days about anyone being held hostage."

"But we're not *American* hostages," the journalist protested. "We're hostages in our own country."

"We'll say we're Americans. This will bring all the media down here and then General Caesar will have to open his jails to prove we're not. Once the American public sees what Caesar has been doing to us, Haig may have to deal with the human rights issue here whether he wants to or not."

The journalist said, "It's worth a try. I'll smuggle out a letter to Amnesty International saying General Caesar is holding 500 Americans hostage in his dungeons."

The opposition leader said, "Make it 52. That number has more meaning for Americans."

"Haig's going to blow his top when he finds out it was all a trick to get the United States to recognize human rights."

The poet said, "Yes, but for him it will just be his blood pressure, for us it means our fingernails."

Percival the Playboy

If inflation keeps rising the way it is now, this is the kind of story we can expect to read on our society pages soon.

"Percival Flagstone, scion of the Flagstone chewing gum fortune and noted playboy, checked into Peppermint Hospital yesterday for a gall bladder operation. In keeping with his reputation for free-spending, Percival demanded a private room. He told reporters laughingly, 'I'm going to stay for two weeks and I may blow half my trust fund, but what the hell, I might as well go first class.' When asked what his operation would cost, Percival just chuckled and said, 'If you have to ask what an operation will cost, you can't afford one.'

'The young millionaire has been noted for spending money like water. Last month he took a movie actress to dinner and they both had T-bone steaks. When the papers got wind of it, Percival was indignant and said, 'It's my money and I can do anything I want with it. Just because most people can't afford T-bone steaks is no reason why I can't eat one if I feel like it.'

"Percival was left a fortune of $20 million which his bankers estimate is now down to five. One of the trustees told this reporter, 'The man has no idea that if he keeps spending at the present rate he won't have anything left in two years. He had strawberries for dessert three nights in a row, and he bought two pairs of shoes this year. No matter how much a person has, he can't keep up that pace and not use up all his principal.'

"But Percival has no intention of slowing down. He told this reporter, 'There are no strings attached to my inheritance and I'm even thinking of buying a new tuxedo this year. My theory about money is that if you've got it, flaunt it.

" 'I was terribly criticized when I bought a new azalea bush for my house last year,' Percival told this reporter, 'but I happen to like azaleas, and although there are only about 100 people in this country who can still afford them, we are giving work to greenhouses and florists, and it angers me when the papers make such a big deal of it.'

"Percival just bought a two-bedroom split-level brick house on a quarter-acre of land in Washington, D.C., that is

estimated to have cost him $5 million. The estate, which was
once owned by a conductor on the Penn Central Railroad, has
two bathrooms, one on the top floor and one in the basement. It
also has a dining room. 'They say I went wild when I bought it.
But I consider it a very good investment. In two years the
house will be worth $7 million, and then I wonder how many
people will say I threw away my money.'

" 'Is it true you're buying a four-door Toyota?' I asked him.

" 'I haven't made up my mind yet, but someone has offered
me one at a very good price and I might get it. Ever since I was
a kid I've wanted a car, and I may sell the AT&T bonds my
grandmother left me if I can break the trust. No one said
anything when the Rockefellers bought a VW last summer for
$2 million, yet when they hear I put in a bid for a Toyota it's a
front-page story.'

" 'Perhaps,' I said, 'it's because you do everything with a
flair. Is it true that after your operation you are thinking of
going to London on Laker Airways?'

" 'Yes, I am. But it's not just for pleasure. I hope to visit our
plant in Manchester while I'm there. Everyone thinks I fly
Laker just for pleasure, but many times I use it for business.'

"Percival is known for the lavish gifts he gives the women
he is seen with around town. Just the other day he bought a
14-karat gold necklace from J.C. Penney for $800,000, and
last month he gave a well-known model a rhinestone-covered
compact from Montgomery Ward's worth $600,000. 'To me
they're just trinkets, but to most of the women I date they're a
month's salary.'

"My final question to Percival before he was wheeled into
his private room was, 'Percival, you seem to have done it all.
You've eaten a T-bone steak, bought an azalea bush, you own
a two-bedroom house and you've flown Laker Airlines. Is
there anything you still want to buy?'

"He thought for a moment and said, 'Well, I've always
wanted to own a crate of California lettuce, but even for
someone like me that's out of the question.' "

Creation Vs. Applebaum

The battle being waged in the schools has pitted the Creationists (those who believe the Bible's version of how man appeared on Earth) against the Darwinists, who claim that man walked out of the sea millions and millions of years ago and eventually developed into the human being that we know today.

But there is a third theory which combines the two, and this one should also be taught in the schools.

Professor Heinrich Applebaum has been researching it for years and here is what he has come up with:

"I believe God did create Adam, and then made Eve from one of his ribs, but I can't buy the story of why they were driven out of the Garden of Eden."

"What do you think happened?"

"Well, Adam and Eve were living happily in the Garden when some geologists came along and suspected there was oil under it. They recommended that some test wells be drilled. Adam protested that the Garden of Eden was a perfect paradise, and oil companies would destroy it if they started putting up rigs on the property. Adam pointed out that God had set aside Eden as a place where man and woman could commune with nature. He said he would take them to court if they tried to drill on it."

The oil companies took their case to the secretary of the interior, who was charged with protecting public lands.

He accused Adam of being an environmentalist and trying to stop the human race from developing its natural resources.

"We can't just let the oil sit there under the ground to protect a Garden which only two people are using," he said on *Meet the Press*. "Our job is to see that we use our natural resources for the benefit of all mankind. Besides, I have no intention of giving permission to the oil companies to drill all over the Garden. I'm setting 20 percent of the land aside for drilling, and the rest will be kept in its present natural state."

Adam complained to God, who said, "The oil lobby is much

more powerful than I am. There isn't anything I can do to stop them."

The Interior Department auctioned off the leases, and it turned out there was not only oil but gas on the land.

The next people to apply for permission to dig were the coal companies. The secretary of the interior decided to let them go ahead, despite Adam and Eve's protests, because the coal had a low sulphur content. But he said he would permit them to mine on only 30 percent of the Garden, which gave Adam and Eve plenty of room to enjoy the view.

Consolidated Edison decided to build a plant in the Garden because it was cheaper then hauling the coal across the continent. Then the copper and nickel companies erected smelters to take advantage of the cheap energy.

Adam developed sinus trouble and Eve's eyes were tearing all the time. The final straw came when a snake gave Eve an apple covered with insecticide and she got sick to her stomach.

"That does it," Adam said, packing his few belongings. "We're getting out of this hellhole and moving to New Jersey."

"Off We Go"

One of the major reasons the U.S. armed forces are woefully short of every type of military equipment is that we have such a big heart, and we keep giving it away to countries that claim they need it more than we do.

If the U.S. military believes that the new Reagan appropriation requests are going to beef up their forces, they're in for a surprise.

I was at one of the larger fighter aircraft companies, where several Air Force officers were eagerly waiting for the planes to come off the assembly line, when I saw the following scene:

A brand-new fighter came rolling out of the hangar, and one of the U.S. pilots jumped on the wing.

"What the hell do you think you're doing?" a company foreman said.

"I'm just looking over our new plane."

"That plane doesn't belong to you. The State Department has promised the first 20 to Saudi Arabia."

"When do we get ours?" he said.

The foreman looked over his order list. "After Saudi Arabia, the next 12 go to Chile, 14 have been set aside for Argentina, the following 15 have been allocated for Taiwan, and if we have any left over we're to ship them to South Yemen."

"Wait a minute. We came all the way from the East Coast to pick up these planes. We can't go back empty-handed."

The foreman checked over his list. "What military service did you say you were with?"

"The U.S. Air Force. You know, 'Off we go into the wild blue yonder.'"

"I don't see anything here for the U.S. Air Force. Are you sure you're supposed to get American fighter planes?"

"That was the whole idea of giving the Pentagon more money. Who's in charge around here?"

"There's a fellow from the State Department over there. You might talk to him."

The head of the Air Force delegation went over to a man

wearing striped pants and a tailcoat. "How come we're not getting any fighter planes from this plant?"

"What country do you represent?" Striped Pants asked.

"The United States, dummy."

"You don't have to be rude. We have certain priorities when it comes to the allocation of fighter planes. We have to see that our friends get them first."

"I don't get it. I thought the U.S. was trying to play catch-up with the Russians. What are we doing giving all our stuff away?"

"If we don't let the Third World have our best planes, the Soviets will start supplying them with MIGs. Therefore, it's in our national interest to see that every country in the Free World gets all the military equipment it asks for."

"What are we giving Chile and Argentina planes for?"

"They both have military governments and need them to stay in power. With some countries it's a question of defense, with others it's a matter of prestige."

"What about Taiwan?"

"We've always sent fighter planes to Taiwan. It's an old American tradition."

"Look, fellow, the basis of American foreign policy is to be able to face up to the Russians anywhere, any place. How do we do it if you keep giving away our new military equipment?"

"We're aware of the problem, but no self-respecting military junta will take hand-me-downs. They want only the best military hardware that money can buy. If we gave the U.S. armed forces our newest equipment before we gave it to the Third World, they would be very insulted."

"So where does that leave the U.S. Air Force?"

"I think you'll get yours after Pakistan, or is it Jordan? I know your name came up as a possibility for fighters somewhere along the line."

"Isn't there any way we can get planes before Chile?"

"Colonel, it's absolutely out of the question. Where would we be today if we hadn't given Iran our first-class fighter planes years ago?"

It's Great to Be Rich

Anyone who has been to the grocery store lately knows what a rare and expensive delicacy peanut butter has become.

Therefore it came as a real surprise when the Brokaws brought out an entire jar of it for cocktails the other evening. The jar, which weighed at least a pound, contained the extra-crunchy kind that you can find in only the finest restaurants. It was sitting in a carved figure of ice surrounded by toast and pats of jelly.

"I didn't know this was a special occasion," one of the guests said.

Meredith Brokaw replied, "It isn't, but every once in a while Tom and I get the urge to splurge and we treat ourselves to a luxury."

I whispered to my wife, "There must be money on her side of the family, because I know Brokaw could never afford a jar of peanut butter on what he makes."

She said, "Hush, they'll hear you. Anyway, what difference does it make? You only get to eat peanut butter once in your life. Let's make the most of it."

We all gathered around as Mrs. Brokaw started spreading the golden substance on toast and passing it to her guests.

Some people asked for jelly with theirs, but a few purists like myself wanted it without any condiments.

We all "oohed" and "ahhed" as we tasted it.

"This is the real stuff," I said. "Where on earth did you find it?"

"We have a connection at the United Nations," Brokaw said. "He gets it through the diplomatic pouch."

"Did you know it takes three pounds of peanuts to make one jar of peanut butter?"

"No wonder no one can afford it," I said.

One of the guests said, "I remember when I was a kid, my mother used to keep a jar in the closet and after school we used to spread it on bread like butter."

Another one said, "I recall those days. I didn't know what I had and used to trade my peanut butter and jelly sandwiches at lunch hour for ham on rye."

"Help yourselves," Meredith Brokaw said. "We don't want it to go to waste."

We didn't need to be asked twice. I put two large teaspoonfuls on a piece of toast.

"Don't make a pig of yourself," my wife whispered. "You act as if it's the first time you ever ate peanut butter."

"It's the first time in months," I whispered back. "If they're crazy enough to serve it, why shouldn't we get our share?"

"I was once on the *Queen Elizabeth* and they gave you all the peanut butter you could eat."

"They always make a big deal of that on luxury liners," someone else said.

We all laughed as we kept digging into the jar.

One of the guests said, "Does anyone here remember when we used to feed peanuts to the elephants at the zoo?"

"I recall when we used to eat them at baseball games."

Mrs. Brokaw brought out more toast and jelly.

"I went to a bar when I was in college and you'll never believe this, but there was a bowl of peanuts on each table," I said. "We used to throw the shells on the floor."

By this time the jar was empty and the toast and jelly were gone.

I tried to lick the inside of the top, but my wife stopped me.

It was an evening I'll never forget. I've been to houses recently where there have been a few canapes of peanut butter mixed in with the smoked salmon sandwiches. But I've never been in a home where someone actually brought out an entire jar of it and passed it around like it was caviar.

Anchors Away

The United States is going into a crash program to build up its military might. We want to be in a position to match the Soviets on land, on sea and in the air. There is only one problem. Once we get all the new helicopters, planes and ships built, where do we find the people to man them?

The Navy, for example, does not have enough crewmen to handle the ships they're supposed to keep on the high seas now. If we take the *New Jersey* and *Iowa* battleships out of mothballs, as Defense Secretary Weinberger wants to do, this is what might happen:

"Captain, as admiral of the North Atlantic Forces, I turn over the command of the battleship *New Jersey* to you and your fine crew."

"Thank you, sir. Where's the crew?"

"They're standing over there."

"Six men for a battleship?"

"That's all the bureau of personnel could spare. I asked for ten but they said they needed the others to man a missile cruiser that will escort you to sea."

"Begging your pardon, sir, and meaning no disrespect, but a battleship calls for a complement of 4,000 men."

"I'm aware of that, Captain. But we're going to have to make it with what we've got. I'm sure with proper training your six-man crew can do the job. They'll just have to double up on their watches."

"You actually want me to take this battleship out of harbor with six people?"

"Captain, may I remind you that getting command of a battleship is one of the highest honors that the Navy can bestow on one of its officers."

"I'm aware of the honor, sir, and it's been my dream to command a ship like the *New Jersey*. But I always thought when I got one this size, the crew would go with it."

"I assure you, Captain, once you get the hang of it, you'll be amazed at how few people it takes to run a battleship. We've put in an automatic steering system, so you won't need anyone at the wheel, and all your meals have been pre-packaged so you won't require a mess crew, and the engines have been fitted with computers so you won't need anybody in the boiler rooms. And when you press this button you can fire your guns fore and aft. So actually the only thing your crew will have to do is scrape and paint the ship when it pulls into port."

"It sounds very reassuring, Admiral. I imagine my first job will be to brief the officers."

"Officers? You're it."

"You mean I have to eat by myself?"

"Don't feel bad. Your only chief petty officer has to eat by himself also."

"What are my orders, sir?"

"You're to seek out the enemy and destroy him at will. But first check with Washington before you engage in action."

"By radio?"

"We couldn't spare a radioman. Here is a bag of dimes. There's a pay phone on the bridge."

"Thank you, sir. That's very generous of you."

"Money isn't our problem, Captain. We have more of it than we know what to do with. Our problem is that the more ships the Defense Department wants to put to sea, the more we have to stretch our manpower. After I leave here, I have to recommission the aircraft carrier *Oriskany* with three squadrons of Grumman fighters."

"That should beef up the fleet."

"Not quite. They only gave me two pilots."

"Would you like to address the crew, sir?"

"No, Captain. I believe you'd better pull up anchor right away before they find out they're the only ones on board. We can't afford to have any of them jump ship."

How Playboy *Did It*

Playboy magazine has just done a lovely take-out on Rita Jenrette, the wife of the former congressman from South Carolina.

Apparently, *Playboy* was searching for an in-depth feature on the typical congressional wife, and by chance came across Mrs. Jenrette while she was making love to her husband on the Capitol steps.

This is how the story came about. A *Playboy* editor, who was on his way to see his senator to protest the higher mail rates for magazines, tripped over the couple and said, "This is a great honor for me. I never thought I'd meet a congressman and his wife in the flesh."

Then he explained that *Playboy* was planning to do a long spread on the trials and tribulations of what it was like to be married to a congressman.

"Congressional wives lead an awfully dull life," Mrs. Jenrette protested. "We just go to parties given by lobbyists, where other politicians proposition us, and sometimes people attempt to put drugs in our drinks, and other times a governor might try to grab us in the shower. But it doesn't seem worth a whole story in *Playboy*."

"To you it might sound dull, but to the average reader sitting at home reading the hi-fi ads in our magazine, it sounds very exciting. After all, you're at the seat of power."

"We're just like everyone else," Mrs. Jenrette said. "We attend our husband's trial when he's caught in an FBI sting operation, and we keep a stiff upper lip when he goes off the wagon, and we hide our cash in a shoebox."

"That's just the point of our story," the *Playboy* editor said. "Despite the glamour and the heady atmosphere of Washington, you're still just plain simple folks at heart. Let me ask you something. Do you always make love on the Capitol steps?"

"Not always," said Congressman Jenrette. "Sometimes we wait and do it at home."

"Terrific," the editor said. "It shows that a congressman's

wife understands his work and, if he can't get home, she's willing to spend time with him on the Capitol steps."

"Are you planning to illustrate the story with pictures?" Congressman Jenrette asked.

"It would be nice to show Mrs. Jenrette around the house when she wasn't all dressed up to go out. It would depict the human side of a congressman's wife."

"That would be fun," Mrs. Jenrette said. "No one ever wants to photograph me at home when I'm in something real comfortable."

"Well, honey, I think it could help my career and make everyone forget about ABSCAM," Congressman Jenrette said. "If Jerry Falwell can appear in *Penthouse*, I don't see anything wrong in you appearing in *Playboy*."

"Then you'll do it?" the editor asked.

"If you think it will help the readers of *Playboy* understand how our government works, I don't see why not," Mrs. Jenrette said.

"Great. I'll have a photographer call you tomorrow morning."

Unfortunately, by the time the article was scheduled to appear, the Jenrettes broke up, so the idea of how a typical congressman's wife lives in Washington went out the window. The *Playboy* editors decided to change the theme of the story to how difficult it was for a congressman's wife to stay married in Washington. Fortunately, they didn't have to shoot any new art work to go with the feature.

The New Class

President Reagan hasn't been in office for long, and he's already created a new class of people. Before Reagan we had the rich, the middle class and the poor. The new class is now called the "Near Poor."

The President and his advisers decided they needed another class because the government was putting too many people in the poverty class. Instead of dealing with poverty as previous administrations had, the Reagan people made the decision to eliminate a percentage of the poor people by promoting them to Near Poor. In order to do this, they raised the requirements for what it took to be declared "poor."

I know a struggling mother who used to think of herself as poor, since she had to work and raise her children without the help of her husband. I thought she would be delighted with the news that she was no longer a poverty case, and was now considered by the government as a Near Poor person who did not require federal assistance.

But it turned out that she wasn't too thrilled that she had achieved upward mobility through an OMB directive.

"I'd rather be poor than Near Poor," she told me. "At least when you're poor, you know where your next meal is coming from. Now I'm on the razor's edge. I'm just over the new poverty line so I'm in worse shape than I was before."

"But," I said, "just think of your social status. Now your friends will respect you because you're no longer in the lowest class of our society. You can look at the poor people with scorn."

"I know it sounds good on paper," she said, "but the Near Poor are the ones who really have to take it on the chin under Reagan's economic plan. We have all the problems of the poor but none of the benefits. I'm not entitled to food stamps, or rent subsidies, day care or even a tax cut, because in my bracket there is nothing to cut."

"Ah, but you forget the trickle-down effect of supply economics. When the rich get their tax cuts, they will use their money to invest in the country and that will trickle down to the poor and the Near Poor. I wouldn't be surprised in a year or two if the Reagan people promote you to the middle class, and then you'll be in really great shape."

"How do I keep my kids in shoes until then?" she wanted to know.

"You tighten your belt. That's what the middle class and rich people have to do."

"If I tighten my belt any more, I won't be able to breathe. I've talked it over with my social worker, and she doesn't think I can make it as a Near Poor person."

"What did she suggest?"

"Her only solution was to quit my job and go on welfare."

"You mean you're willing to take a demotion from being Near Poor to poor, just to feed your family?" I asked in astonishment.

"I'm not thrilled with the idea, but I'm discovering there really isn't that much advantage to being Near Poor."

"I hate to say this, but it's people like you who are going to make it very difficult for Reagan to turn this country around. He raised you above the poverty level by declaring that you were no longer poor, and all you talk about is going back on welfare."

"I guess," she said, "I don't have what it takes to appreciate Near Poverty, though God knows I've tried."

"Would it help if the Reagan people changed your category from Near Poor to Lower-Lower Middle Class?"

"Do you think they would?"

"I'm sure of it. They'll call you anything you want as long as they don't have to help you out."

Hope for Detroit

I am not as pessimistic about the American automobile industry as most people. The one thing that makes the U.S. consumer buy something is if the product is different from anything his neighbors have. This is particularly true of cars.

Americans consider their automobiles status symbols: something not only to drive, but to use to put down their friends and relatives.

For a long time, the foreign car has been the ultimate status symbol for someone living in the United States. At first only a few people drove them. But in recent years it has become impossible to impress anyone with an imported model because everyone has one of his own.

But the pendulum may be swinging back, and because they are so rare, an American car is the fashionable thing to own.

Just the other day, at a party, Jeffrey Doranz drove up the driveway in a strange-looking vehicle and honked his horn.

We all rushed out of the house to look at it.

"What is it?" someone asked.

"It's called a Citation," Jeffrey said proudly.

Bob Elliott, who was the first one on the block to own a Toyota, was livid with jealousy.

"Where was it made?" he asked.

"In the United States," Jeffrey said. "It was built in Detroit. I have this friend who lives in Grosse Pointe, and he tipped me off. He said it's going to be the car of the future."

Mrs. Elliott, who owned a Mercedes-Benz sports car, whispered to Bob, "Do you think it's true?"

"I don't know," Bob told her. "I heard they were toying with the idea of making cars in Detroit, but I didn't realize that they had gone into production."

Burberry, who owned a Volvo and a Volkswagen, opened the door of the Citation and looked inside.

"Would you like me to take you for a spin in it?" Jeffrey asked. "It's amazing what American engineers have put in a little car this size."

Jeffrey and Burberry took off, while the rest of us stood around depressed and sick that Doranz had put one over on us.

The wives were particularly furious. One said to her husband, "I thought you told me that the BMW was the new status car in the country."

"It was, for a year. How did I know Americans would start making automobiles again?"

"I'm going to top Doranz," Elliott said. "I hear the Ford Motor Co. has a new car called the Escort. If we move now, I'll be the first one on the block to own one."

My wife asked me, "What do we do with our Mazda?"

"We sell it before Doranz makes a fool of us. I saw on television the other night that Chrysler is putting out a Dodge Aries. I'll make enquiries. But mum's the word. We don't want anyone in the neighborhood to get wind of it."

Doranz came back with Burberry. "Anyone else want a ride?" he said pompously.

We all declined, though the curiosity of driving around in an American-built car was killing us. Most of us left the party as soon as we could because we couldn't stand the smug look on Doranz's face.

Who would have dreamed that in such a short time the thrill of owning a foreign-made car would be gone?

The Stranger Amongst Us

Anyone in the public eye, whether it be a movie star, a television personality, a politician, or even a columnist, has a better idea than most people of what happened in front of the Washington Hilton Monday afternoon.

Somewhere out in this country are sick people, who, though complete strangers, harbor bitter grievances against well-known individuals who have never done them any harm. But for some reason they have decided that a particular person is responsible for their pain.

The mail arrives and among the letters are the anonymous scrawls of anger and hate. The scrawls can be threatening or they can make no sense at all. You tend to laugh them off because you don't want to admit to yourself that somebody out there has chosen you as the target for their discontent.

The letters are either thrown into the wastebasket or placed in the increasingly large "nut file" that you've built up over the years. Sometimes the mail continues for months and even years. Other times one letter is sufficient to relieve the person of whatever is bothering him.

The hate and the anger and the frustration are not only transmitted through the mail, but also over the telephone. The stranger tells you what you have allegedly done to him and asks what you are going to do about it.

The trick is to talk calmly and assure him that whatever his grievance is, you will look into it. You try to persuade him that you are not responsible for whatever is hurting him, and you end the conversation as quietly and gently as you possibly can.

Fortunately, very few people act out their fantasies of "getting even" with the person they have chosen as the one who is tormenting them.

But every once in a while, someone decides he or she must take action.

The most obvious person in this country to take action against is the President of the United States. It doesn't matter what party the President belongs to or what his political philosophy is. The stranger has decided to have his day in the sun.

The problem of obtaining a gun to carry out the fantasy is no problem. In almost any state you can buy a weapon. You can get one for as little as $20 or one for $200, and in many places you can buy a gun with no questions asked.

Stalking a President is also no problem in a country where Presidents mingle with the people. The opportunity to fire the gun is a matter of luck and daring. No Secret Service or umbrella of police personnel can protect a person from the stranger who is intent on shooting someone.

And sometimes the deed is carried out, as it was on Monday, when a smiling President waved to a friendly crowd on the streets of the capital of the United States.

But Presidents are not the only targets for the sick people who walk the land. The victims can also be John Lennon or a little black child in Atlanta.

And every time it happens, the American people rise up in anger and say, "What can we do?"

Stop the sale of handguns? It might be a good beginning, but the gun lobby will never let it happen. Lock up every sick person in the country? It can't and shouldn't be done.

The truth of the matter is that there is very little that can be done.

The brooding stranger who dreams of taking his revenge is always amongst us. But until the gun is fired, nobody knows his name.

Don't Ask

It used to be if a person owned a boat and was queried, "How much does it cost to run?" the response was, "If you have to ask, you can't afford it."

With the arrival of spring, the same answer could go for someone owning a house.

I came home the other day to see a man standing on my roof.

"What are you doing up there?" I asked him.

"Four thousand dollars, which doesn't include the gutter work."

I was about to say something when a truck drew up and two men started throwing mulch on the lawn.

The driver said, "You're lucky it was a warm winter. The grass looks in pretty good shape."

"How good?" I wanted to know.

"Two thousand and six dollars, if you want us to prune the trees."

A car parked behind him. The man got out holding a clipboard and a ruler, and started to measure the retaining wall next to the garage. "What's up?" I asked.

"Your wife called me and asked me to give her an estimate on what it would cost to repair your wall."

"I know how much it will cost," I said.

"How much?"

"Three thousand, two hundred and twenty-five dollars."

"How did you know?"

"I have psychic powers."

A large van pulled up in back of the retaining-wall man's car.

"Where do you want the patio furniture?" the burly man asked.

"You sure you got the right house?"

The man checked his order slip. "It says, 'Patio Furniture, $4,500.' "

"You've got the right house."

I sat on the stoop and lit a cigar. Two men in overalls came around from the side of the house. "It's had it."

"What's had it?"

"The air conditioner. The motor is shot. You need new bearings and the cooling unit has to be replaced. You would be better off buying a new one than having us fix the old one."

"Don't I know it," I said. "What are air conditioners going for these days?"

"If you want one that will last, start thinking $6,000."

"That's what I was thinking," I said.

"You have to order one now in time for the summer," one of them said, handing me the slip.

I was about to go into the house when the painters arrived. They kept staring up at the window and writing numbers on a pad.

"There's a lot more trim on those windows than you think," one told me. "Also your front door is warped. You better have that fixed before we paint it."

"I'll bet you couldn't paint the windows for less than $3,000," I said.

"We could, but you'd be wasting your money. They should have at least two coats."

My wife called down from the porch, "Don't let the painters leave until they look at the cracks in the basement."

"Why would I want them to leave?" I said.

The roofer was putting his ladder back on the truck, the mulchers had finished their mulching, the retaining-wall man had left, and the painters were in the house talking to my wife.

My son drove up in his car. "What's up, Dad?" he asked.

"Sit down, Son. I have something to tell you. Someday," I said, pointing at the house and grounds, "all this will be yours."

"When, Dad?"

"How does today suit you?"

They All Sniff Mace

Don't believe what you read about Hollywood. From the recent stories in the newspapers and magazines, everybody in show business is into cocaine. It's not true. They're into Mace. For those who don't follow self-defense, Mace is a gas that can paralyze an attacker for as long as three hours.

To hear people out in Los Angeles tell it, Southern California is now more dangerous than El Salvador, and no one knows when he or she is going to be assaulted.

On my visit there last week, all the table conversation had to do with burglar alarm systems, private police services, but mostly Mace.

There are hundreds of classes being held all over town in the use of the gas, and you have to go to school for 2½ hours before you can be licensed to carry a Mace can in your handbag or your pants pocket.

I didn't realize how nervous everyone was until I went to visit a producer friend of mine named Alain Bernheim at MGM Studios.

His secretary asked suspiciously, "Do you have an appointment?"

I said, "No," and she took a can out of her desk and gave me two squirts in the face. I hit the floor for an hour and a half. When Bernheim finally revived me, he apologized. "I'm sorry," he said. "She's new on the job. She is supposed to use a karate blow to your neck first."

He took me to lunch in the studio commissary.

The headwaiter asked us if we had a reservation and Bernheim said, "No, I forgot to call."

The headwaiter whistled twice and two Doberman pinschers leaped out of the kitchen and went for our throats. Fortunately, Billy Wilder, the director, who speaks German, called them off and let us sit at his table.

"Things are really tough out here," I said.

"You have to be on your toes," Walter Matthau said. "Last week they let in a guy without a reservation and he mugged two stuntmen right in front of the salad bar."

Jack Lemmon came over to the table, and I got up to shake hands with him. Two private security guards jumped me from behind and wrestled me to the floor.

"It's OK, boys, he's a friend," Jack said. "But nice work anyway."

Bernheim excused himself to call his house to find out if everything was safe, and then came back to the table. "Marge maced the grocery delivery boy by mistake and had to take him to the hospital."

"How many squirts?" Matthau asked.

"Two."

"We always give our grocery boy three," he said. "Everyone in the neighborhood squirts him when he comes to the back door, and now two shots from the can don't even faze him."

After lunch, I decided to go shopping in Beverly Hills. I went to a very fancy store on Rodeo Drive.

"Can I help you?" a salesman asked.

"I'm just looking," I said.

He took out his can of Mace and was about to let me have it.

"Wait," I cried, "I have a credit card."

He took the card and said, "It better be good or you're a dead duck."

I left the store as fast as I could and went back to the Beverly Wilshire Hotel. They were holding a Mace class in the ballroom and I signed up for the course. In 2½ hours I had my own Mace can. I went upstairs and waited patiently. At five the knock came on the door.

"Who is it?" I said.

"It's me, honey," my wife said.

I put the chain on the door and opened it two inches and went "Squirt, squirt, squirt."

When she finally woke up and asked me why I did it, I told her, "In L.A., it's every man for himself."

A Lawyer Has to Eat

It goes without saying that when it comes to book, film and TV rights, a notorious crime has a great deal more value than a run-of-the-mill one that hardly got into the newspapers.

There was a time when the person who was thought to have committed the offense received the lion's share of the money for telling his side of the story. But now, with legal fees so high, lawyers are demanding they get their cut of the action.

Recently, an accused murderer revealed that his lawyer would take his legal fee out of the potential proceeds of a book contract.

The D.C. Bar Association is looking into the matter because the arrangement could violate the District Bar Code of Ethics.

The reason why the District doesn't approve of lawyers sharing in the literary fruits of their clients' alleged crimes (although many states do) is that a lawyer might be more interested in how the book comes out than the trial. He could even knowingly or unknowingly tailor the defense to make a better story.

This fictitious conversation could take place in many states where a canon forbidding a defense lawyer from sharing in literary rights does not exist:

"Lefty, as you know, we're in the second week of the trial and I think I've made a pretty strong case for you."

"I ain't complaining. You gave the DA a run for his money. I got a feeling the jury is going to come back with a Not Guilty verdict."

"That's what my editor thinks too, Lefty. Originally, when we worked out the outline of the book, we thought it would make a better story if I got you off at the end. But now that the press keeps referring to our case as the Crime of the Century, we believe it would be better if you got the electric chair."

"Are you crazy or something? Why would it be better if I got the chair?"

"It's more dramatic if after a great defense the jury still finds you guilty. A Not Guilty verdict makes the book anti-climactic and a big letdown, particularly if we're going for a Book-of-the-Month deal."

"Wait a minute. I don't mind you taking your fee out of the literary rights to my trial, but I don't want to fry for it."

"Listen, Lefty, when you came to me you didn't have a dime. You chose me because I was the best criminal lawyer in the country. But I'm not in this business for my health. I don't want you to go to the chair any more than you do. But if I don't make any money on this book, I'll have wasted six months of my time."

"Can't you figure out some other way of ending the book without me going to the chair?"

"I could get you life, but every major Hollywood studio is interested in making a movie from the trial. We can't make a big deal unless you get capital punishment. My agent said the difference between you getting life and the chair is worth a half a million bucks."

"So what are you going to do?"

"I've got to persuade the jury in my summing up that all our witnesses have been lying through their teeth, and society would be much better off if you paid the ultimate price for your heinous crime. But I have to be subtle about it. I don't want to hurt my reputation in the legal profession."

"I think the whole thing stinks."

"Look, Lefty, I'll even throw in an appeal to the Supreme Court for nothing for you. But my first obligation is to my publishers. After all, they're the ones who are paying me."

"I could have done better with a public defender."

"You know you don't honestly believe that, Lefty. Have you ever heard of a public defender who has won a Pulitzer Prize?"

We Need Students

With education tuition soaring, student loans being cut to the bone, and the 1960s baby boom coming to an end, many colleges are desperately looking for warm bodies to fill their freshman classes.

For the first time schools are advertising for students in newspapers, magazines and on television.

An advertising agency recently made a presentation to the board of Desperate Tech University, which had decided to spend a million dollars trying to attract students.

Honeybee, the account executive, said, "Gentlemen, our surveys indicate that today's students are interested in sleeping late, partying and not being bugged about their studies. We have to go after this market and persuade them to come to Desperate Tech."

"How do you propose to do it?" a board member asked.

"First we need a catchy slogan. How does this grab you? We show a TV commercial with John Belushi throwing food at his fraternity brothers while they're teaching the science lab. A voice-over says, 'If you liked the movie *Animal House*, you'll love the real thing at Desperate Tech.' "

"Won't that put Desperate Tech in a bad light?" one of the board members asked.

"Gentlemen, we have to resort to a hard sell. Our competitors are offering free cars to the kids, two-week paid vacations in Fort Lauderdale, and remedial rock music classes. If you expect to get a share of the freshman market, you're going to have to top them. Now here is a magazine layout I believe has tremendous student appeal. As you can see, it shows a coed in a wedding gown in front of the student chapel. The text reads, 'I went to Desperate Tech to get an education, but I wound up with something much better—a husband. He is going into his father's oil business, and we will start married life on a 10,000-acre ranch just outside Dallas. If I hadn't gone to Desperate Tech I might have wound up working in a massage parlor. There are many men like Ted and you won't have any trouble finding Mr. Right, if you just fill out the coupon on the bottom of the page!"

Honeybee continued his presentation. "Now, I think we should also go into newspapers in a big way—on the comic pages. Here you see a puzzle. It is a series of numbered dots and the copy reads, 'If you can connect all these dots to each other, and make a football player out of them, then you've passed your entrance exam to Desperate Tech. If you fail to do it, we'll permit you to take a make-up exam in next week's comic pages.'"

"What else do you have?" someone asked.

"Well, this is another TV commercial. We show the president of the university standing in front of the administration, like Lee Iacocca does for Chrysler. He says, 'Desperate Tech is now offering the largest close-out sale in university history. We have to get rid of 100,000 college degrees by April 15th. That's why we're offering $700 rebates to every college freshman who applies this month. Whether you're looking for a BA or a BS, or just want to waste four years of your life, stop into one of our showrooms today and see why so many students are turning to Desperate Tech as an alternate to book-guzzling schools like Harvard.'"

Have You Got a Minute?

Jason Robards was in his office gently snoozing when Robert Redford, his assistant managing editor, came in to see him.

"Have you got a minute?" Redford said.

"What is it?" Robards asked in his gravelly voice.

"I've got good news and bad news," Redford told him.

"The good news is that one of our reporters won the Pulitzer Prize."

"That's great," said Robards. "Put it on the front page. What's the bad news?"

"The bad news is the story she won it for isn't true."

"On second thought, you'd better put it in the food section."

"I don't know what happened," Redford said. "She swore every fact was true."

"Why didn't you check it out with me first?" Robards said.

"We did. You were the one who okayed the story. Don't you remember, we came to your house late at night and you came out on the lawn in your bathrobe and read it under the street lamp."

"Oh, my God. It's coming back to me now. Isn't that the girl who graduated Magna Cum Laude from Vassar?"

Redford said, "Would you believe Magna Cum Nothing Laude from the University of Toledo?"

"I need a drink," Robards said. "Who else knows about this?"

"Just myself and Dustin Hoffman," Redford said.

"Well, that gives us time anyway."

"I'm not so sure. Dustin now works for ABC and they're going to lead with it tonight on the evening news."

"Okay, we blew it," said Robards. "But I don't want a cover-up. I want us to play this story straight down the line. Put your best reporters on it, dig up all the facts, talk to everyone you can, get statements from everybody from the Pulitzer Committee to the mayor of Washington, D.C."

"I gotcha, boss. If there's a smoking gun, we'll find it," Redford said.

"Do you still see 'Deep Throat'?" Robards asked.

"All the time. He works in the garage where I park my car."

"Well, see what he knows about the Pulitzer gang. Find out where the money's coming from for the Prize. Talk to all the wives of the editors and find out where they were the night the story was printed. One of them has to break."

"I just thought of something. I used to date a girl who worked in the city room. Maybe she knows how the article got into the paper."

"Good idea. Take her to dinner and whatever."

The secretary came in. "President Nixon's on the phone."

Robards picked it up. He listened for thirty seconds and hung up.

Redford said, "What did he say?"

"Nothing. He just gave me a Bronx raspberry."

"At least you know who your friends are when you make a blooper," Redford said.

"People forget so soon," Robards said. "Okay, let's get back to business. I won't accept any facts on how we blew it unless they're confirmed by two sources."

"Don't worry, boss. We won't rest until we get to the bottom of this. I have a friend at the FBI who owes me a favor. He might be willing to open his files on us."

"Good," Robards said. "If anyone asks you what you're doing, tell him you're working on a story about how many husbands Governor Carey's wife really had."

"I'll get on it right away," Redford said. "What are you going to do now?"

"Me?" said Robards. "I'm going to call my agent and see if I can get out of this lousy movie."

Ban the Bullet

The Handgun Control lobbyists maintain that guns kill people. The Right to Bear Arms crowd says that guns don't kill people—people kill people. Both groups are wrong. According to Arnold Crocus, a lethal weapons expert, bullets kill people.

To back up his theory, Arnold invited me to his laboratory, where he had an array of guns on the wall. He took one off the rack and told me to point it at a target and pull the trigger.

I did, and the gun went "click."

"Nothing happened," Crocus said, "therefore we know that guns don't kill people. Now pretend the target is someone you really hate."

I thought of someone, and stared at the target with all the anger I could muster. Once again nothing happened.

"This proves," said Arnold, "that people, at this distance, cannot kill people. Now I am going to place a round of ammunition in your gun, and I want you to pull the trigger."

I did as I was told. There was a loud explosion and the bullet went right through the target's heart.

"Well," said Arnold, "what do you conclude?"

"The only conclusion I can come to is that the bullet was the deadly weapon."

"Right. Now it's true that the bullet would not be able to penetrate the target unless it was fired through the barrel of the gun. And it is also true that the gun could not have been fired unless someone pulled the trigger. But without the bullet, the target would not have suffered any injury."

"That means," I said, "that the real problem America faces is not the plethora of handguns in this country, nor the people who use them, but the ammunition that is available to anyone who wants it."

"You got it. What this tells us is that it may be possible to satisfy both the Right to Bear Arms crowd and the Handgun Control people at the same time. By permitting the sale of guns, but prohibiting the manufacture or sale of ammunition, you make both sides happy."

"But the gun lovers will say that there is no sense owning a firearm if you can't fire anything out of it."

"Let them say it. They don't have a legal leg to stand on. There is nothing in the Constitution that says Americans have a right to bear bullets.

"The mistake the Handgun Control people have been making is that they keep trying to take handguns away from the people. This won't fly in Congress, because you have too many congressmen and senators from the South and the Western parts of the country who would be committing political suicide if they voted for such restrictions. But they could, in good conscience, vote to forbid the sale of any kind of ammunition to fit the guns. We wouldn't see any immediate results from the prohibition because most people have a stock of ammunition in their houses now. But it would either be used up or go rotten on them in time."

"What I like about your idea," I told Crocus, "is that the people who make handguns couldn't complain, because they could still sell them. And those who wanted to buy a gun could still obtain one without too much trouble. The only flak you'd get is from the bullet makers. How do you deal with them?"

"They can always make suppositories for duck hunters with the same equipment."

"Have you suggested this compromise to the Handgun Control people and the gun lobby?" I asked.

"Yes, I have," he replied. "The Handgun Control people are willing at this stage to try anything to stop the slaughter in this country. But the gun lobbyists are asking for more time to think it over. Without ammunition, they are afraid people might lose interest in owning handguns, and then they would all be out of jobs."

"Maybe they could join the U.S. Marine Corps. They're always looking for a few good men."